THE GUIDE TO
MYSTERIOUS
LOCH NESS
AND THE INVERNESS AREA

THE GUIDE TO
MYSTERIOUS
LOCH NESS
AND THE INVERNESS AREA

GEOFF HOLDER

This one's for Roger Zelazny, not least because of
The Doors of His Face, The Lamps of His Mouth.

First published in 2007
Reprinted 2012

The History Press
The Mill, Brimscombe Port,
Stroud, Gloucestershire, GL5 2QG
www.thehistorypress.co.uk

British Library Cataloguing in Publication Data.
A catalogue record for this book is available from the British Library.

ISBN 978 0 7524 4485 7

Typesetting and origination by
The History Press
Printed in Great Britain

CONTENTS

ACKNOWLEDGEMENTS

I would like to thank: the Local Studies staff at the AK Bell Library, Perth and the staff of the Inverness Library Reference section for their diligence and help; Adrian Shine of Loch Ness 2000 and Robbie Bremner, Ali Matheson and the staff of the Drumnadrochit Hotel (www.loch-ness-scotland.com); Joe Gibbs of Belladrum Estate (www.belladrum.co.uk); Iain Cameron, Katie Ellam and Frank Ellam of the South Loch Ness Heritage Group (www.southlochnessheritage.co.uk); Catherine Niven of Inverness Museum & Art Gallery (www.invernessmuseum.com); Kelvin Hunter of the Highlanders Regimental Museum, Fort George (www.historic-scotland.gov. uk); Isabel and Graeme Steel of the Old Parsonage Guest House, Croachy (www. bedbreakfast-scotland.com); Don Davidson of Abriachan Nurseries (www.lochness-garden.com); John and Ann Forsyth of Foyers; Janet and Tim Honnor of Westhill House B&B, Culloden (www.scotland-info.co.uk/westhill); James Williamson for designing the maps; and Ségolène Dupuy for driving, trike-care and cheerleading.

All photographs are by the author.

For more information visit www.geoffholder.co.uk.

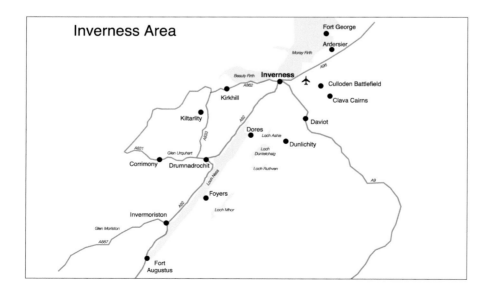

1

INTRODUCTION

It is a vertebrate that leaves no bones, a monster that cannot be dredged, a shape without a fixed design – a dragon of dreams, half-seen across the loch among mist spilled down from the hills… if there really were a monster, Loch Ness would still be the best place to hide it.

Richard Fortey, *The Hidden Landscape*

In Scotland, more boggles are seen and heard of than there are in all the rest of the world… *warlocks* without end, *worricows, kelpies, spunkies, wraiths, witchies* and *carlines*… Accounts of these supernatural beings will… show that the Scots are a nation not only famous for religion, war, learning and independence; but also for superstition.

John MacTaggart, *The Scottish Gallovidian Encyclopedia*, 1824

I shall be accused of having assembled lies, yarns, hoaxes and superstitions. To some degree I think so, myself. To some degree I do not. I offer the data.

Charles Fort, *Lo!*

A WELCOME TO A WORLD OF MARVELS AND WONDERS

This book ranges wide across many kinds of human and natural phenomena, mysteries and curiosities. As a general introduction, it could be said to include the following:

Encounters with and stories of non-human entities, typically ghosts, demons, fairies, spirits and loch monsters.

Death and the afterlife. This includes graveyards, tombstones carved with symbols of mortality, and prehistoric burial sites.

Religious phenomena, such as miracles, holy wells and superhuman saints.

Prehistoric ritual monuments – stone circles, standing stones and the like.

Mythological personages such as Fingal (Finn MacCool) and his war band the Fianna/Fionn, the Irish equivalent of King Arthur and the Knights of the Round Table.

Strange nature, such as out-of-place animals – especially big cats – or hot rain.

Aerial phenomena, from meteorites to UFOs.

Witchcraft and all kinds of magic.

Folklore (defined as broadly as you wish).

Tall tales, hoaxes and unlikely assertions.

Strange beliefs, curiosities of literature, and other oxbow lakes of culture.

Gargoyles, Pictish stones and other strange and marvellous sculpture.

The book is organised geographically. You can find everything mysterious and weird about one location in the same place, and the places flow logically with the traveller in mind. The book starts with Inverness and proceeds in an anti-clockwise route around the area. Cross-references to other locations are shown in CAPS. Things worth seeing are asterisked, from ★ to ★★★.

A FEW KEY CONCEPTS

Apotropaic. Protective against evil.

Fairies. Place names featuring the Gaelic word 'sith' (pronounced 'shee') are generally taken to mark an association with the fairies. 'Sithean' and 'Sidhean' ('shee-an') usually indicate fairy knolls or hills. Note that, in contrast to the Victorian idea of sweet-natured diminutive creatures, most of the fairies encountered in this book are duplicitous at best, and at worst dangerous, even lethal.

Liminality. That which is betwixt and between, a transition, a threshold. Very important in magic and encountering the supernatural. Liminality can apply to places (caves, bogs, rivers, boundaries) or times – holy wells are visited at Beltane (1 May), the dead can return on Hallowe'en, and Hogmanay has its own set of peculiar customs. Weddings, births and funerals are also liminal events.

Magical Thinking. 1. Certain things (a saint's relics, water from a special source, an unusual stone) have power. 2. This power can be accessed through proximity to the source. (So rich people paid large sums to be buried in church, the closer to the altar – the power source – the better.) 3. Things which have been connected once are connected for ever ('sympathetic magic').

Simulacra. Natural formations in trees and rocks which we, pattern-seeking apes that we are, interpret as faces, animals and 'Signs From God'.

Storytelling. Our species is misnamed – *Homo sapiens* (wise human) should be *Pan Narrans*, the storytelling ape. It is in our nature to take a chaotic series of events and turn it into a story. We do it all the time in our daily lives. Paranormal or strange events are often random and confusing, but they quickly become transformed into a ghost story or a monster sighting. Moral: don't depend on stories if you're looking for truth. See 'truth', below.

'Tradition.' Also known as 'it is said that', 'they say that', and other get-outs used by writers to bring a spurious *gravitas* to tall tales. Treat with caution.

Truth. Just because a respected chronicler from a previous age has written something down, doesn't make it true. And I'm often reporting the words of storytellers, fantasists, liars and journalists. *Caveat lector.*

Nessiemania: Plesiosaurs at Loch Ness 2000 (above) and Brachla Harbour (below).

Left: The Original Loch Ness Exhibition.

Opposite above: Plesiosaur at the Clansman Hotel.

Left: Fort Augustus.

Opposite below: Under the A9 at Brachla.

THE LOCH NESS MONSTER

There are marten cats and badgers
and foxes in the Enchanted Woods,
but there are, it seems, mightier creatures,
and the lake may hide what
neither net nor line can take.

W.B. Yeats, The Celtic Twilight

The main theories surrounding Nessie are:

1. The monster is real, and is a prehistoric reptile or similar creature.
2. The monster is real, and is either an animal already known to science (such as an eel or a sturgeon), or a similarly-sized aquatic animal either unknown to science, or known but not suspected to live in the loch. In this scenario, there is no 'monster' as such, although the animal may be larger than most other specimens of the species.
3. The monster is a manifestation from some Otherworld of the spirit or of demons.
4. There is no unusual creature in the loch – all sightings can be explained as hoaxes, known animals, misperception, boat wakes, natural if strange water phenomena, and the expectations of visitors (that is, you see something moving in a loch famous for its monster, and jump to certain conclusions). 'This business [of Loch Ness] serves as a kind of mirror reflecting human behaviour.' (Tim Dinsdale, monster hunter).

Is there a monster in Loch Ness? I have no idea. But for food for thought on points 2 and 4, I recommend the Loch Ness 2000 exhibition and Adrian Shine's book *Loch Ness*. For more on supernatural Nessie, see LOCHEND and URQUHART CASTLE. And as for Jurassic Nessie... a large reptile... in a cold nutrient-poor Scottish loch only formed in the Ice Age? It's not the most likely of scenarios.

The 'monster' of Loch Ness was created in 1933. In that year the creature was mentioned for the first time in national, as distinct from local, newspapers. In a short period reports went from describing a 'strange fish' (journalistically dull) to a 'monster' (journalistically very exciting). The 'journoverse' – the universe of press deadlines, newspaper competition, a story that runs and runs, and witnesses succumbing to the glamour of media attention – produced a heady, intoxicating 'cultural moment' which, to an extent, we are all living in the shadow of. Pre-1933 encounters were dusted off. People who had kept quiet for decades came forward with their stories. Nineteenth-century sightings surfaced. It is impossible to tell how much of all this was absolute scratch-glass-with-it true coin, and how much was encouraged by the heightened atmosphere of those days. Other monsters were also in the news – *King Kong*, with its animated dinosaurs, was doing great business – and soon the fateful word 'plesiosaurus' was used. The humped, long-necked, finned, small-headed plesiosaur, denizen of the oceans of the Jurassic and Cretaceous until sixty million years ago, became the received wisdom as to the monster's nature – despite many sightings being at variance with this.

I offer an analysis of the Loch Ness phenomenon based on a book by Michel Meurger, *Lake Monster Traditions: A Cross-Cultural Analysis*. Meurger, a Canadian folklorist, suggests all monster-inhabited lakes have in common a series of themes, themes which are shared across cultures and which make up what Meurger calls 'the mythical landscape' of the lake. This mythical landscape – which Meurger identifies with lakes in France, Germany, Switzerland, Austria and Canada as well as in other parts of Scotland – somehow strikes a deep chord within our psyches. In other words, if the themes are in place, then something in the human mind says, 'This is a place where lake monsters live.' Meurger's themes are:

Dark Water. Loch Ness is notoriously dark, with underwater lights being needed at even shallow depths. And if you can't see through the water, you can only imagine what could be there.

The Bottomless Lake. Within the loch is a place 'where all lost things go… an abyss, deeper than any other abyss in all of Scotland… [home to] an unshapely black mass dreaming of evil.' (Otta Swire, *The Highlands and their Legends.*) Swire records that when the soundings in advance of the construction of the Caledonian Canal failed to find bottom, the local people considered this to be a vindication of their beliefs. 'If you gaze long into an abyss, the abyss will gaze back into you.' (Friedrich Nietzsche).

The Lake That Does Not Give Up Its Dead. When she was a child Swire heard that the bodies of drowned people were never found. In 2007 several people told me the selfsame story. The case of Mary Hambro (see GLENDOEBEG) is a classic example of this motif.

The Terrified Divers. Once again, see the Hambro case, where the divers supposedly returned with fear-whitened hair. The motif may be seen as the consequence of the violation of a taboo – 'If you fathom me, I will swallow you.'

The Sucking Currents. These are held responsible for both drownings and the retention of the dead.

Underwater Caverns. In legend the loch has a vast subterranean cavern in which hide 'blind, white and viscous' monsters (Baumann, *The Loch Ness Monster*). The cavern also explains the lack of monster bones, because it is where Nessies go to die. The fact that there are no great caves under the waters of Loch Ness is irrelevant to the motif: here we have the stereotype of the dragon in its underground

Loch Ness from Borlum Bay.

lair. The media fuss over the discovery of 'Nessie's Cave', a 30ft (9m) hole in the surface of the loch floor, is the living echo of this theme.

Connecting Lakes. Any monster-lake worth its legend has to have a convenient network of passages and tunnels. For one example, see ALLTSIGH. For a connection between the loch and the volcanoes of southern Europe, see FORT AUGUSTUS.

The Eye-of-the-Sea and the Underwater Hell. This is a variant of the 'Connecting Lakes' motif, in which the lake is connected by a great hole to the uttermost depths of the ocean, an Otherworldly rather than geographical location. Through this hole demons erupt into our world. For an example of this motif in action, see the exorcism of Loch Ness at LOCHEND.

Meurger does not deny that eyewitnesses encounter strange things, or even that there may be real lake monsters, but notes that '*reality only proves the myth*, or rather, *with time the event becomes myth itself.*' So, for example, with the 'Terrified Diver' motif: 'The lengthening of the years removes the particulars from the truth – e.g. the names of the divers and other details – in order to raise it to the level of a *fixed model*, an intangible "Terrified Diver".' Any modern person encountering what might be the Loch Ness Monster does so through the lens of both this 'mythical landscape' and the constantly evolving contemporary 'aquatic legend' of the monster itself, where '*facts* have been integrated in the web of the fable.' (Original emphasis throughout).

To summarise all the records of sightings would take an entire book (and indeed there are several excellent books which treat the subject in depth – see the bibliography). What I have done in the main text is to include especially interesting episodes – of all kinds, from sightings to hoaxes and Nessie-ania – related to a particular place. Each Nessie entry is marked by the ᵕₙᵣ icon.

> Kelpie: this British and Irish water demon can take various shapes… The world's largest kelpie is found in Loch Ness, Scotland. Its favourite form is that of a sea serpent. International Confederation of Wizard observers realised they were not dealing with a true serpent when they saw it turn into an otter on the approach of a team of Muggle★ investigators and then transform back into a serpent when the coast was clear.
>
> Newt Scamander (J.K. Rowling), *Fantastic Beasts and Where To Find Them*

★Muggles – ordinary humans without magical powers.

ARCHAEOLOGY

> Grey recumbent tombs of the dead in desert places,
> Standing stones on the vacant wine-red moor,
> Hills of sheep, and the howes of the silent vanished races,
> And winds, austere and pure.
>
> Robert Louis Stevenson, *Songs of Travel*

When discussing prehistoric archaeological sites I have concentrated largely on ritual and funerary monuments. Pre-eminent among them are the many chambered cairns – stone-built structures with a central chamber for the deposition of bodies. There are two major classifications of chambered cairns in the area, known to archaeologists as Orkney-Cromarty and Clava-type cairns. The former tend to be found on upland areas and have subdivided rectangular burial chambers, while the latter are usually in river valleys, and typically have circular chambers with corbelled roofs and, most spectacularly, a ring of standing stones around the cairn, hence the usual term 'ring-cairns'. *The* book on the subject is Henshall and Ritchie's *The Chambered Cairns of the Central Highlands*. The best 'Clava' sites to visit are at CORRIMONY, GASK and the CLAVA CAIRNS themselves. Also featured are sites with prehistoric rock art, typically 'cupmarks', the purpose of which remains a matter of speculative discussion – choose from agricultural, astronomical or ritual functions, communication with the dead or the gods, or mundane calculations. Archaeological terms used include:

Neolithic – *c*. 4000-2500 BC

Bronze Age – *c*. 2500-800 BC: the Neolithic and Bronze Ages were the periods of the chambered cairns, standing stones and cupmarked stones.

Iron Age – *c*. 800 BC to the early centuries AD: this was the period of the historical Druids.

Picts – Dark Ages peoples, from the early centuries AD to the tenth century.

THE SAINTS

There are numerous legends that various undeniably ancient churches in the Great Glen were originally founded by Dark Ages saints such as Ninian, Merchard, Drostan, Baithan, Cumine, Adomnan and Columba. Unfortunately all we have to support this are long-standing traditions, with no documentary and archaeological evidence. The only exception to this is St Columba, who is described visiting the area (possibly in around AD 565) in St Adomnan's *Life of Columba*, written in around AD 700. Adomnan mentions several place names around the loch, and although elsewhere the *Life* takes on the fabulous forms of Dark Ages hagiography – Columba performs miracles and magic, bests Druids and overcomes wild beasts, all to prove the superiority of Christianity over paganism – the geographical details Adomnan provides suggest he may well have been describing a genuine journey or series of journeys.

Even here, however, no mention is made of Columba founding specific churches, so it is impossible to assess the historical claims of those sites in the area for which a Columban origin is mooted. Many works suggest Columba came to the Great Glen to convert Brude, king of the Northern Picts. A close reading of Adomnan makes it clear Brude did not convert to Christianity; rather, Columba had journeyed from his outpost of Christian civilisation on Iona to conduct a diplomatic mission to his powerful neighbours to the north. For Adomnan's description of Columba's triumph over a monster in the River (not Loch) Ness, see LOCHEND.

THE BRAHAN SEER

> Highlanders, seeking an explanation for momentous events, find it in prophecy. People searching for answers to sorrow and tragedy find comfort in the fact that they were pre-ordained… Coinneach Odhar is both scapegoat and prophet… he was created out of a need and he is kept alive for the same reason.
> Elizabeth Sutherland, *Ravens and Black Rain*

There are a number of references in the book to the prophecies of the so-called Brahan Seer, Coinneach Odhar. Many of the prophecies were collected – or imaginatively reconstructed – by Alexander Mackenzie in his book *The Prophecies of the Brahan Seer*, first published in 1877 and perennially popular. Mackenzie places the seer in East Ross-shire in the seventeenth century. There was a historical Kenneth or Keanoch Ower, but the records show him to be the (probably gypsy) leader of five other men and twenty-six women accused of witchcraft in 1577, that is, a century earlier.

The folkloric relationship between the little-known but documented sixteenth-century sorcerer and the famous but undocumented (and possibly fictional) seventeenth-century seer is extensively discussed in William Matheson's 'The Historical Coinneach Odhar and Some Prophecies Attributed to Him' (*TGSI*) and in Sutherland's book, quoted earlier. It is clear that, even if the seer did exist, he did not utter all the prophecies attributed to him, and many 'prophecies' were only written down after the events they describe came to pass. 'Coinneach Odhar is no more than a collective name for a number of *taibhsears* [seers], a magnet that has drawn to itself the whole of Highland prophetic history. There was a man called Coinneach Odhar; there are a host of prophecies. From these two facts, folklore has woven its own rich and colourful tapestry, a living, growing mystery that cannot properly explained.'

⚘ Prophecies attributed to the seer continue to circulate and be invented, often in the press. On 5 September 1984 the *Glasgow Herald* quoted a hitherto-unknown prophecy of the seer: 'When the Loch Ness Monster is captured, Inverness will be engulfed in flame and flood.' In 1984 there was a much-publicised attempt to trap Nessie in a large underwater cage: the journoverse strikes again.

THE CLANS

Highland clan society before the Battle of Culloden is often simplified as a 'warrior culture'. In some descriptions this becomes a code for honour, fidelity, courage and martial prowess. From the victims' point of view, a culture that valorised cattle theft, murder, abduction, church-burning and endless vendettas may be viewed less favourably. As with so much else, the way you view clan history will depend on your own perspective. But I recommend leaving any rose-tinted eyewear behind.

THE BATTLE OF CULLODEN

The Jacobites were supporters of the Stuart claim to the throne (from *Jacobus*, Latin for James, this being James II of England/VII of Scotland, who was deposed in 1689). Following the inconclusive 1715 rebellion led by James' son James Edward Stuart, the Government increased its military presence in the Highlands. In 1745 the third generation of Stuart claimants, Charles Edward, known to supporters as 'Bonnie Prince Charlie' (BPC from hereon) landed in Scotland from exile and instigated the final sorry chapter. BPC – a poor leader and a man with an archaic view of governance – didn't deserve the devotion the clansmen lavished on him (the First World War phrase, 'lions led by donkeys' comes to mind). After some considerable military success the Jacobites were comprehensively defeated at the Battle of CULLODEN in April 1746. The battle and its aftermath is a major factor in the folklore of the area. The victorious Hanoverian government embarked on a brutal campaign: prisoners were executed, and Jacobites and non-partisans alike were persecuted, burned out, raped and murdered. Prominent Jacobites went into hiding – the caves where they allegedly hid are scattered around the area – and BPC led the troopers a merry dance through the heather before slipping away to the Continent to eventually degenerate into a disappointed drunk. The visible symbols of Highland culture – bagpipes, tartan – were banned, and, over time, the entire quasi-medieval, semi-feudal nature of Highland clan society was dismantled.

ALEISTER CROWLEY

Crowley owned BOLESKINE House on the south shore of Loch Ness between 1899 and 1918. In the relatively little time he spent there during that period he practised magick (spelt with a 'k' to distinguish it from stage illusion) and allegedly raised demons. Until his death in 1947, Crowley remained the twentieth century's most publicly visible master of the dark arts, but despite his intellectual energy, his exploration of altered states, his extensive writings and his claim to be the founder of a new religion which would sweep away Christianity, he was known not for magick, but for immorality. Crowley craved recognition, but what he achieved was simply notoriety. Having been brought up within the strict Plymouth Brethren, his psychology included a lifelong need to attack Christianity and conventional morality, no matter how childish the means or negative the consequences for both himself and those around him. It is not my intention to be an apologist for Crowley – there is a great deal about him that is repellent and vile – but it is perhaps worth putting a few things in perspective, including his oft-quoted label, 'the Wickedest Man in the World'.

Crowley described himself as 'The Great Beast 666', which is standard Crowleyan Christian-baiting, but 'the Wickedest Man' phrase was the title of one of a series of articles on Crowley by the right-wing publication *John Bull*. (The piece came out on 24 March 1923; the titles of its previous two vitriolic attacks, 'The King of Depravity' and 'A Wizard of Wickedness' have had no such shelf life.) By May 1923 (when *John Bull* published a piece called 'A Man We'd Like to Hang') Crowley had been expelled from Sicily – by Mussolini's fascists. So, on the one hand we have an egomaniac who was deeply unpleasant to his friends and supporters, and on the other one of the most brutal dictators of the twentieth century. Somehow the name 'the Wickedest Man in the World' seems to be misapplied.

I know arguing from analogy is philosophically unsound, but I suggest another way of evaluating Crowley may be to compare him with John Lennon. Lennon was responsible for placing Crowley on the cover of *Sgt Pepper's Lonely Hearts Club Band*, thus introducing him to a new generation for whom Crowley's sex-and-drugs lifestyle was not a bad thing. Although he never reached Crowleyan levels of abuse, Lennon frequently behaved appallingly to those close to him, but his reputation rests with Lennon the artist, not Lennon the man. The popular perception of Crowley, in contrast, is of the man and not the magician. And it is this reputation that continues to distort the cultural space around Crowley – and around Loch Ness. Al has become the *de facto* local bogeyman, fatuously invoked any time something comes up that even hints of black magic, ritual or sacrifice. For examples of this, see ABRIACHAN, BUNLOIT and BOLESKINE.

SOURCES

Many references come from the *New Statistical Account* (*NSA*), published in 1845, where each parish was described by its Church of Scotland minister. A number of articles cited as *TGSI* are from various years of the learned *Transactions of the Gaelic Society of Inverness* (see the bibliography for full details). Where the source is given as 'Field Club', this refers to the book, *The Hub of the Highlands*, published by the estimable Inverness Field Club in 1975.

Much more on archaeological sites can be found on the online 'Canmore' database of the Royal Commission on the Ancient and Historical Monuments of Scotland, www.rcahms.gov.uk. For a peek into the contemporary megalithic community, I recommend www.themodernantiquarian.com.

MAPS AND EXPLORING

The best maps for trying to track down obscure sites are definitely the Ordnance Survey 1:25000 Explorer series, particularly 415-417, 422 and 431. If you are heading onto the moors or hills, be prepared for volatile and vicious weather. Loch Ness is cold, deep and dark, not a place for swimming, and on a bad day venturing out on a boat can feel like being at sea. Note that walking or cycling along the A82 on the north shore of the loch is very dangerous. The Great Glen Way offers an alternative, although it's pretty boring between Drumnadrochit and Fort Augustus, with the forestry plantations hiding the loch.

THE SCOTTISH OUTDOOR ACCESS CODE

Everyone has the right to be on most land and inland water, providing they act responsibly. Your access rights and responsibilities are explained fully in the Scottish Outdoor Access Code. Find out more by visiting www.outdooraccess-scotland.com or phoning your local Scottish Natural Heritage office.

The key things are to take responsibility for your own actions, respect the interests of other people and to care for the environment. Access rights can be exercised over most of Scotland, from urban parks and path networks to our hills and forests, and from farmland and field margins to our beaches, lochs and rivers. However, access rights don't apply everywhere, such as in buildings or their immediate surroundings, or in houses or their gardens, or most land in which crops are growing.

Many sites in this book are near houses and other private property; always ask permission – it's simple good manners. Don't disturb animals (wild or domestic). Respect the countryside and the sites – do not scrape away lichen, leave offerings, do any damage or drop litter (even better, pick litter up – it's good karma).

2

INVERNESS

Thou dost frighten me with dreams
And terrify me with visions.

Job 7:14

There are a number of stories and events that have no more precise home than simply 'Inverness', so I have collated them at the start here. They also act as a taster of the wonders, marvels and oddities that populate this book:

Weird nature: Inverness and the Great Glen is an active seismic zone and over the years a number of minor tremors have been recorded. On 30 June 1819 there was a small earthquake, the immediate consequence of which was that hot rain briefly fell on the town.

Second sight, dreams and visions: In 1892 a young Inverness policeman dreamt he was at the Northern Meeting Games the next day. There, he was handed a telegram informing him that the Duke of Sutherland, who was expected to attend, had died at 10.30 p.m. the night before. The policeman woke up and related the dream to his family. Then the phone rang: it was the chief constable, telling him that the duke had died the night before at 10.30 p.m. (Source: James Robertson, *Scottish Ghost Stories*.)

Two seers both visited the manse of an Inverness minister. One, 'a common fellow', cried out that a woman five miles away was either dead or dying. The second seer, of gentler birth, disagreed. 'Can't you see her covered in her winding sheet?' said the first. 'Aye,' replied the gentleman, 'I see her as well as you do, but do you not also see that her linen is wet with sweat? She will soon be cooling of her fever.' (Source: John Aubrey's seventeenth-century *Miscellanies*, quoted in Sutherland, *Ravens and Black Rain*.)

Strange powers: Blood-staunching at a distance required a gift called in Gaelic *casg fola*, blood-stopping. It was essential to know the exact name of the patient or the charm would not work. A girl in the neighbourhood of Inverness had a tooth extracted. The doctor could not help with the copious bleeding so a friend contacted a farmer who had the *casg fola*. The healer immediately went into a closet and uttered a charm. It was 10.15 p.m. He came out and told the friend the bleeding had stopped. On his return the man found the girl's wound had stopped bleeding at the exact time. (Source: Francis Thompson, *The Supernatural Highlands*.)

Legends, magic and the mythologised landscape: in 'Highland Superstition' *(TGSI*, 1888) Alexander MacBain relates how the great medieval Scottish wizard/intellectual (take your pick) Michael Scott nearly dammed up the mouth of the River Ness with a mound of sand built by 'the little men he commanded.' The mound 'is still to be seen.'

Strange things in the sky: two large, bright lights that looked like stars, sometimes stationary, but occasionally moving at high velocity across the sky. (Source: *London Times*, 19 September 1848, quoted in Charles Fort's *Book of the Damned*.)

Hauntings and spirits: Dane Love in *Scottish Spectres* records a haunted Inverness B&B where Helen MacLellan awoke in the middle of the night to see man at the foot of her bed. He seemed to be washing his face; he disappeared when the light was put on. Other times, footsteps were heard coming from empty rooms. The house formerly belonged to a guard on the railway. Norman Adams (*Haunted Scotland*) briefly mentions an actor, a cast member of the pantomime showing at the time, *Aladdin*, who said she had been spooked by an old female ghost at her Inverness lodgings. Please resist the temptation to cry, 'She's behind you!' etc.

Fairies: There was a fairy well somewhere in the town. If a poor woman had a sickly child she would leave it there with a small offering such as some milk. In the morning the elf child would be gone and her own healthy child restored. (Source: J.M. McPherson, *Primitive Beliefs in the North-East of Scotland*.)

Witchcraft and magic: An old woman in Inverness, aggrieved at her minister because he had denied her Holy Communion, made a corp crèadha, an image of the man. As it decayed, he became very ill. The image was eventually discovered and the minister recovered. (Source: McPherson again.)

Bodysnatching, and things gruesome and ghoulish: in the early nineteenth century a woman begged a lift when a cart passed her at Abriachan. There were two or three men in the seat. Near Inverness she looked around and saw a toe protruding from the loose covering, which she could now clearly see was in the shape of a corpse. She kept silent and counted herself lucky not to have joined the body. (Source: Alexander MacDonald, *Story and Song from Loch Ness-Side*.)

A child of Dr John Inglis Nicol died and was buried in a grave next to that of another child. After the funeral Dr Nicol was seen to place a mark on the second child's grave. The child's father investigated and after dark saw a luminous sign on the gravestone, which he swapped onto the grave of the doctor's child. Later that night Dr Nicol and an associate lifted the body. His wife recognised her child's clothes, and died of the shock. (Source: Leonella Longmore, *Inverness in the 18th Century*.)

Religious phenomena and odd beliefs: On 9 June 2001 the *Scotsman* reported that twenty-four women from a religious community in Inverness took out insurance against immaculate conception before the millennium. The cover was meant to pay for the cost of bringing up Christ if one of the women had a virgin birth. According to Goodfellows, the insurance company that provided the £1 million policy, more than 15,000 women around the world, particularly those called Mary or Maria, believed that not only was the Second Coming due at the millennium, but that they themselves might be the mother of the next messiah.

An item on the BBC News website on 22 June 2006 took the story further – the insurance company had been forced to cancel the cover following complaints by the Catholic Church. By this date the company had changed to Britishinsurance. com and the number of Inverness virgins continuing to make plans for bringing up the baby Jesus had shrunk to just three siblings. The women had renewed the £100 annual policy since 2000, and the burden of proof that the child was Christ had rested with them. The Catholic Church declined to comment.

If you thought this story could not get any stranger, the original 2001 article also listed the other hazards Goodfellows would insure you against: alien abduction, being impregnated by an extraterrestrial, having an alien microchip inserted into your body, injury caused by a Yeti, Bigfoot, Loch Ness Monster, ghost or poltergeist, and being transformed against your will into a werewolf or vampire.

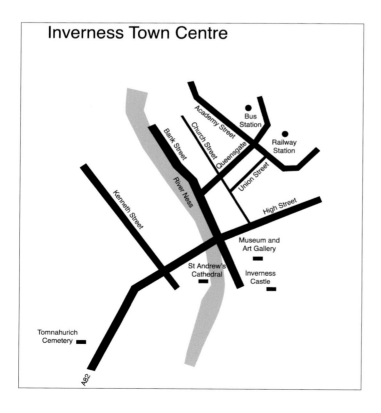

Carved head on Highland Rail
House, Inverness.

INVERNESS – MYTHICAL ORIGINS

As with many other Scottish cities, Inverness lays claim to be not merely historic
but ancient, with a pedigree stretching back to Classical times. For example, the
sixteenth-century writer Hector Boece says the city was founded by Evenus II,
the fourteenth King of Scotland, who died in 60 BC. William Mackay, in his
editorial comments on *The Letter-Book of Bailie John Steuart of Inverness 1715-1752*,
notes that a petition presented to the people of Inverness in 1626 by James VI
states the town's 'foundation was long before the birth of Christ.'

Boece's *History of Scotland*, once highly regarded, is now seen as a mix of fantasy
and fiction; there is no historical basis for the founding myth, nor for the story,
propagated by several writers down the ages, that a Roman fort was established
at Bona, where the River Ness exits Loch Ness. Gerald Pollitt (*Historic Inverness*)
mentions another tradition without a basis in reality, where the Beauly Firth
supposedly did not exist and the rivers Ness and Farrar formed a single super-
river flowing through what is now the Firth, joining the sea somewhere east of
Chanonry Point.

The actual foundation of Inverness is obscured in the uncertainties of a poor
historical record. The Pictish king Brude had a stronghold in the area in the sixth
century; this could have been on Auldcastle Hill in the Crown area of the city,
although there are several other just as likely candidates further afield. By the
tenth century there may have been some sort of township here. A century later
Macbeth may have had his fort on Auldcastle Hill as well, but all later fortifica-
tions of the Middle Ages were set up on the present Castle Hill, around which the
town developed.

Inverness Castle.

INVERNESS CASTLE★

The current castle (occupied by the Sheriff Court, so not usually open to the public unless you sit in the public gallery during trials) dates from 1836, on a site occupied by several castles since the twelfth or eleventh century. Its strategic position overlooks a fording point (later replaced by a bridge) across the River Ness; controlling the river crossings here meant controlling the area. Whoever was in charge in a given year had a tendency to fix the heads of enemies on the castle walls. King William the Lion did it with the rebellious Donald Ban MacWilliam's head in 1181, and in September 1562 Mary Queen of Scots repeated the act with the severed head of the garrison captain, who had refused her admission to the castle (the rest of the tiny garrison got off with perpetual imprisonment or, on Mary's whim, were just released without punishment). In the 1720s, when the castle was being rebuilt, three soldiers dug up a corpse near the door: when touched it fell to dust and the troopers fled. Edward Burt, an officer in the English military, remarked to one of the townsmen that it was strange the body should be so close to the door. The Invernessian replied, 'Troth, I dinno doubt but this was ane of Mary's lovers.' The next day the man tried to take back his unguarded words to the English visitor, which only confirmed Burt's impression that there was a local tradition about the fate that awaited anyone who ventured into the bed of Mary Queen of Scots. The episode is in Burt's *Letters*. Roddy Maclean (*The Gaelic Place Names and Heritage of Inverness*) mentions Alasdair Beag of the Huagh who regularly met the silent ghost of an officer in a small workshop in the castle.

INVERNESS MUSEUM & ART GALLERY★★★ (CASTLE WYND)

Every museum of any substance has within its collections items that speak of magic, ritual, or customs and beliefs, and IMAG is no exception. Here's a quick guide to the best of the displays:

First floor: A small case on 'Myths, Legends and Fantastic Creatures' includes:

'The Bernera Goddess'★★ – an impressively large whalebone, crudely carved with eyes and mouth, reputedly found in a burial mound on the Hebridean island of Bernera.

Six polished witchstones★ used to cast curses, and a linen bag of pebbles used to cure cattle.

A medieval spindle whorl pierced for use as a pendant, a talisman against the Evil Eye.

A wooden ladle used to remove the Evil Eye. 'The sufferer drank water from the ladle, which contained a piece of silver, whilst standing under a bridge.' You can find descriptions of this practice in the entries for KILTARLITY, ABRIACHAN and GLENMORISTON.

'Elf's arrow' pendant – a Neolithic arrowhead mounted in silver, used as an amulet.

Three sea beans – tropical beans washed up on a West Highland beach and thought to protect sailors from drowning. Also two polished pebbles that imitate the look of sea beans and hence offered the same protection.

A gold and a copper luckenbooth heart, either given as tokens of love or sewn into a child's bedding or clothes as protection against fairies. The name comes from 'locked booth', the wooden booths or shops clustered around Edinburgh Cathedral.

Several heart-shaped charms worn by nineteenth-century Highland soldiers at FORT GEORGE; they provided invulnerability in battle.

An ivory horseshoe and a silver brooch topped with a cross.

In other cases:

Ring brooches. The largest has three animals whose tails branch into foliage.

A modern silver brooch of the Ardross Wolf (see below).

Carved wooden quaiches with silver mounts, inspired by the Arts and Crafts movement and decorated with interlace and oak leaves. One has a fierce toothed foliaceous beast in the foliage and serpents for handles. Another has luckenbooth-style silver lugs.

Two gold and one silver luckenbooth brooches.

Numerous Jacobite items clearly regarded as 'relics' by those who owned them, including fragments of BPC's hair and plaid, and a copy of BPC's death mask.

More interesting are examples of covert Jacobite propaganda and communication, such as a dice box and silver caskets with concealed portraits of BPC, inscribed drinking glasses to secretly toast the 'king over the water' (the rose is code for King James, and the word 'Fiat' means 'may it come to pass') and tartan silk garters woven with the messages, 'then we will fight in armour bright to pull usurpers down' and 'God bless the Prince who had long since a right to the crown'.

Other relics refer to Charles I, including a pendant with his hair and a fragment of his execution block decorated with a tiny skull and crossbones, and, quite bizarrely, a medallion from the 'Society of King Charles the Martyr', a still current Anglican organisation who regard Charles I as a saint, a sentence which one feels deserves at the very least one exclamation mark, if not two.

There is also a portrait of Oliver Cromwell★ displayed upside down as it was by its original owner, who clearly cared little for the regicide.

Ground floor: There is a good collection of carved Pictish stones featuring symbols such as 'mirror and combs', 'double discs' and 'crescent and V-rods'. The best stones are the Ardross Wolf★★ and Lochardil Bull★★★.

Ritual objects include an eighth-century cannel coal pendant★ with a Christian cross on one side and pagan entwined serpents on the other (clearly designed for the person who wants to stay on the good side of any currently active gods) and two Neolithic carved stone balls★. These latter items are truly mysterious – great effort was required to carve them, but they have no obvious function. Suggestions include badges of office (chiefship or priestship) or 'talking stones' – only if you hold the stone can you speak at a tribal gathering, or address the gods.

Other archaeological curiosities and marvels include a cupmarked stone★ from CLAVA, a piece of vitrified rock from CRAIG PHADRIG, a tiny bone sword★ (toy or charm?), a twelfth-century zoomorphic buckle gripped by two grotesque beasts★, and a Bronze Age urn with cremated bones and a bone toggle, from the Neolithic cairn at RAIGMORE. My favourite item is a pot quern★★ from the Dominican Friary, with a grotesque human face through whose mouth the flour poured. And we can't forget 'Felicity'★★, the puma caught near Cannich in 1980, living (or now, stuffed) proof that out-of-place big cats roam the Highlands (see KILTARLITY and ARDERSIER).

Two very different walking tours leave from in front of the Tourist Office on Bridge Street – a gruesome horror walk led by 'Davy the Ghost', and a story walk run by Highland storyteller Greg Dawson Allen.

TOWN HOUSE★ (CORNER OF CASTLE AND HIGH STREETS)

This imposing late-Victorian municipal building has a superb single gargoyle poking out onto Castle Street and, on the opposite side, a coat of arms taken from the now-gone 1686 bridge. The front façade features the arms of the former Royal Burgh of Inverness – a crucifix on a shield under a cornucopia, all flanked by an elephant and a camel. There is another version on the glass of the front door, with the two beasts standing awkwardly on their hind legs. It's not entirely clear why two African animals should be on the Inverness coat of arms, but perhaps the undignified poses they were forced into influenced their being dropped when the arms ceased following the demise of the Burgh title in 1975. The building was part-funded by a bequest from Duncan Grant of Bught, hence the burning rock of the Grant crest on the centre windows in the hall, and the Macrae crest, a hand brandishing a short sword (Mrs Grant was a Macrae). The windows in the hall feature the crests of Highland clans, with the Campbells and MacDonalds being as far apart as possible.

BRIDGE STREET – MARKET CROSS

This stands outside the Town Hall. The present unicorn-topped structure, restored several times, was put up in 1768. The earlier cross was somewhere in this area, and formed the very centre of old Inverness. In December 1643 it was the site of the burning of 'ane Idolatrous Image called St Finane', formerly kept in a private house in DUNLICHITY. In 1746 Duncan MacRae of Kintail, suspected of spying for the Jacobites, was hanged from an apple tree growing in front of the Town Hall. Traditionally, the tree immediately withered and died. At the foot of the cross is Clachnacuddin, the stone of the tubs and the symbol of Inverness. Other cities have an omphalos or fulcrum stone associated in legend with a saint, warrior or mythical founder: in Inverness it's a stone where housewives rested their baskets of washing while they stopped for a blether after climbing the slope from the river. (Although Roddy Maclean suggests an earlier, grander origin, in which the stone was the inauguration stone when the Lords of the Isles were installed as Lords of Lochalsh.) Invernessians were known as Sons of Clachnacuddin; great numbers of pieces were chipped off the stone for use as amulets when travelling, so in 1900 it was protected by being lowered and made flush with the pavement.

HIGH STREET – THE ATHENAUM*

This now mostly-ignored 1815 building, opposite the Town House, is carved with a number of Biblical quotations. Dr John Mackenzie, Provost of Inverness between 1867 and 1873, refrained from alcohol on religious grounds. Finding himself thus in a minority of one on the council, he had the words from the Bible put up as a rebuke to his fellow councillors, who would hardly miss them from the main steps of the Town House. Some are obviously about the evils of drink, while others show Mackenzie's moral stance on other matters. They include:

James II.19–20 'Thou believest that there is one God, thou doest well: the Devils also believe, and tremble. But wilt thou know, O vain man, that faith without works is dead.'

James IV.7 'Resist the Devil, and he will flee from you.'

Habakkuk II.15 'Woe unto him that giveth his neighbour drink, that puttest thy bottle to him, and makest him drunken also.'

Revelation XXI.8 'All liars shall have their part in the lake which burneth with fire and brimstone.'

I Corinthians VI.9–10 'Be not deceived: neither fornicators, nor adulterers, nor thieves, nor drunkards, shall inherit the Kingdom of Heaven.'

BRIDGE STREET – THE STEEPLE

This tall spire on the corner of Bridge Street and Church Street used to be the steeple of the old jail or tollbooth, 'the most dirty and offensive prison in all of Scotland'. Mhairi MacDonald, in *By the Banks of the Ness*, relates how in September 1709 the town clerk paid for a cart of peats to be burnt in it to try and remove the smell. The 'thieves' chamber' for incarcerating criminals opened into the court and smelt so bad the judges were at times almost overcome. In 1690 a stone spire was added to the tower, with spikes on the battlements for criminals' heads. In 1791 a new jail was erected but this one was just as inadequate as its predecessor. The steeple dates from this period. The foundation stone was laid with full Masonic honours by the brethren of two Lodges wearing black coats, vests and breeches with white stockings and gloves. The spire was damaged by an earthquake on the 13 August 1816, twisting it out of alignment *à la* the crooked spire of Chesterfield. This became something of a tourist attraction, so there was adverse comment when the damage was repaired in 1828. The lower and larger of the three balls on the spire contains a time capsule – holding coins, newspapers, photographs and a pint of Millburn whisky.

WITCHCRAFT

For this is man's nature, that where he is persuaded that there is the power to bring prosperity and adversity, there will he worship.

George Gifford, *A Discourse of the Subtill Practices of Devilles by Witches and Sorcerers*, 1587

In the sixteenth, seventeenth and early eighteenth centuries post-Reformation Scotland went through a socio-religious spasm in which ordinary people were seen to be in league with malign demonic forces bent on subverting both Protestantism and the kingdom itself. Satan and his hundreds of imps were omnipresent. This mindset encouraged the searching out, interrogation and execution of those deemed guilty of the crime of witchcraft. Torture, which was legal in Scotland, was widely used to extract confessions. The tollbooth held the instruments – thumbkins, bootkins, branks, cuckstool, stocks and pillory. Where the episodes below do not have a specific credit, the information has been collected from a variety of sources, notably Roy J.M. Pugh, *The Deil's Ain*, Alexander Polson's *Scottish Witchcraft Lore*, Leonella Longmore, *Inverness in the 18th Century*, and the *Survey of Scottish Witchcraft* database at www.arts.ed.ac.uk/witches.

The first notice in the town records is from 7 March 1558, when Sandy Macillmertin was 'judged in amerciement for saying in open market to Henry Kerr, elder, that his servant had put witchcraft in his net.' On 26 July 1572 Agnes Cuthbert had to apologise in church for saying she had put witchcraft into Christina Dingwall's ale so she could not sell it. Neither of these resulted in any kind of serious punishment, but things were soon to change. On 2 December 1603, Donald Moir Macpherson/Mackferquhar was found guilty of 'having visited Robert Stuart, baker, who was ill in bed in his workhouse and having charmed him with enchantment and devilish witchcraft.' Donald had also used a spell to kill his victim's dog. He was burnt on the Haugh. In 1655 Malcolm McConel suffered some kind of non-capital punishment (such as branding and/or banishment), and Andro McGibbone either died from torture or suicide, or escaped from prison. On 26 June 1662 Issobell Duff was executed; on 30 September of the same year, a witchpricker called John Dickson was arrested and revealed to be a woman, Christian Cauldwell or Caddell. She had pretended to be a burgess from Forfar and had worked for officials in Moray, where the pay was 6 shillings a day and £6 for every witch who was found guilty, and she had also pricked witches in Elgin, Forres, Nairn, Inverness, Ross and Sutherland. It is possible she sent fourteen women to their deaths. Cauldwell worked alongside Issobell Dick, and claimed to be able to spot witches by sight, simply by looking into their eyes. Her mentor had been John Kincaid, a witchpricker from the Lothians. In July of the same year another female witchpricker dressed as a man had been involved in the horrific torture of up to seventeen people who were simply the inconvenient tenants of a grasping laird; for the story, see KIRKHILL.

A great deal of folklore has accumulated about the execution of Creibh (or Cré Mhór) and her sister. In 1842 John Maclean, 'the Clachnacuddin Nonagenarian' described how Cré/Creibh lived with her sister in the Millburn valley (a mile east of Inverness), a sinister place still notorious for witches and ghosts in 1745. Cré made a living selling charms. Some children found a corp crèadha stuck with pins in the burn. One of the children said she often saw her grandmother, Creibh Mhor, make such things. The effigy was identified as that of Cuthbert of Castle Hill, a prominent merchant in the town. Gossip spread and Creibh was arrested and tortured. She denied the accusations but her sister, similarly violated, confessed, and both were burnt at the stake. Before her death Creibh indicated that many of the rich women in attendance to see her burn had been customers for her charms. Hugh Barron in 'Verse, Story and Fragments from Various Districts' in the *TGSI*, citing the anonymous 1891 work *The Witch of Inverness and the Fairies of Tomnahurich*, says Creibh fled to Flichity in Strathnairn. Before being burned in Inverness she cursed Flichity (for a different version of this story, see FLICHITY).

Alexander Polson (*Scottish Witchcraft Lore*) says at the stake she cried for water. An onlooker went to get some but when 'a so-called wise man' learnt it was for her he poured it onto the ground. Creibh cursed the crowd and said, 'if only I had gotten a mouthful of that water I would have turned Inverness into a peat bog.' The *Celtic Annual* for 1913 repeats an old song sung about the witch: 'Be you treated like a victim of Big Cré in Inverness; what agony she suffered, she richly deserved it; She would put the saddle on the man of her house; The marks of the hooves that turned back into hands; and the bit of the reins ground down on his mouth.' The folkloric Creibh and her sister are probably the same people as the two married women called McQuicken and McRorie burned in 1695, the last women executed for witchcraft in Inverness. John Noble, in *Miscellania Invernessiana*, notes that George Cuthbert of Castle Hill, sheriff-depute of Inverness-shire, who had persecuted many witches, and may have been the intended victim of the corp crèadha, fell off his horse and died in 1748. The spot was the Millburn, Creibh's stamping ground: 'With the characteristic weakness of popular superstition, Mr Cuthbert's death was, and is, looked upon as the retributive act of those weird sisters whose companions had suffered by his command.'

In 1704 George and Lachlan Rattray were convicted of 'Maleficium', one of the standard descriptions of evil witchcraft. The proceedings dragged on for two years, with the executions reprieved several times. Many authorities say they were burned but it appears that at the last minute their sentence was commuted to banishment. It is hard to tell what was going on, as there are no details given, but it may be that doubts about the reality of witchcraft were starting to creep into the judicial mind. The last execution for witchcraft took place in the 1720s; by 1736 the crime had been taken off the statute books.

In the 1740s a man at Millburn, aggrieved at thefts from his field of peas, kept watch at night. A group of pranksters dressed up as witches and scared him into fainting.

The *Inverness Courier* of 3 May 1837 reported the discovery of a clay corp crèadha in a burn near Inverness. The head was carefully sculptured and fastened to the body and arms by red silk threads, and the whole thing was pierced by several pins and needles.

J.M. McPherson, in *Primitive Beliefs in the North-East of Scotland*, quotes the *Macclesfield Courier* of 22 December 1883 about a case at the court in Inverness. An elderly Highland woman called Isabella Macrae or Stewart, from Muirton Street, Inverness, was charged with assaulting a little girl:

> Towards the close of the case, great amusement was caused in court by the accused producing a clay image or corp crèadha which she believed was made by a so-called witch. The legs had been broken off the image, and since then the prisoner believed that her own legs were losing their strength. A gentleman who wished to purchase the image after the accused had left the court was promptly told that on no account would she part with it, for if anything happened to it in this gentleman's possession, she might die and she was not prepared to die yet. She therefore wished to keep the image in safety, so long as it would hold together, for so long as the image lasted she believed its baleful influences upon her would be ineffectual. The image was about four inches in length: green worsted threads containing the diabolic charm were wound about, while pins were pierced through where the heart should be.

In the 1880s a woman and her daughter, taking the Kessock Ferry to Inverness, encountered a reputed witch, who said: 'What a pretty little mouth you have got.' Almost at once the girl's face twisted to one side and stayed that way for a month (Alexander Polson, *Scottish Witchcraft Lore*).

Man crowned with cornucopias: Iguana
Wana, Church Street.

CHURCH STREET

In 1830 workmen digging a sewer found many trunks of fossil oak and several
deer's horns, one of which had prehistoric tool marks. When the former well at
Nos 29-33 was excavated, curious dark brown soft stones resembling ginger-nut
biscuits were found. It was speculated they may have been healing stones. The
corner with Union Street (Iguana Wana restaurant) features eight different carved
human heads. Both bearded men are crowned with cornucopia and two of the
women have anchors and maritime symbols. Dunbar's Hospital★, built in 1688,
has a series of inscriptions on the pediments of the six attic dormer windows.
Binoculars and good light reveal them to be (from left to right): 'This poor man
cryed'; 'And the Lord heard him, and saved him out of his tryel'; 'A littl that a
rightious man hath is beter nor the'; 'Richis of manye vikid men'; 'He that giveth
to the poor leneth to the'; 'Lord and Hie vil paye them sevean tyms mor.'

The first pediment has a figure of a bearded man with cloak and stick, presumably the 'poor man'; above him are two dragons with forked tongues, wings and
curled tails. Over the entrance door a tablet bears the arms of Provost Dunbar and
the legend 'Alexander Dunbar, Provost of Inverness, the rent thereof payable be
the master of the weyhouse to the Treasurer of the said Hospital.' At the north end
of the street is Leakey's vast secondhand bookshop, once a church, thus swapping
one kind of heaven for another. John Maclean's *Reminiscences* tell that the bodies
of the drowned were left in the church for claiming, including a fisherman whose
death was foretold by the Revd Morrison, the Petty Seer (see PETTY).

OLD HIGH CHURCH★★

Although the current church only dates from the 1770s, the site, called St Michael's
Mount, is one of the many places claimed to be an early church foundation by

St Columba in the sixth century. Certainly there was a stone church dedicated to the Virgin Mary here by 1171. By the eighteenth century the medieval church had fallen into disrepair and had to be replaced. The most striking structure is the large pillared mausoleum of the Robertsons of Inshes★★, carved with crossed bones, sexton's tools, hourglasses, bells, coffins, winged souls, coats of arms and, best of all, bewigged skulls. Inside the mausoleum, on the east wall, is a memorial with a winged soul, sexton's tools, hourglass and a skull and crossed bones tied with ribbon. At the top is a curious carving of a hand emerging from below holding what appears to be a triple set of dividers. There are further carvings of mortality on other stones in the main graveyard, as well as a spectacular military monument with a bearskin and crossed weapons. *Nessie's Loch Ness Times* for 30 December 2000 reported the discovery of human bones when workers installed a wheelchair ramp to the front door. The bones, dated to the fourteenth century, were surrounded by cockleshells, apparently a medieval ritual. In 1746 Jacobite prisoners were executed in the graveyard. South of the west door are two stones, nine paces apart in a direct line, one with two curved hollows and the other with a V-shaped groove. The blindfolded prisoner sat or kneeled on the former and the musket rested in the groove of the latter. Killing still goes on in the graveyard – on my visit I found the bones of dozens of pigeons and gulls, victims of some avian predator.

FRIARS' STREET, OFF FRIARS' LANE

The small Greyfriars graveyard here is all that survives of the Dominican friary founded in 1233 and dissolved in 1542. There are several interesting stones but the graveyard is usually kept locked. Note the Dominicans were Black Friars, not Grey. Gerald Pollitt in *Historic Inverness* says a house on the northeast side of Friars' Street has a monk's cell in the cellar.

CHAPEL STREET – CHAPELYARD CEMETERY★

Once associated with a long-lost fourteenth-century chapel dedicated to the Virgin Mary, this large graveyard has stones dating back to the seventeenth century and a number of carvings such as winged souls, crossed bones, skulls, coffins and gravedigger's tools. The paths were laid over the graves of the victims of a nineteenth-century outbreak of cholera. The area west of here, between Glebe Street and the river, was known as The Maggot, probably from an early chapel of St Margaret on the site. Writing in the nineteenth century, John Maclean, the Inverness Nonagenarian, says high tides uncovered the dead in the burial grounds of The Maggot.

ACADEMY STREET★★

This street is home to a superb collection of carvings. Deeno's Sports Bar: the Victorian building above the bar sports a fantastic collection of sea monsters, bearded dragons, wyverns, lions, long-necked Nessieform creatures, humans, eagles, merpeople and gryphons, all merging into foliage and/or waves★★★. It is easily one of the best sights in the area: high up are modern frescos extolling the dignity of industry and working men.

Corner of Academy Street/Queensgate, William Hill bookmakers: at entrance, superb Green Man★★, foliate monster★★, two cherubs with foliate tails. On Academy Street side: four foliate dragons★★, two excellent Green Men★★, one with a crown. On projection above: four foliate monsters★, four foliate eagles★ emerging from leaves and thistles. At very top of building: arms of the Lancashire Insurance Company containing three lions and topped by a crown and two winged dragons with spiralling foliate tails. On opposite corner, P.J. Mackenzie Gents' Outfitters: several friezes of figures, including foliate angels confronting foliate dragon heads and cherubs, and a woman in Classical robes sitting by a column, foliate human and lion heads★.

Opposite above: Inshes Mausoleum, Old High church.

Right: Foliaceous winged dragon and fish-swallowing Nessieform monsters above Deeno's Sports Bar, Academy Street.

Above: Foliaceous monster above Deeno's Sports Bar, Academy Street.

Left: Weary foliaceous figure. Deeno's Sports Bar, Academy Street.

Queensgate
south side.
Foliaceous
angel and
monster.

Arcaded entrance to Victorian Market: two foliate rams' heads, one bull's head★★. Georgian building opposite (currently Seconds and Firsts): bearded head. Fornari Hair Stylists: Foliate monkey, human and lion heads. On opposite side of road, above 'Restaurant' sign: eagle of the Highland Railway sheltering a crucifix and the Lamb of God under its outstretched wings. Highland Rail House, next to railway station: bearded man.

LIBRARY, FARRALINE PARK

The *Inverness Courier* for 8 July 1840 reported workmen digging up nine entire skeletons here (the library building was formerly Bell's School, built 1841, and after that a theatre, police station and courthouse). 'The bodies did not seem to have been regularly interred and they were probably the remains of men who had fallen in fight.'

QUEENSGATE★★

More amazing carvings, usually ignored in the bustle. At No. 6 Queensgate: two foliate lions at entrance. Osbournes pub: foliate lions and sea monsters★★, Green Man★★ and Green Woman★★, all excellent. Primo: fantastic male foliate head★★, foliate winged soul, Classical frieze above. Above entrance to Victorian market: Classical frieze with foliate cherubs, above, two large bearded foliate heads★★.

UNION STREET

Female head above arched doorway to west of MacCallums pub. Four sets of three lion-headed corbels along north side of street. Gerald Pollitt tells a story from 1975, when a Manchester firm were contracted to clean the stonework of the Royal Bank of Scotland building, but, not knowing the difference, actually cleaned the façade of the Bank of Scotland. Both banks have now vacated their premises.

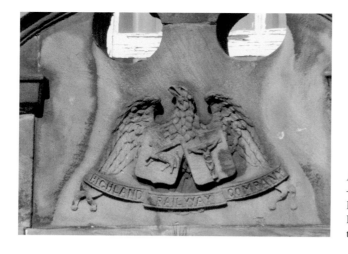

Academy Street
– symbol of the
Highland Railway.
Note the crucifix and
the Lamb of God.

Victorian market,
Academy Street
– rams' heads and
bull's head.

Corner of Academy
Street/Queensgate
– Green Man.

Corner of Academy
Street/Queensgate
– Green Man spewing
foliage.

Corner of Academy
Street/Queensgate
– foliate monster and
cherubs.

Queensgate south side
– Green Man.

Inverness railway station – wild men and heraldry.

RAILWAY STATION

A Victorian plaque listing the names of directors of the railway features two wild men dressed in loincloths and holding branches, an arm emerging from cloud holding a ring of foliage, a mounted knight in armour, and a lion wielding a sword.

HIGH STREET

Former Caledonian Bank★: the portico of this elegant cream-coloured building has a symbolic set of figures. In the centre, Caledonia holds the Roman fasces, a symbol of power. To the left the female River Ness generates a tributary stream in the form of a child. Further left, two children row a boat laden with packages, signifying commerce. On the right, Plenty pours out the rich contents of her cornucopia, and cherubs cut corn and look after sheep. Tiso/Phones4U: four female heads on top floor. Topshop: huge thistle high above.

INGLIS STREET

Lloyds TSB Scotland – coat of arms with lioness and stag. High up on west side of street, huge thistle.

Above left and right: St Mary's church, Huntly Street. Note her ruff and hat and the eyebrows on both faces.

THE RIVER NESS

In *By the Banks of the Ness*, Mhairi MacDonald described the dismal prison cell built into the third pier of the stone bridge constructed in 1685. Near the wall of the bridge was a trap-door and a few steps down from it an iron door and then a few steps into the narrow cell, which was just 6ft high and 10 by 7ft in plan. On the sides were a stone seat, a small window and two apertures to dip for water. In 1720 two of the occupants complained of the conditions. The prison was infested with rats, there was no shelter from the rain and they were often waist-deep in water and feared being drowned.

The Brahan Seer predicted that when seven bridges were over the river 'much bloodshed would ensue.' The seventh bridge was built in 1939. In February 1932, Miss K. MacDonald saw a 'crocodile-like' creature in the river, swimming towards Loch Ness. It had a short neck and long snout, and some reports suggested tusks.

HUNTLY STREET

St Mary's church was built in 1837 in the Gothic Revival style. It has crude male and female heads at the entrance; on the arch above is a woman with cap and ruff, and a bearded man, both with expressive eyebrows. Over the British Red Cross is a carved female head. Roddy Maclean (*The Gaelic Place Names and Heritage of Inverness*) mentions an ancient barn behind the domed west church which was

Columba Hotel, Ness Walk. Note the boot, which someone has managed to throw onto the very top of the hotel.

built in one night by the fairies of Tomnahurich and which was avoided after dark. *Nessie's Loch Ness Times* (20 May 2000) reported a ghostly encounter in Balnain House. Administrator Jane McMath was looking in the mirror in the toilet on the way back up from the basement when she saw a young girl dressed in old-fashioned clothing standing very close behind her. 'I felt a cold draught below my knees as if the door was opening but I didn't see it move nor hear any sound… I glanced again and the girl was small and appeared to be in black and white. When I looked back she had gone.' The house was built in 1726 and later divided into flats. The article also mentioned a haunting by a Green Lady and that a former resident of the flats was too frightened to go into the cellar alone. 'She said she'd rather freeze than go down by herself for coal.' The property was saved from demolition by the Inverness Civic Trust, was a traditional music centre from 1993 to 2001, and is now offices for the National Trust for Scotland.

NESS WALK

Above Rocpool are four reptilian monsters★ on two dormer windows, whilst on the Columba Hotel you can see carvings of the dove of Columba, a lion(?) holding a saltire in a shield, and four animals (cats? dogs?) on the spires. The gable spires of the Tower Hotel have a lion with a shield and what looks like a bear howling at the moon.

St Andrew's Cathedral. Angel.

SAINT ANDREW'S CATHEDRAL★★

Nineteenth-century cathedral with superb collection of gargoyles, angels, monsters, animals and other carvings: look out for the insect with large eyes. On the arch of the east-transept window is a wheel and horse. The story is that the horse turned the pulley system which raised the stones, until the day when one of the stones slipped and killed the horse. The nave has sculptured heads of St Margaret, Charles I, Dr Ross (Alexander Ross, the architect of the cathedral and neighbouring Ardross Street and Terrace, and his 1865 home Riverdale, now Ach-an-Eas Old People's Home) and Bishop Eden (bishop 1850-1885, who built the cathedral). I am grateful to Gerald Pollitt's *Historic Inverness* for these identifications. The choir stalls have wooden carvings of the symbols of the four Evangelists (bull, eagle, angel and lion) and the font is a kneeling angel holding a giant clamshell.

EDEN COURT THEATRE, BISHOPS ROAD

This centre for the arts incorporates part of the old Bishop's Palace. Norman Adams (*Haunted Scotland*) identified two phases of ghostly phenomena. The former palace garden was haunted by a little girl 'to the terror of the people about the place' – this sounds like a much earlier haunting than the episodes reported in the 1970s, soon after the theatre opened. An Afghan dog belonging to a staff member refused to cross the threshold, and the owner himself saw a 'strange

St Andrew's Cathedral. The cow
that turned the wheel.

St Andrew's Cathedral. The wheel
that lifted the stone that killed the
cow.

St Andrew's Cathedral. Insectiform
gargoyle.

shimmering figure' in the corridor to the Green Room, which incorporated the chapel where a woman was supposed to have hanged herself. Val Falcon was in the first circle with two colleagues when they saw a woman in green walk with her back to them upstairs from the stalls foyer. When the staff looked around there was no one there. On another occasion Val heard the click of stiletto heels across the brick forecourt, long after all customers had left. Footsteps were also heard in empty rooms and corridors. At lock up two female staff saw someone entering the gents' toilets – a check showed they were empty. Other phenomena included sparkling lights, cold spots, framed pictures falling from the walls and smashing, and tapestries slipping from hooks. It remains to be seen whether the hauntings will survive the recent major refurbishment of Eden Court.

NESS ISLANDS

ᴧᴵ In 2000 a 'Millennium Time Capsule' was buried on the islands. As well as newspapers, a child's handprint, home-shopping catalogues and an old £1 note, the capsule contains a scale model of Nessie.

The stone canopy of the General's Well can be found near the bridge to the west bank. It was reputed to cure whooping cough and rickets. A silver coin was thrown into the well and the 'silvered' water used to wash the child's ribs and shoulders.

GLENURQUHART ROAD

The foyer of the Highland Council Building houses the Knocknagael Boar Stone★, an excellent Pictish carving of a boar, with a disc symbol above. The stone was originally at Knocknagael, south of Inverness, but after suffering erosion and vandalism (it was used as target-practice for bottles thrown from speeding cars) it was moved here. The stone is illuminated at night and the glass-sided foyer means it can be visited out of hours.

GLENURQUHART ROAD – TOMNAHURICH CEMETERY★★

The very conspicuous hill of Tomnahurich…was in ancient days used as a watch or ward hill, and a place for dispensing justice; and, being the great gathering hill of the *fairies* in the north, its broad and level summit and smooth green sides waving with harebell, broom, and braken, afforded them ample space and seclusion for their elvish orgies.

NSA, 1845

…the fairies within it are innumerable, and witches find it the most convenient place for their frolics and gambols in the night-time.

Edward Burt, Burt's *Letters*
(NB Burt was writing with despair at the 'weak credulity' of the locals.)

Above left: Tomnahurich Cemetery.

Above right: Tomnahurich Cemetery. Foliaceous lion, sword embraced by a snake and, at top, the worm ouroborus encircling a butterfly.

Knocknagael Boar Stone.

The prominent Tomnahurich hill is a glacial esker, where soil and rock were deposited over many years by a stream under the great mass of ice. Prehistoric burials have been found at its base. In the seventeenth century it was the focal point for horse races which ran round the base of the hill. In 1864 it became a commercial burial ground, which was acquired by the town council in 1889.

Although there are none of the carvings of mortality found in older grave-yards, a stroll around its very extensive woodland paths reveals Victorian and later statues of beautiful youths and grieving women, carvings of greybeards and ser-pents, angels, and the occasional 'worm ouroborus', the snake that eats its tail, an alchemical symbol of eternity.

Many meanings have been applied to its name: the 'hill of the yew tree', the 'hill of the fairies' (supposedly derived from an alternative or corrupted name, Tom nan Sithichean), and the 'hill of the boat', or the 'boat-shaped hill', the latter possibly from the legend that St Columba laid the foundation of the hill by turn-ing his boat upside down here.

As the above mention of 'elvish orgies' shows, this is a place with a folklore that stretches back long before its use as a cemetery. The most commonly-told story is that of the Fiddlers of Tomnahurich. The version here is taken from Donald Anderson's 'Local Folklore' (Field Club). After a poor day busking in Inverness, Farquhar Grant and Thomas Cumming, two itinerant fiddle players, met a small man dressed in a red tam o'shanter and green jerkin and breeches who invited them to play at his party. At the top of Tomnahurich hill they entered a little door which led to a narrow tunnel and then to a large warm hall. They played all night and were rewarded with a bag of gold, at which they said, 'In the name of God we thank you.' The man promptly disappeared. Back in Inverness people laughed at them because of their clothing, and everything was unfamiliar. They went to a church for assistance but as they crossed the threshold the gold turned to brown leaves and they themselves to dust, having been gone for 100 years.

Janet and Colin Bord, in *The Enchanted Land*, tell of the fairy queen who desired a young and handsome piper. The piper refused her advances, as he wanted to return to his wife and child in Inverness. The queen said he would never find them again, but he still refused to be her consort or eat fairy food so she released him into the world. At home he found his family had been abducted. A sympa-thetic fairy told him to go to Tomnahurich and sing a certain song which she taught him. The piper did so and his wife and baby son were pushed out of the door. In other versions the piper is Big Angus, a shepherd, who learns the song by secretly eavesdropping on the fairy queen's private singing sessions. Yet another tradition is described in Gerald Pollit's *Historic Inverness*: Thomas the Rhymer, having spent three years in Elfland as the fairy queen's lover, re-emerged into the world with the promise he would return if called. In 1297 the call came and he followed a stag and a hind into the forest to re-enter Elfland through the agreed route, Tomnahurich. Another story has a kind of pied piper who led the fairies into the hill.

Then there are the sleeping giants, heroes asleep under the hill, awaiting the call to assist Scotland at its hour of need. A shepherd boy entered an opening in the hillside, found a bugle and blew it twice; three huge figures stirred and rose to their elbows. The boy fled without blowing the final summoning blast. Donald Mackenzie, in *Scottish Folk-Lore and Folk Life*, quotes a poem by MacCodrum, the Uist bard: 'When the hosts of Tomnahurich come, who should rise first but Thomas?'

'Strange as it may seem to you this day, the time will come − it is not far off − when full-rigged ships will be seen sailing eastward and westward by Muirtown and Tomnahurich, near Inverness… The day would come when Tom nan Sithichean would be under lock and key, and the fairies secured within.' This double prediction by the Brahan Seer has come true: ships pass Tomnahurich along the Caledonian Canal, opened in 1822, and the hill has become a municipal cemetery, locked up at night. No one has seen the fairies recently, but the hold Tomnahurich had on the Inverness imagination can be seen in M. Dick's fictionalised childhood memoir, *Erch in Urchinage*. 'Erch' and 'Andy', both nine years old in 1924, venture into the graveyard on the 'Hill of the Leprechauns' at night, despite the various ghosts − the marching tinkers, the Stewart kings of Scotland, and the Provost in his red robes and cocked hat. After a few minutes the two boys are spooked by an owl and run all the way home.

THE NORTHERN PART OF THE CITY ᴖ

Cromwell's Fort, on Cromwell Road, is in an industrial estate. Only a very small part of the rampart remains of what was once a huge pentagonal citadel built by Oliver Cromwell's Commonwealth Army between 1652 and 1657. The building stone was taken from churches in Inverness (Greyfriars and St Mary's Chapel) and from the monasteries of Beauly and Kinloss, all of which were demolished for the purpose, so 'it was a sacrilegious structure and therefore could not stand.' (J. Cameron Lees, *A History of the County of Inverness*). Lees records that when the citadel was destroyed at the Restoration, the minister of Kirkhill gleefully noted that a great thistle was seen growing out and obscuring the Commonwealth arms carved over the gate, 'to the admiration of the beholders. This was a presage that the Scots should therefore eclipse.' Similar omens were related at the destruction of other Cromwellian forts across Scotland.

Caledonian Thistle football stadium is on the ground where public executions took place. On 16 October 1835, 8,000 people watched the hanging of John Adam, the last public execution in Inverness. In the eighteenth century a Highlander, unable to pull a pair of expensive shoes from a dangling corpse on the gibbet, simply cut the feet off at the ankles. The site of Macbeth's eleventh-century wooden castle may well have been on Auldcastle Road.

There is a large plastic Nessie in the forecourt of a garage on Longman Road.

THE EASTERN PART OF THE CITY

The Broad Stone★ at Broadstone Park on Kingsmill Road is a very large flat stone with a central oblong hole cut right through it. Suggestions for what it is include a burgh boundary stone, a marker for a nearby well, and, the most likely candidate, the base of a large freestanding cross. The Mill Burn, which flows to the east of Diriebught Road, was once notorious for witches (see WITCHCRAFT). Of the burn, the Brahan Seer prophesised, 'The day will come when thy wheel shall be turned for three successive days by water red with human blood; for on the banks of thy lade a fierce battle shall be fought, at which much blood shall be spilt.' This day appears not to have come. At the junction of Perth Road and Culcabock Road is King Duncan's Well, apparently named after King Duncan's Grave a short distance to the southeast, the reputed burial place of Duncan after his fictional murder by Macbeth. Not surprisingly, an archaeological evaluation in 2002 found no archaeological support for this claim.

The well is covered over and is a bit dull. Kenneth MacRae, in *Highland Ways and Byways*, claims the association with King Duncan is false – the well was actually named after a Duncan Robertson of Inshes. Dane Love (*Scottish Spectres*) mentions the ghost of Culcabock House: in 1645 the owner, one of the Grants of Glenmoriston, lost the house at cards. He returned to haunt the room where the game took place, but is supposed to only appear to a Grant who is about the take part in a battle.

North of Raigmore Hospital (behind the Community Centre on Ashton Road) is Raigmore Chambered Cairn★ (NH68784549). This impressive cairn was re-erected here in advance of the new road, which runs over the original site. The excavation revealed some intriguing findings: the cairn was built on the site of an earlier timber building; and pits and cists continued to be dug into the cairn long after its original use had passed. These pits contained cremations, pottery and, of great interest, a cupmarked stone and a second-century Roman brooch, demonstrating that people were tapping into the power of this site more than 2,000 years after it was built. The grounds of Raigmore Hospital itself have a whooping-cough well.

THE SOUTHERN PART OF THE CITY

Norman Adams, in *Haunted Scotland*, reports that in spring 1996 the Scottish Society for Psychical Research was asked to investigate the BBC's Inverness studios at No. 7 Culduthel Road. A Grey Lady had been seen in the private car park and once crossed the foyer to vanish behind the fax machine. Investigator Daphne Plowman encountered ghosts of the living – doppelgängers of two members of staff were seen working in the studios late one evening when it was known they were not on site. In his blog (www.bbc.co.uk/scotland/radioscotland/jzdiary) on 31 October 2006, Jeff Zycinski, Head of Radio Scotland, noted that plans were afoot to demolish a back stairwell which was the favoured spot of the newsroom phantom: 'every old BBC building seems to have its own ghost. They tend to materialise in the run-up to Christmas when news is a bit thin on the ground, which is helpful.'

Opposite, at No. 5, Ardkeen Tower is the site of Tom nan Ceann, the 'hill of the heads', where execution by beheading took place. The building is a former school and charitable institution; the tower was used as an observatory. There are male and female heads at the doorway of 30 Old Edinburgh Road, and the Hermitage, 7 Annfield Road, is inscribed with the Clan Robertson motto *Vertutis Gloria Merces*, 'Glory, the reward of Valour'. Aden House Rest Home, next door at No. 5, has the motto of the Cook family, *Tutum monstrat iter*, more usually rendered *Tutem monstrat iter*, 'He showeth a safe road' or 'He leads the way.' The letters AO EN are on the banner below.

In 1925 numerous skeletons were found on the east side of Muirfield Road, the site of a former gibbet. The contractor building the new houses quietly dug a deep pit and deposited the bones in it. Houses now occupy the site. When Alexander MacKintosh of Borlum, probably innocent of his crime, was executed at Muirfield: 'with mingled feelings of sorrow and horror the multitude slowly and silently dispersed, many, if not most of the company, placing a small piece of bread under a stone, which, according to a superstitious tradition, would prevent after-dreams of the unfortunate Alexander MacKintosh.' To dream of the dead was to invite them to return as revenants; the apotropaic rite appears to have been specific to witnessing an execution. (Source: George Henderson, *Survivals in Belief Among the Celts*, quoting from *Celtic Monthly* in *Inverness Northern Chronicle*, 16 August 1905.)

THE WESTERN PART OF THE CITY

Gruach, Lady Macbeth, is imprisoned in the hill fort of Torvean (NH64374315). Unable to sleep, she paces back and forth and washes her hands in the River Ness. Across the river, Duncan has been seen parading in his kingly regalia. Ah, Shakespeare, how your fictional ghosts do still walk amongst us! Somewhere near Dunain Hill (NH626433) is Fuaran a' Chragain Bhric, the Well of the Spotted Rock, a fairy well where changelings could be exchanged for the original child, with the offering being a bowl of milk. In 1982 the Morrises (*Scottish Healing Wells*) described it as being adorned with rags and pins and the water gifted with white pebbles and shells.

In the area called Muirtown is Duff's Well, also known as Fuaran Allt an Ionnlaid, 'well of the washing burn', or 'the anointing well', with a vague association with Druids, and yet another well supposedly consecrated by St Columba. In the nineteenth century it was still being used as a healing well for gout, rheumatism and skin diseases, but it lost its powers when a soldier's wife, hoping for a quick cure, immersed her scurvy-ridden child in the waters – the *genius loci* fled in disgust. In 1830 H.R. Duff of Muirtown House added a stone inscribed *Luci Fontisque Nymphis*, 'to the nymphs of the grove and fountain'. Without the description in Roddy Maclean's *Gaelic Place Names* book I would never have found the well; it is now a dismal, muddy patch to the east of Clachnaharry Road, just before a corner on the way to Inverness (NH651461).

On a hill south of the main A862 as it leaves Clachnaharry is a storm-damaged monument erected by Major Hugh Robert Duff in 1821 to the fallen of a battle between Clan Monro and Clan Chatten (MacKintosh). In the 1930s there was a report of a Grey Lady who haunted the area but nothing more was heard of her. Various sources give the date of the battle as 1333, 1341, 1378 or 1434; the RCAHMS 'Canmore' website comes down firmly on the year 1454. Close by at NH644465 is Priseag Well, said to have been blessed by St Kessog and useful for treating sore eyes and countering the Evil Eye. Drinking from it each day or carrying some of the water protected against demons and fairies.

Donald A. Mackenzie's *Scottish Folk-Lore and Folk Life* relates an eighteenth-century folktale from the area. Simon Lord Lovat ejected his tenant John Fraser (or Barron) from a mill and land near Beaufort Castle: Fraser moved to a farm and mill on the estate of Robert Chevis of Muirtown. The two landowners quarrelled, and in December 1746 Chevis gave evidence against Lovat at his trial before the House of Peers. Fraser prospered and his cows supplied very good milk: then it dried up, the milk famine lasting a year. One summer evening Fraser was beside a rowan tree near his mill and saw a strange dwarfish man in odd clothes. His face was old but his hair was young, and over his shoulder was 'a long tapering sapling of hawthorn that seemed as if it would break beneath the load of some invisible burden that was attached to its slenderest end.' He did not speak when he reached the tree. Fraser knew something was up and cut off part of the hawthorn with his knife: unconcerned, the old man 'disappeared over the rising ground towards the Leachkin... as he vanished from the sight of Fraser, a rushing sound came from the cut twig that had fallen... Rich, creamy milk flowed as in a stream – it overspread in all directions...' even milkifying the River Ness. As well as the released milk all the cows now gave more than before and the field where it happened gave a rich crop of grass. With minor variations, this same story is told about STRATHERRICK. The implication in the Fraser version is that the powerful Simon Lord Lovat had hired the dwarfish man to steal the *toradh*, the substance, of his neighbour's lands.

CRAIG PHADRIG FORT★

This fort and forest walk is signposted from Leachkin (pron. Larkin) Road. From either car park the tracks up the east side to the fort pass the Giant's Chair, whose name is obvious when you see it. One of the paths is suitable for wheelchair users. The fort is notable for three things: the views from its summit, its vitrification, and its association with St Columba. In Adomnan's seventh-century *Life of Columba*, the saint was refused admittance to the Palace of Brude, King of the Northern Picts. Columba approached 'the folding-doors with his companions, and having first formed upon them the sign of the cross of our Lord, he then knocked at and laid his hand upon the gate, which instantly flew open of its own accord, the bolts having been drawn back with great force.' In the later *Life of Comgall*, Columba is accompanied by Saints Comgall and Cainnech. Comgall makes the sign of the cross and opens the gates of the *'castrum'*, and then Columba does the same to open the door of the *'domus regalis'*, the royal dwelling.

In the tenth-century Old Irish *Life of Columba*, Columba is challenged by Brude's son Maelchu and a Druid – he kills both with a curse. In the *Life of St Cainnech* a drop of Cainnech's blood cures Brude's daughter, who is blind, deaf and dumb. Columba very probably did visit Brude on a diplomatic mission, possibly to ensure safe passage for other missionaries travelling through the King's territories. But all tales of miraculously-opening doors and Druid-besting contests should be understood in terms of their purpose – to demonstrate the wonder-working abilities of the early Christian saints, and thereby to make clear Christianity's superiority over paganism.

The exact location of Brude's fortress has eluded certainty. Reeves, the editor of the nineteenth-century edition of Adomnan's *Life of Columba*, was certain it was Craig Phadraig. Later editors were more cautious. Excavation found that in the sixth century, that is, the period of Brude's rule, the site was domestic only, not military or royal. Other candidates include Torvean, Auldcastle (also possibly the site of Macbeth's castle), the dun over which Urquhart Castle was built, and the junction of the loch and River Ness.

Craig Phadraig is a 'vitrified' fort, that is, part of its stone walls have melted under intense heat. There are numerous vitrified forts in Scotland. Speculation as to the cause has centred on whether it was: a) burned in an attack; b) set alight in a ritual when the fort was abandoned; c) a design feature to increase the strength of the wall; d) accidental. Alan Small, in 'The Hill Forts of the Inverness Area' (Field Club) conclusively demonstrates through experimentation that the answer is d). Wooden buildings inside the ramparts caught fire, spreading into the timber lacing of the rampart. A draught funnelled through the gap like a blast furnace. The intense heat in the core caused the rock to shatter and the revetments to collapse, forming heat-shattered rubble heaps which created a heat blanket around the lower part of the wall, thickening the wall here by several yards and increasing suction. At this point vitrification occurred – the rocks in the core melted. The end product is a rampart about half its original size buried in a mass of rubble on both sides, useless for defence. No fort has a continuously vitrified rampart. Vitrification 'is due to the accidental circumstances of low-melting point rocks lying in a part of the wall which attained a sufficiently high temperature for them to reach a fluid state. Many forts which show no signs of vitrification may have been built by exactly the same techniques and may also have suffered burning, but a sufficiently high temperature was never attained to melt part of the core.'

Vitrified material can be found in other circumstances. In the nineteenth century a farmer in Kirkhill found that during land reclamation the peat was scraped off the surface, piled into heaps and ignited, leaving vitrified fragments beneath.

3

WEST OF INVERNESS: THE AIRD AND GLEN CONVINTH

Some account of the Barrows or artificial mounts; of monumental stones, whether those inscrib'd with Letters, or other carving; or those plac'd in a circular order, or vast stones placed on the tops of others pitch'd in the ground. An account of the Amulets and charms &c. viz. Adderstones, Toadstones, Cockknee-stones, snail-stones, mole-stones, Leag, Elf Arrows and the like; with any other *Relations* that may fall under this Head.

Request from Edward Lhuyd, keeper of the Ashmolean Museum in Oxford, to the Revd Mr James Fraser, Minister of Kirkhill, 18 December 1699

BUNCHREW

'Prodigious signs, apparitions, spectres, and strange sights presaging war and revolutions – such as men fighting in the air, horse and foot retreating and returning – were all visibly observed... Two of our fleshers [going one morning into Inverness], saw an army, foot and horse, marching before them, and heard the rattling noise of their arms till they came and entered into the woods of Bunchrew.' It was the year 1644, a time of political and military crisis, and signs and wonders were abroad:

Another evening, three men going to the ferry of Beauly saw an army marshalled, horse and foot, the very colour of their horses and clothes, kettle-drum and ensign, apparent... Two prodigious whales came up the firth with a high spring-tide, the one pursuing the other, and fastened both upon the shallow sands. They were so big and high that the people made use of small ladders to reach the top. There were also two porpoises that ran up the Ness under the bridge, and reached the Isle a mile above the town, where they were killed. Some conjectured that the two whales were an emblem of the king and Parliament pursuing one another; but, alas! These things portended no good. Another wonderful event happened above Beauly three several evenings – two parties fighting, so that men saw the glistening of their swords slashing at one another.

All these accounts are from a seventeenth-century local historian quoted in J. Cameron Lees's *A History of the County of Inverness.*

Bunchrew House★ (NH62174591), now a prestigious hotel, is a seventeenth-century mansion, extensively altered in 1896. The moat and drawbridge have sadly long since vanished. The hotel's website makes much of the resident ghost but this is just a fantasy touch of Auld Scotland, concocted around a painting of the scary-looking Isobel Ogilvie in the front hall (personal communication from the hotel, 9 March 2007).

1.25km NNW in the Beauly Firth (NH61754730) is a large mound of stones and timbers which may be a beacon-stance. What may have been two others were visible in 1793; 'urns' are said to have been found in the largest mound. The site is submerged every high tide. A little to the west, the damaged Phopachy Crannog (NH60254670) sits on a sandbank 250m from the shore: the Fuaran a' Chladaich, well of the beach, is on the shore. At low tide the water can be seen bubbling out. It was once enclosed by a causeway, and was much resorted to during outbreaks of cholera, on the basis that its waters would be uncontaminated. At Ladystone Farm is a double stone row (90m long) and standing stone (NH622433).

LENTRAN

Archie MacRae of Lentran told Kenneth MacRae (*Highland Doorstep*) that one night he and a friend were approaching an old bridge on one of the Lentran House entrances when they were joined by a mysterious lady all in black, who walked with them in silence, then faded into the night. Another night, walking home in the dark, he heard footsteps walking in time with him, and the dragging of a chain. When he stopped, so did the footprints. Frightened, he hid in the bushes – to see a goat dragging its loosened chain.

KIRKHILL

The Bogroy Inn, also known as the Old North Inn, on the junction of the A862 and the B9164 to Kirkhill (NH567449), is reputedly haunted by a twentieth-century ghost, a previous owner who died at the top of the main stairs the day before he was due to leave. Another story has two bodysnatchers pausing at the inn for a wee drink, leaving a recently-disinterred corpse dressed in a coat and hat on the seat of their horse-drawn cart. The local magistrate spotted the body and took its place, complete with coat and hat. On continuing their journey one of the resurrectionists said, 'Is it my imagination or is this body still warm?' The corpse promptly replied, 'You would be warm too if you had to sit out in this sun with not a drop to drink.' Cue hasty exit by two terrified grave robbers! The magistrate returned the body to the cemetery at Wardlaw. This may be an example of a well-worn bodysnatching tale – a very similar story is told about Perth (see my *Guide to Mysterious Perthshire*).

The old Wardlaw church★★, also known as St Mary's, sits on a small hillock northwest of the village, Wardlaw meaning 'watch hill'. The church is ruinous

Kirkhill, Wardlaw church tower.

but the later Lovat Mausoleum, built in 1722, is complete outside, and has a spectacular seventeenth-century turreted belfry topped by a weathervane of a crowned creature which may be a basilisk or cockatrice. In heraldry the basilisk is represented as an animal with the head, torso and legs of a cock, the tongue of a snake and the wings of a bat. The snake-like rump ends in an arrowpoint. The basilisk had the head and legs of a cock, a snake-like tail, and a body like a bird's. It seems that the wings could be depicted as either being covered with feathers or scales. Several gravestones have carved symbols of mortality.

In 1662 a notorious witchpricker named Paterson visited the area. He had already brought about the deaths of four women in Elgin and Forres, and Margaret Duff in Inverness, and had made a tidy sum from his services, being able to employ two servants. In the churchyard at Wardlaw he was presented with fourteen women and one man brought by Alexander Chisholm of Comer, and four brought by Andrew Fraser, chamberlain of Ferintosh. The victims had nothing to do with witchcraft – they were Chisholm's tenants on his estates at Conveth (CONVINTH), and he simply wanted to get rid of them. Paterson stripped the victims naked, cut off their hair and hid it in the recess of a stone wall, then rubbed his hands over each victim's body and 'pricked' them, inserting a brass pin up to its head into parts of the body supposedly touched by the Devil, and therefore insensitive to pain: 'with shame and fear being dashed, they felt it not, but he left it in the flesh, deep to the head, and desired them to find and take it out!' Without looking, none of the victims could identify the location of the pin in their flesh, thus 'confirming' their guilt. It has been suggested the pin may have been a retractable fake, but this remains unproved. The incident was recorded by Revd James Fraser of Wardlaw (who was possibly an eyewitness) in the *Wardlaw Manuscript*, and can be found in many later publications, such as Polson's *Scottish Witchcraft Lore*. In *The Deil's Ain*, Roy Pugh gives the victims' names as noted in the Privy Council *Register*: twenty-three names are recorded, although the accounts noted above mention a smaller number:

McLean, Donald
McLean, Hectour
McLean, Jonet
McLean, Margret
McConchy (Vic Conchy), Mary Nein Alaster
McEan (Ninian) Dowie Vic Finley, Baike
McEan (Nean Ean) Duy Vic Conchie Vic Goune, Cormule
McEan (Vic Ean), Cristian Neil (Nein) Ferquhar
McEan (Nein Ean) Cheill, Jonet
McEan (Ninian) Ean Vic Ean Culleam (Vic Connell, Vic William), Kathrin
McEan, Kathrin Nein Ferquhar
McEwen (Vic Ewin), Cristian Nein Ferquhar
McEwen (Nyn Owan) Vic Omnoch, Kathrin
McFinlay (Nean Finlay) Vic Ean Vic Homas, Beak
McFinlay Vic Comes, Mary
McFinley (Vic Finley), Beak Nein Ean Duy
McGilliphadrick (Nein Giliphadrick), Muriall Duy
McGown (Nein Goune), Mary
McInnes (Viv Innish), Mary Muarn
McNish, Baik
McPhail (Nein Phaill), Cristian
McPhail (Vic Phaill), Donald
McRory (Ninian Rory) Mie Buy, Jonet

These people were Macleans, and despite having left Mull 300 years earlier, clan ties were still strong. When the husband of one of the women appealed to their chief, Sir Allan Maclean of Duart, on Mull, Sir Allan successfully petitioned the Privy Council for the release of his kinsfolk. However, by this time the women had been tortured further – denied sleep, suspended from the jail ceiling by their thumbs, had the soles of their feet burnt, and been dragged through the streets by horses. One died in prison: another went mad. The grim psychopathology of the witch trial era is further underlined when Paterson was later revealed to be a woman in disguise.

Revd Fraser also describes the proceedings when the body of Donald Mackwilliam Chui or Dhuibh was discovered below the high water mark. The corpse was taken to Wardlaw church, stripped naked, and placed on a bier. Every one of the parishioners, some 600 or 700, were required to touch the body. When John Mackeanvore laid his hand on the corpse blood issued out, a clear sign of guilt. Mackeanvore was imprisoned but a second suspect, John Mackeanire, fled the area. 'John Mackeanvore, the capital murtherer, being in the pit at Inverness, laid fast in the stocks, continued there but about a fortnight, and both his feet down from the ancles dropt off as if by amputation. When he was brought forth he had a foot in every hand like a shoe last, cursing and imprecating.' Mackeanvore spent two years protesting his innocence and begging on his stumps, but then Mackeanire was caught and confessed, but implicated Mackeanvore, and both men were hung near the Kirkhill parish church.

R. Macdonald Robertson (*Selected Highland Folktales*) tells the story of Crunar Fraser, born about 1625 at Kingellie in Kirkhill parish. Crunar grew to be strong – very strong – and cruel. Eventually he was commissioned as an officer in the army and sent to fight in Ireland. His stepmother, secretly relieved to be free of him, gave him a *sian*, a charm which would guard him against sword and bullet 'How long will the charm last?' asked Crunar. 'Until you see my face again,' she replied. Crunar decapitated her on the spot, ensuring the charm would last all his days. He died of natural causes at an old age, after a life of murder and violence. His house was thereafter haunted, but any manifestations have long since vanished. (For another example of this sian, see CULLODEN BATTLEFIELD.)

Henderson in *Survivals in Belief Among the Celts* (1911) describes Craobh Pareig, a cherry tree near Cononbank, west of Kirkhill, planted in remembrance of Pareig, a murdered woman.

> It was an uncanny place. A grey beast used at times to be seen there; it was cat-like in appearance, and thought by some to be a *tannasg* or *tasg*, 'apparition, ghost'. Such a creature followed in the track of a cart which was going to town at an early hour. My informants said it followed them until dawn, when, on coming to a bridge, it gave an unearthly yell, it being a property of the ghost or apparition to give a loud cry as it passes over running water.

The Winery at MONIACK CASTLE★ (NH55194362) is a popular visitor attraction. The rockery between the castle and the road mimics an arrangement of prehistoric megaliths. The furthest west of the stones is a Class I Pictish symbol stone. In the *Proceedings of the Society of Antiquaries of Scotland* for 1881-2, W. Jolly describes the carving as a man holding a stick, and fourteen cupmarks:

> one of which has been mistaken for the eye of the figure…This stone was brought from a spot where it stood for a time, close to the old parish school of Kilmorack, near Kilmorack Free church. It was however, removed to this place between fifty and sixty years ago, from a spot 100 yards further west, when the ground was them reclaimed.

This places the original location somewhere near Balblair (NH5045). The man is hard to see and only three cup marks are now visible. Jolly also reported a second cupmarked stone in the rockery, but this has long vanished.

Reelig Glen.
Tigh-an-Aigh,
built by fairies or
a benevolent laird.

REELIG GLEN★ (NH557432) has a delightful series of walks from the Forestry
Commission car park. Taking either route alongside the Moniack Burn brings
you at the end of the walks to a modern bridge, a mossy, humped stone bridge
and the overgrown atmospheric ruins of Tigh-an-Aigh★ (pron. 'Tan-eye') the
'house of good luck or fortune'. Kenneth MacRae in *Highland Ways and Byways*
says that this folly was built in the 'hungry times' of 1846 during the potato famine. The benevolent laird had it constructed to provide work for his tenants, but,
the story goes, he threw it down every night so the work could continue; this is
possible, or it may just have been that the structure was poorly designed. Popular
belief blamed the fairies, which may have led to a later idea that the building was
inhabited by a brownie. If you take the uphill path west from the car park you
reach a Bronze Age burial cairn, which may, or may not, be the 'Fairy Hill' identified somewhere near here in 1936. 'Reelig' is from the Gaelic word for graveyard,
and there are certainly a number of other prehistoric funerary monuments in the
immediate area, although few are really worth visiting. In *Scottish Healing Wells*,
Frank and Ruth Morris identify an ancient well said never to run dry at Cabrich
(NH539433), near a disused quarry, but I could not locate it.

KILTARLITY AND AREA

Kiltarlity has had its share of 'Alien Big Cat' reports. Several issues of the *Kiltarlity
News* in 2000 catalogued the incidents. Between October 1998 and the spring
of 1999, Eskadale keeper Neil Lyon lost more than twenty sheep, with the carcasses showing clear signs of big cat predation. In late May 2000, Boblainy farmer
Davie Maclean lost a ewe and two lambs overnight on rented grazing at Hughton
(NH477415). Once again, the predation was not typical of fox or dog attacks. A
neighbour heard the sound of a beast caterwauling from the location on the night

Highland Liliums Garden Centre,
Kiltarlity. Statue of monk(?).

of the attacks. Loaneckheim resident Caroline Hutchinson saw a 'large black panther' twice on the banks of the River Beauly. The first time she watched it from across the river, but on the second occasion it crossed the road near Groam Cottage. As she got out of the car to follow it, she could smell its distinctive scent. In February 2000 Sam Ferguson had a similar encounter with a large black cat that 'seemed to take up the whole width of the single-track road' by the new houses in Belladrum. The next day Sam and his father found paw marks in soft ground by the woods where the beast had vanished from sight. There was also a report of a local driver colliding with a mystery animal on the A833 between Kiltarlity and Drumnadrochit. Alan Sime, a vet then with the Scottish Agricultural College, sent hairs from the bumper for analysis in Edinburgh. The tests found that they belonged to no known British mammalian species. In 1980 a puma was caught not far away at Cannich (see INVERNESS MUSEUM.)

Alexander Carmichael's collection of folklore, *Carmina Gadelica* (1899), includes a charm to counteract the Evil Eye, collected at Kiltarlity. Take a clay vessel, go to running water over which the living and dead cross (that is, a bridge to a grave-yard). On the lower side of the bridge go down on the right knee, lift a palmful of water in the hollows of the hands and put it in the dish, saying:

I am lifting a little drop of water
In the holy name of the Father;
I am lifting a little drop of water
In the holy name of the Spirit.

Rub a little of the now-blessed water into the two ears of the victim of the Evil Eye, or on the part, or down the spine of the animal, saying:

> Shake from thee thy harm,
> Shake from thee thy jealousy,
> Shake from thee thine illness,
> In name of the Father,
> In name of the Son,
> In name of the Holy Spirit.

The name of the person must be mentioned at the same time as the water is applied. Then pour any remaining water over a grey stone or fixed rock, so that the holy power of the water cannot be abused. Many of the charms and practices recorded by Carmichael dated back to at least the eighteenth century. Francis Thompson in *The Supernatural Highlands* mentions a late twentieth-century bearer of the tradition, Mrs Annie Fraser, a Kiltarlity resident with the power to lift spells, a gift inherited from her parents and grandparents. The process involved gathering water from a burn close to 'the Bridge of the Living and the Dead' and adding her wedding ring and a silver coin, blessing it all with the words 'I, Mrs Fraser, sprinkle this water on [name of person]. In the name of the Father, Son and Holy Spirit I bless you and may all evil depart from you.' This had to be performed before sunrise, and gold and silver had to be together in the water.

In 'Some Notes on the Parish of Kiltarlity', an article in the *TGSI*, Hugh Barron recorded some events of great interest, such as an example of second sight which took place during the incumbency of the Revd Dr Ronald Bayne in Kiltarlity (1808-1821). Donald Fraser of Easter Clunes asked the congregation to pray for his father, who was very ill. In those days, notices were usually read out after the singing of the opening psalm and just before the first prayer. The precenter read out the notice but Revd Bayne did not mention Donald's father in his first prayer, or the second or last. After the service Donald asked for an explanation. 'My dear Donald,' said the minister, 'before the first prayer your blessed father was in glory, beyond the need of our prayers.' Donald went home to find his father had died at 11 a.m. – the time the morning service had begun. Donald told Bayne's words to Barron's father, who passed them on to him.

Barron also discusses Alasdair Hutchan (*d*. 1846), a pious, godly man and a pillar of the Church: 'He was also a seer and extraordinary things were told of him which one might perhaps better forget, but one of a few preserved in my own family I think I should tell you, as I think it may be unique.' Barron's granduncle Donald Maclean took up the farm of Lienassie in the Braes of Kilmorack, and built a new byre, but each year several cattle mysteriously died. Donald went to see Alasdair Hutchan. Alasdair prayed for insight and told Donald his new byre was under a spot where evil angels expelled from heaven were suspended in the air. Donald took Alasdair's advice to build a new byre on a different spot, and the deaths ceased.

Barron's article also describes an incident from around 1820, when the husband of a recently deceased woman was keeping watch with some friends in the old burial ground at Fanellan (now the site of an industrial operation, NH489428). The body lifters enticed the watchers away but missed the concealed husband in the bushes. He shot one of them, said to be a medical student from Inverness.

Then there's the Bodachan Allt Speic, the spirit who haunted the Allt Speic, the small stream flowing into the Allt Mor south of Belladrum (NH4152). It irritated a traveller so much he shouted, 'Get out of my way, splasher of the pools.' The Bodachan, insulted, was never more seen or heard. The Clach a' bhodach, the Bhodach's Stone, is apparently close to the south side of the burn, although I have been unable to identify it – it may be another name for Meg's Stone (see below). In some cases 'Bhodach' seems to be a catch-all term for any paranormal entity, and has been used for disembodied spirits that haunt a particular stretch of road or a certain burn, as well as fairy, little man, demon, gnome, or anything similar. Sadly we have as yet no Linnaeus to classify supernatural Scottish species and sub-species, and DNA analysis is utterly lacking. And perhaps the entire phylum has become extinct.

I am indebted to Joe Gibbs of Belladrum Estate for much of the following. Except where noted, the information is taken from personal communication with Joe on the 21 June and 9 July 2007. The estate hires out a folly, the beautiful Belladrum Temple, for weddings. Another folly, the neo-Gothic castellated Tigh Romach, can be rented for a self-catering holiday. The proprietor of Belladrum (James Merry, Joe's great-great-grandfather, who came here in 1857) sent a friend to Edinburgh to buy the neighbouring estate of Ballindoun. To Merry's fury, the friend bought it for himself. Merry built Tigh Romach with one wall rough and rocky, so every time his former friend came past, who he called Mucaidh (piggish), he could stop and claw himself. It has served as a laundry and, during the Second World War, an ammunition dump. The house was said to be haunted but Joe thinks that this was a story his great-grandmother put about to keep courting couples away from it when it was a ruin. Archie Merry, James's son, is said to haunt the Italian Gardens, occupying a spot where he always sat on a bench, and a White Lady lurks around Dalnamien Bridge on the road below Phoineas.

Kenneth MacRae (*Highland Doorstep*) records other ghosts: on New Year's Eve a coach and horses could be heard passing Phoineas House in the middle of the night, and Ballindoun House, now gone, had a Dark Lady, a black woman whom the laird married abroad but abandoned when he returned home, only to be haunted by her ghost after her death. In 1953 one recent tenant told MacRae that several times she saw a bearded head (with no body) peering at her from the foot of the bed. Joe's children and others have seen more ghosts at Phoineas House, including a man writing at a desk reflected in a mirror and a young groom in a bowler hat. Nearby, at Belladrum Home Farm (NH52054161) is a now-derelict farm building with a central tower aping the style of a large nineteenth-century church. The buildings were aggrandised in the 1850s when David Bryce remodelled Belladrum House.

Meg's Stone, Kiltarlity. Witch's stone? Coffin stone?

Near where the minor road that passes the farm rejoins the A833 (NH515412) is a single standing stone, Meg's Stone. It used to be part of the drystane dyke on the opposite side of the road to where it is now before the local council changed the road layout in the 1970s and moved the stone. Joe Gibbs recalls that, 'When we were children, we were told that Meg, a witch, had been buried under it and if it was ever moved she would fly out and claim us for ever.' There is no record of any supernatural comeback on the council workers. Joe also recalls a theory that it had been a coffin stone, and a funeral party rested a coffin here while visiting the hostelry that once stood on the site. They then got too bladdered to take the corpse any further, and the name of the deceased – Meg – became attached to the stone. It has to be said that the current upright stance of the stone – with the pointy bit upwards – is not one on which you could easily place a coffin.

The graveyard of the current parish church at NH51274137, just southwest of the main village, is dominated by the mound of Tom na Croiseige, Tomnacross, the Baron Baillie's Court. The church itself was built next to the site of hangman's noose – the hanging tree was cut down in 1925. The old medieval parish church, now ruined, with interesting gravestones, is actually 4km to the northwest, just south of Black Bridge on the River Beauly (NH49744392). There is confusion about the history of this church. The dedication is said to have been to St Thalargus, Taraglainn or Talorcan, a disciple of St Donnan. Another version is St Tarrail, whose grave was said to be marked by Clach Tarrail, a stone, now lost, about 1km southwest of the church (see also GLEN CONVINTH). The *Third Statistical Account* of 1985 claimed the real name of church was Comar Kilbeathan, dedicated in the sixth century to St Baithen, also reputedly the name-giver to Kilvean (Cill Bheathain) next to Inverness and Torvean (Torr Bheathain). The same account also says the churchyard is popularly called Clachan Chomair, the Clachan of Comar. The old churchyard once contained two stones with deep, large cupmarks. These were known as the holy water stones of St Baithean, 'and were probably used for baptismal purposes.' They are now lost.

For Sale: prehistoric burial monument, only one previous occupant. Culburnie Ring-Cairn. (It is the cottage that is for sale, not the cairn.)

The area is rich in prehistoric remains:

Lower Bog Chambered Cairn (NH52364038), the ruinous chamber of an otherwise destroyed Orkney-Cromarty cairn.

Belladrum Home Farm Chambered Cairn (NH51604158), possibly of Orkney-Cromarty-type: five upright stones in a ploughed field which are very difficult to access.

Belladrum Chambered Cairn (NH51424210), a Clava-type chambered cairn. All that remains is a typical kerb of irregular, heavy boulders. It is possible to visit from the A833 by keeping to the woodland and avoiding the crops; it is badly ruined but spectacular in May when covered in bluebells.

Bruiach Ring-Cairn★ (NH49954143), a large Clava ring-cairn, but all that remains is the kerb and the outer circle of standing stones, the rest having been dug out for a pond, now dry. Two of the kerb stones are cupmarked, but you'll be lucky to find them as in summer this is a jungle. It is easy to visit as it is next to the road west of Kiltarlity. The massive hole of the former pond actually makes it a site with an unusual atmosphere.

Culburnie Burn, modern cairn (NH497418): a curious large stone-built platform at the side of the road, heavily overgrown, with no obvious dedication or purpose.

Culburnie Clava Ring-Cairn★ (NH49164180). Despite (or because of?) being incorporated into a garden by the side of the road, this is still a very impressive site, with a ring of large standing stones. Aubrey Burl in *Circles of Stone* notes the mason who supposedly removed the missing northeast stone died a sudden death – the traditional folk-memory punishment for such violations. Ask permission to visit at the croft.

Nine-Holed Stone★, cupmarked stone, (NH46653994).

Clach Bhan, a cupmarked stone (NH50313991): possibly impossible to find.

GLEN CONVINTH

This is the area from lowland Kitarlity south along the A833 into the high hills above Glen Urquhart. The ruined former parish church★ west of the road at NH51203746 has an attractively lonely atmosphere, although a carved stone of a horse and rider, and two cupmarked stones, both reported in the 1880s, have disappeared. Hugh Barron, in 'Some Notes on the Parish of Kiltarlity', tells a story of the gravestone marked 'EF 1783', which is next to the large beech tree called Croabh na banaraich, the dairymaid's tree. After the burial of Elizabeth Fowler ('EF') a stranger on horseback gave her son, who was the butler at Belladrum, a young tree to plant at the side of the grave. For some reason he did not do it straightaway but waited till night, got up and planted it (there is clearly a backstory here but we can only guess at it). A bodysnatcher was buried somewhere near the tree – it was said his bones kept coming to the surface. Across the road, and visible from the graveyard, is Cnoc an t-Sidhean, the fairy hill.

The historian of witchcraft P.G. Maxwell-Stuart, in *An Abundance of Witches*, notes that on 26 July 1662 the Privy Council granted a commission to try eleven women and one man from the area around Buntoit who had already 'confessed themselves to be guilty of the horrid crime of witchcraft.' There are no more details of their fate.

Hugh Barron in 'Some Notes on the Parish of Kiltarlity' (*TGSI*) describes the Clach nan sleagh, a stone marked 'AF' and 'NR', 'in a croft near the main road on the east side of Allt Ramh-raidh which runs into the Belladrum Burn.' The traditional story says a wolf-hunting party sharpened their spears on the stone. I have been unable to locate it.

DOCHGARROCH TO CAIPLICH

Kenneth MacRae (*Highland Ways and Byways*) reports the murder of a woman by her husband when he came home to find her in the arms of another, at Wester Altourie (NH572400). Before she died she managed to crawl for help to the neighbouring house. Later tenants claimed to hear her knocking in the middle of the night. MacRae was told: 'We never heard anything unusual, but I remember once seeing a strange light hovering in a hollow nearby. It seemed to rise in the air to a height of four feet, then suddenly faded out.' The landscape nearby has been folk-mythologised: a point on the ridge between Lochend and Caiplich is Suidhe Churadain, where St Curadan rested, and nearby is Glaic Oisein (Ossian's Hollow) and Uaigh Bhran, the grave of Bran, Fingal's finest dog.

4

THE NORTH SHORE OF LOCH NESS I: FROM DOCHGARROCH TO DRUMNADROCHIT

Proceed with great caution in your Loch Ness work. We are caught up in a series of games which must be played by 'their' rules. Anyone who tries to invent his own rules, or breaks the basic patterns, loses his mind or even his life.

John A. Keel to Ted Holiday, *The Dragon and the Disc: An Investigation into the Totally Fantastic*

Note: the A82 along the lochside is dangerous for pedestrians (there is no pavement) and cyclists should take great care in the fast and heavy traffic.

DOCHGARROCH ᵢₙ

Since Loch Ness lies 52ft (15.8m) above sea level there are a series of locks on the Caledonian Canal. The first is at Dochgarroch, just beyond the Dochfour weir where the canal branches away from the River Ness. In 1996 a member of the Girls' Brigade, Karen Wood from near Dores, wrote a report called *The Folklore of South Loch Ness-Side* as part of work undertaken for the Queen's Award. Much of the material came from published sources, but Wood also included stories that had been passed down the generations in her family. Wood describes how sometime in the 1970s two water bailiffs sitting in a boat at Dochgarroch Locks heard, felt and saw what looked like a large sea serpent moving under their boat. They got the impression it was angry, as if it had been thwarted by the closed lock gates (see FORT AUGUSTUS for more detail).

In 1960, Hector Whitehead, in a letter to the *Scotsman* of 17 September, related an incident where he and a fellow boat fisherman struggled to land a huge unseen 'something' near Dores. After several hours the line broke. Some weeks later their lure was found embedded in a large waterlogged timber which had blocked the Dochgarroch locks.

In around AD 565 at the River Ness, St Columba supposedly 'drove away a certain water monster.' One of Columba's followers was attacked as he swam across to collect a boat from the other side. The saint 'formed the sign of the cross in the empty air,' saying, 'Think not to go further nor touch thou that man. Quick! Go back!' The beast 'fled backwards more rapidly than he came.' Many commentators have treated this account as if its source – Adomnan's *Life of Columba*, written around a century after the saint's death – is an entirely reliable historical document. It is not. It is a hagiography, designed to demonstrate the superiority of Christianity, as evinced by miracles. In *The Guide to Mysterious Iona and Staffa* I wrote of the *Life*: 'First-time readers of this astonishing irruption from the Dark Ages Christian mind are often surprised to find it is explicitly supernatural in both tone and content… In the oldest and most authoritative book we have on Columba, we find telepathy, remote viewing, teleportation, telekinesis, precognition, exorcism, fairy-tale wizardry, death curses, illumination, sympathetic magic, angelology, demonology, weather, love and battle magic, remote healing, New Testament miracles, apotropaic rituals and mastery of life and death.' Context within the book is important: the defeat of the river monster is part of a section showing Columba's power over brute and dangerous nature, such as his slaying of a terrible wild boar with just the spoken word. Is the account in the *Life of Columba* the first report we have of a monster in the Ness Valley? Yes. Is it a credible report? Who can tell?

The church at Bona (Kirkton, NH602385, south of Dochfour House) is at the old churchyard of Cladh Uradain, the site of the ancient church of St Curadan. There is a nineteenth-century watch house and a number of interesting gravestones.

LOCHEND ᴌᐡ

As Lochend is where Loch Ness actually begins, it is fitting that fantasy and misidentification are first on the agenda. In 1845 the *NSA* identified a square feature on the peninsula between Abban Water, Loch Dochfour and Loch Ness as a Roman fort, the colonisation of an existing Iron Age fortification, Boness, aka Bonessia. Sadly for Romanophiles the legions never made it this far north, so the structure was probably the fragmentary remains of Bona Castle, aka Lochaleg Castle (NH602378), a fifteenth-century towerhouse that was already in ruins when the builders of the Caledonian Canal robbed it of its remaining stones (finding human bones in the process). Around 1450 a clan battle took place between Cameron of Lochiel and Hector Buie Maclean, Seneschal of Urquhart Castle. It ended with the multiple murders of hostages: Maclean displayed dead Camerons from the battlements of Bona Castle and Lochiel hanged two of Maclean's sons and other Glenurquhart men in view of the castle. From thereon it was deemed to be haunted and was called Caisteal Spioradain or Spiordan, the 'castle of the spirits'. What little is left of the castle hides under a tree-covered mound east of the lighthouse, in a location showing how it dominated the ford across the River Ness. Thinking of the ghosts, author Richard Frere (*Loch Ness*) asked George Reid, owner of the lighthouse, if he ever heard cries or groans. Reid pointed to the bare places on the larches which overhang the canal from the mound in a spooky manner, saying on windy nights the trees rub together to make strange noises.

In 1976 an underwater sidescan sonar survey found large round heaps of stone just off the lighthouse. The find was immediately compared to Stonehenge, which is several degrees of preposterousness above even the usual standard, not least because the putative temple builders would have been working in 30ft (9.1m) of water. Fortunately wiser counsel prevailed after it was learned that one of Telford's dredgers had dumped hundreds of tons of stone in the loch, something confirmed when a diver compared samples with an old canal quarry. As Frere noted in *Loch Ness*, 'It is a mercy that this truth was discovered before an Official Neolithic Exhibition took root near the site.'

In 1852, on the 1 July, the *Inverness Courier* reported 'A Scene from Lochend'. Two strange animals were seen swimming across the loch. Some 'thought it was the sea-serpent coiling along the surface, and others a couple of whales or large seals.' The inhabitants prepared to defend themselves with agricultural tools. One man putatively identified the creatures as a pair of deer, fetched his gun, and was about to fire, when he threw it down and shouted in Gaelic, 'God protect us, they are the Water Horses.' In the end, the animals did turn out to be horses, but actual not paranormal: two ponies from the Aldourie Estate less than a mile away across the loch. If anything, the story demonstrates the dread with which supernatural loch creatures were regarded.

In the 1970s several researchers came to the conclusion that Nessie behaved not like a natural creature but a supernatural one. Some saw the monster simply as an elusive spirit; others, most notably F.W. Holiday (*The Goblin Universe*), went further and regarded Nessie as outright malevolent, a manifestation of evil. This view came to be shared by the Revd Dr Donald Omand, one of the foremost exorcists in the Christian Church, with an international reputation for exorcising circus big tops and wild animal cages. In *Experiences of a Present-Day Exorcist* he wrote: 'What has been seen, and is still visible to some on occasion, is not a concrete present-day monster, but a projection into our day and age of something which had its habitat in Loch Ness and its surroundings, millions of years ago… What they [modern eyewitnesses] saw was not something that was taking place at that precise moment… It was something seen out of time. The so-termed Loch Ness Monster is not physical but psychical, a spectre of something which existed in the waters and on the shores of the vast lake in the dim recesses of the past.' Revd Omand received confirmation of his ideas at a meeting of the Swedish Organisation of Enquiry into Psychical Disorder. One of the presentations was on the terrible mental effects suffered by those who saw the monster of Lake Storsjon. Lake monsters, it seemed, were demonic. And they needed exorcising.

Along with fellow exorcist Revd Dom Robert Petipierre, a monk of the Anglican Order of St Benedict, Revd Omand drew up a plan based on a cross drawn over a map of the loch; on 2 June 1973, accompanied by Holiday, Dr Omand travelled by land to each of the four points of the cross. Lochend was the site of the first ritual. The participants knelt and received the sign of the cross in holy water on their foreheads, before Omand read out the first part of the exorcism, which included the lines, 'Grant that by the power entrusted to Thy unworthy servant, this highland loch, and the land adjoining it may be delivered from all evil spirits; all vain imaginations; projections and phantasms; and all deceits of the evil one. O Lord, subject them to Thy servant's commands that, at his bidding, they will harm neither man nor beast, but depart to the place appointed them, there to remain forever.' The group then visited a spot between Inverfarigaig and Dores, followed by Fort Augustus and near Urquhart Castle. At the end of the day they rowed out in a small boat to the middle of the loch where, over the centre of the imaginary great cross, Omand performed the final exorcism: 'I adjure thee, thou ancient serpent, by the judge of the quick and the dead, by Him who made thee and the world, that thou cloak thyself no more in manifestations of prehistoric daemons, which henceforth shall bring no sorrow to the children of men.' After the ceremony Revd Omand almost collapsed – something he had come to expect with every exorcism.

The exorcism is described by Holiday in an article in *Flying Saucer Review* (Vol. 19, No. 5 September-October 1973) with more detail in his book, *The Goblin Universe*. During the drive around Loch Ness and the various services, Holiday became increasingly aware of a tension building up, which appeared to affect all participants with the exception of Omand. He wrote: 'Personally, I expected the appearance of the monster or – much worse – something coming up under the boat.' Neither Nessie nor demon surfaced, but in the days following Holiday experienced a bizarre set of paranormal phenomena (see STRONE POINT and FOYERS), which Omand regarded as some kind of consequence of the exorcism.

THE 'WELLINGTON' LAYBY★ ⌂

The sonar which found the 'submerged Stonehenge' (above) also located the wreck of *R for Robert*, a Second World War Wellington bomber, which was finally raised in 1985. Information panels on the operation and a cairn marking the raising of the aircraft can be found in this long layby, the most northerly on the loch.

In 2001, from 23 April to 5 May, Operation Cleansweep, led by Jan Sundberg of the Global Underwater Search Team, sonar-searched the whole of the loch but without any result. They also deployed a large trap in an attempt to capture what they thought might be a candidate for Nessie-hood, a large eel. It was no coincidence that, on 2 May, following the publicity for the 'giant eel hunt', two very large dead eels were discovered on the beach below the layby, one of the most popular viewing points for the loch. Adrian Shine of Loch Ness 2000 identified them as conger eels, an exclusively marine species. Both had been killed by fishing gaffs. The identity of the hoaxers has never come to light, although it's a good bet they were sea anglers.

A second hoax took place two years later on 2 July 2003 when four fossil plesiosaur vertebrae were deposited below the layby. The National Museum of Scotland dated the bones at 150 million years old, and confirmed they were from a different geological region to Loch Ness. Another plesiosaur fossil, a femur, was found nearby in 1985. This wasn't a hoax however – it was a demonstration piece accidentally left behind by a tour guide.

Huge cliffs of granite tower above the next section of road, although the best view of them is from the other shore, from where you can see Creag Dhearg, Red Rock (NH581362), over 1250ft (381m) high, and the large gap of the Pit of the Giant. Somewhere near here is Creag nan Uamh, the Rock of the Caves, outside which is the large stone called the Clach an Fion, Wine Stone, or Clach nan Fiann, Fingal's Stone. Once there was a stalactite-filled cave which could shelter forty sheep or goats, and was much used by tinkers: in this or another cave a nineteenth-century cattle-thief and outlaw called Cameron hid for several years.

R. Macdonald Robertson, in *Selected Highland Folktales*, tells how a tinker took refuge on an autumn night in one of these caves. He placed some brushwood across the mouth of the cave to try and keep out the cold wind. His sleep was disturbed by his dog growling, so he removed the brushwood – only to come face-to-face with a 'huge monster with fiery eyes and long black body'. The dog immediately attacked the creature, and after a long struggle the monster headed for the loch, with the dog's jaws firmly fastened to its neck. Robertson treats this story as a place-legend – the troubled surface of the loch is caused by the endless underwater fight between dog and monster.

ABRIACHAN*** ᴧᴦ

In 1868, the *Inverness Courier* (8 October) reported that a huge fish had been found washed up on the shore at Abriachan. The carcass was identified as a skinned dolphin, presumably caught at sea and 'cast adrift in the waters of Loch Ness by some waggish crew' of a fishing boat passing through the Caledonian Canal to fool 'the credulous natives of Abriachan'. There's a great deal of speculation in this short piece, as it assumes the find was (a) a hoax, and (b) a dolphin, neither of which can be said for definite. The most valuable part of the report is its quoting unnamed residents as saying 'that a huge fish, similar in size and shape, had been occasionally seen gambolling in the loch for years back.' This is the earliest written reference in a modern medium to a monster tradition in the loch.

Rupert Gould's 1934 book *The Loch Ness Monster and Others* describes the experience of Mr D. Mackenzie of Dalnairn, who had seen something from a rock above Abriachan in October 1871 or 1872 coming from the other side of the loch at Aldourie. At first he thought it was a drifting log, but when it reached the midpoint in the water it suddenly appeared to come to life, took on the shape of an upturned boat, and took off at speed towards Urquhart Castle, wriggling and churning up the water. He was sure it was some kind of animal.

Tim Dinsdale's book *The Leviathans* includes a letter written to him in 1961 by Edward P. Smith of Selmeston, Sussex. In it Mr Smith recalled a story told to him by a woman of around seventy years of age whom he met at the Foyers Hotel. When she was a small girl, she and her two brothers had been picnicking one hot summer day.

Left: Abriachan community woodland: the frogs' chorus.

Below: Abriachan Pier: site of a supposed black-magic altar.

They heard a noise and saw coming down the slope:

> an enormous and extraordinary animal, bigger than an elephant, but about the same sort of colour. It had a head perched on a relatively slender neck, and it turned from side to side and seemed to peer at us, passing us a few yards to one side, and waddling down to the lake where it entered the water and disappeared. It had a long tail.

When the children told their father that night he caned them, not for telling a fairy story, 'but for telling a fairy story and pretending it is the truth.' Smith did not learn the name of the woman; he guessed that, based on her probable age, the incident took place in the very late 1870s. The children were 'on one of the northern slopes not far from the old graveyard'; although there are burial grounds at Drumnadrochit and Invermoriston, the best one that fits the description, with the slope behind and the loch visible, is Killianan at Abriachan.

The *Northern Chronicle* for 12 August 1933 reported that 'some 44 years ago an Abriachan mason, Alexander Macdonald, often saw a strange creature disporting itself on the loch in the early hours of the morning.' Macdonald had told a friend he had seen an unusual animal several times in the loch. Once when he was rescuing a lamb from the crags it swam inshore before turning back into the loch and submerging 'with a great commotion.' Macdonald travelled daily on the steamer between Abriachan Pier and Inverness, and would arrive at the pier in the early morning in 'subdued excitement' after seeing what he called 'the salamander'. The name stuck and at the start of the twentieth century the skipper of the ferry would for years shout to the pier-master, 'Seen the salamander today Sandy?' This account has to be handled with a degree of caution, as the anonymous source for the article was Alex Campbell, Nessie's greatest cheerleader, and Macdonald himself could not substantiate any of this because he had died 'a good many years ago.' The story had been handed down in the Campbell family, and may have altered in the re-telling, to be given life anew in the exciting days of 1933. Alex Campbell retold the episode in the *Scots Magazine* of May 1962.

In 1934, at about 1 a.m. on the 5 January, Arthur Grant, a veterinary student, was on a motorbike approaching the Abriachan turn when he saw something in the shadow of the bushes on the right-hand side of the road. As he approached, it revealed a small head on a long neck and made two great bounds across the road and then a great splash as it entered the water. He described it as 'hefty... [with] two front flippers'; there were two other flippers behind. The tail was powerful and rounded off. The total length was 15-20ft (4.5-6m). 'Knowing something of natural history I can say that I have never seen anything in my life like the animal I saw. It looked like a hybrid – a cross between a plesiosaur and a member of the seal family.' The full episode is in Nicholas Witchell's *The Loch Ness Story*.

Immediately south of the turn-off to Abriachan in the A82 is Abriachan Nurseries★, open to the public (with an honesty box). Turning right from the entrance brings you to the ruins of Killianan Burial Ground★ (NH57163466), site of the former church (now vanished), possibly dedicated to the sixth-century saint Finan, although another claim has been made for St Adamnan. The site has a beautifully sculptured medieval graveslab similar to those found on Iona, with an elaborate foliaceous cross and a pair of shears at the bottom, but it has been hidden by turf to prevent erosion. The local tradition is that it marks the grave of a Norwegian princess. Katharine Stewart in *The Story of Loch Ness* quotes local man Angus Grant saying in 1892 that there was a belief that many gravestones had been taken from the graveyard and 'a boat loaded with sculptured stones in the course of removal from Killianan was wrecked on Loch Ness and that, within living memory, the stones could be seen, on a clear day, at the bottom of the loch.' This may be a folkloric re-interpretation of the canal-related dumpings located by the sonar (see LOCHEND). In her book *Abriachan*, Katharine Stewart also claims the graveyard was a preaching site in the eighteenth century, and for many years a sanctuary with a radius of one mile – traditionally, some of the MacDonalds from Glencoe fled here after 1692 massacre. The Sanctuary Stone, which supposedly still stands, can no longer be found.

Abriachan Nurseries:
the 'Font Stone'.

If you walk up the slope through the lovely gardens themselves you come to the
Font Stone★, a large, flat heart-shaped rock rooted deep in the soil. In the centre
is a water-filled hole. The stone is usually called 'St Columba's Font Stone' but
another claim is that it was the foundation stone of St Finan's monastic cell, or just
a post-hole for an ordinary house. The hole is never dry, whatever the weather, and
if it is emptied it fills quickly. The source of the water remains mysterious. What is
certain is that it has long been highly valued for its apotropaic and healing qualities.
In *Abriachan* Katharine Stewart describes how, up until the first part of the twentieth century, infants had a few drops of the water put into their baptismal bowl,
and that it relieved the pain of childbirth. In *A Garden in the Hills* she notes that
'within living memory the women would come to give their babies a surreptitious
lick of this water, though the minister had baptised them officially in church.' J.M.
McPherson in *Primitive Beliefs in the North-East of Scotland* says it was resorted to by
childless women. Alexander MacDonald in *Story and Song from Loch Ness-Side* states
that the water kept the fairies away from infants, and pieces of cloth were deposited
about the stone, which were later kept on the children as anti-fairy talismans.

Elsewhere around the gardens are notices telling tales of local legend and folklore, such as the kelpies, and the protective power of rowan trees. There is also a
reproduction of the carving of a Pictish boar. Further up the hill are a series of
waterfalls. Eona MacNicol, author of *The Hallowe'en Hero*, recalled how during
her childhood the deep pools between the falls were home to lethal kelpies. In
Urquhart and Glenmoriston: Olden Times in a Highland Parish, first published in 1893,
William Mackay relates how in 1803 the factor, Duncan Grant, was so 'beaten and
pounded' by the Devil in the woods here that when he finally made it home he
took to his bed. The local witches then made a clay figure of him, stuck it with
pins and placed it in a stream, where it wore away until Duncan died. Given that
factors were hardly popular with tenants, and Duncan was involved in a local
religious dispute, perhaps something more mundane was the cause.

Several of Katharine Stewart's books refer to a Handfasting Stone located somewhere above the road. It was used in trial marriages, where the couple would ceremonially handfast (join hands) and be provisionally married for one year. If after that time there was no child and they no longer wished to be together, the couple were free to part without consequences, a very sensible arrangement considering the mercurial nature of the youthful human heart. Don Davidson, who runs the Abriachan Nurseries, has never managed to find the stone after years of searching, and the area is so filled with mossy boulders it now seems impossible to identify it. However if you look at the description of the process, the stone is not vertical with a hole that runs right through, but the couple 'would *kneel* and join their hands in *a hollow carved in the stone*' (my emphasis). This sounds to me like a description of the Font Stone, and I wonder if the two have been conflated.

Between the nursery and the Abriachan road-end on the A82 a locked gate leads down a leafy track to a pebble beach and the remains of Abriachan Pier, where once steamers called before the building of the road. 'Devil Worship Altar Discovered', claimed the 9 December 2000 issue of the online newspaper *Nessie's Loch Ness Times*. On the disused pier a couple from Abriachan found something with 'all the appearance of devil worship', a 'large triangular artifact, created from stones. Its internal decorations included standing stones at each corner. Feathers torn out of the bodies of birds were found under one of the central stones. *One side of the triangle appeared to be pointing across the loch at Boleskine House.*' (My emphasis) BOLESKINE is 9 miles (14km) away; at that distance the triangle could just as easily be aligned to the Monadhliath Mountains, or Dun Dearduil fort, or even the power station at Foyers; but no, the couple immediately concluded it could only be pointing at Boleskine – anything 'magical' around Loch Ness is connected to Crowley's celebrity status simply by default. There appears to have been nothing overtly Satanic about the structure – no pentagrams, no sigils, no words written in blood – and the feathers could easily have come from found carcasses rather than actually ripped from living birds, so my guess is that it was put up by a modern pagan. But nonetheless, the discoverers destroyed the triangle and asked the Highland Council to take down the sign indicating the way to the old pier, 'in case the place attracts more weirdos.' Nice place for a picnic.

A similar story is related in Katharine Stewart's *The Post in the Hills*. A countercultural French couple camped in the wood near the bottom of the hill for a summer. Polite, industrious and helpful, they were not unwelcome guests, and the man, creatively good with his hands, made items out of wood, bone and stone. One day after they had left, a visitor out walking came across their former encampment. There was a skull and a scatter of bones, a pattern of stones beside the fireplace, and an old iron pot full of water – the latter a native Indian tradition the Frenchman had picked up in South America, where the custom was to leave shelter (made of branches in this case) water and firing for whomever might next pass by. The visitor immediately interpreted all this as witchcraft, and punted the story to a newspaper. Mrs Stewart spent the rest of the day phoning the paper, eventually getting the editor to agree that it was a story without substance and would not be printed.

Abriachan Community Woodland.

Abriachan, zooform seat on Carn na Leitre hill path.

From the lochside a minor road climbs steeply to Abriachan itself. The words 'Community Woodland' may not strike you as immediately exciting and weighty with mystery, but then you've not encountered the Abriachan Forest Trust★★★, who must be in the running for some kind of Most Innovative Community Award. The best place to experience what they've done is to start from the car park one mile (1.5km) west of the village, where the Great Glen Way crosses the road (NH542356). From here, a series of short paths, including several that are wheelchair-friendly, take you into an otherworld. There's a bird hide on Loch Laide, with its crannog which was said to move about ('One Abriachan woman, not long dead, would not pass Loch Laide at dusk.' Katharine Stewart, *Abriachan*.) There are two tree houses, one with trees still growing through it; sculptures of froggy musicians harumph by a stream. The trees are festooned with child-painted wooden decorations, which are either charming or (at twilight) distinctively spooky in a *Blair Witch* kind of way. One path leads to a reconstructed Bronze Age round house. 'Make yourself at home,' says the sign, 'we are probably out hunting and gathering.'

North of the road is a path to the low hut circles of a Caiplich prehistoric settlement, found after heavy burning of the heather a few decades ago. Best of all are the longer paths, which take a bit of energy but are worth it. The steep Carn na Leitre hill path has welcome seats carved with animals, birds, fish, mushrooms and distorted faces, possibly invoking the spirits of the wood and/or the landscape. The route links to the Peat Path to Fitness, an imaginatively-conceived route dotted with sculptures designed to improve your fitness via peat-related tasks. Along the way you encounter several surreal sights: a giant's peat cutter stuck in the ground; a group of posts carved with nature symbols, standing like stark totem poles in a treeless landscape; and huge cattle horns silhouetted atop a ridge. Then you are invited to 'run like the wind from the sidhe [fairies] who haunted old Pete Bog.' There are sideloops to a reconstructed shieling and an illegal whisky still (formerly belonging to local hero Duncan Fraser, 'the King of the Smugglers').

Nearer the shore the network links up with paths managed by the Woodland Trust. One, the Old Coffin Track to the Clansman Hotel, follows a route once taken by funeral parties. The Abriachan Forest Trust publishes a newsletter: in its spring 2007 issue it described a recent event revisiting this old practice, which involved:

> a morose minister and old Morag MacPhail's last journey from Balchraggan to the boat awaiting her on Loch Ness. The small but sombre band were regaled by many Highland traditions and superstitions from the old crones keeping up the rear. Morag's plaid-covered pauper's coffin was carried by the menfolk and laid on the cairn stones at resting points.

The wooden seats on the path have animal tracks carved into them, as if the wood had once been liquid concrete and woodland creatures had scampered across it.

You will have noticed numerous references to books by Katharine Stewart. For several decades Mrs Stewart has eulogised the Abriachan area, and her books – *A Croft in the Hills, A Garden in the Hills, A School in the Hills, The Post in the Hills, Abriachan, Crofts and Crofting* and *The Story of Loch Ness* – are all highly recommended. All of them contain snippets of folklore and strangeness.

Abriachan in particular discusses several local people touched by some element of the supernatural. In the 1940s Margaret Noble, who lived near the foot of the road to Achpopuli, had second sight, an unwelcome gift, as mostly she saw funerals. In the early nineteenth century a woman lived in what is now a small ruin on the moor just up from the schoolhouse. She was said to know the fairies and, despite her kind nature, rumours circulated that she was a witch. 'Her brother… one day shot a hare, then took malicious neighbours up to see his sister alive, this

Abriachan. The Giant's peat axe.

Abriachan. The cows.

proving she was no witch.' A man from Caiplich had to walk, in silence, for 50 miles (80km) to Speyside to ask a certain person to de-hex him (this was probably Gregor Willox MacGregor, alias Willox the Warlock or Warlock Willie, whose rumbustious life included tricking a kelpie out of its bridle, a highly magical item, and acquiring a mermaid's stone, a small clear crystal more commonly known as the Clach Ghrigair, the Macgregor Stone). A cockerel was buried alive under the doorstep of a house to cure an epileptic child. An elderly man died after being seen casting a shadow on a cloudy day, proof that in his later days he had been accompanied, however unknowingly, by some kind of harbinger of death.

Crofts and Crofting mentions a woman, still alive in the 1960s, whose spell-lifting powers were inherited from her parents and grandparents. Before sunrise

Abriachan 'totem' poles.

she would collect water from a burn which flows under a bridge leading to an ancient graveyard – the 'Bridge of the Living and the Dead'. Into a pail she would put her gold wedding ring and a silver coin, then pour in the water, mentioning the person's name and adding a blessing: 'in the name of the Father, the Son and the Holy Spirit I bless you and may all evil depart from you.' (The exact same ritual is described in another twentieth-century report from KILTARLITY.)

Two men went missing on their way home from the illicit whisky bothy on Creag Dhearg (NH581363); one was found dead in the burn, but the other vanished. Dogs, especially hunting dogs, could once upon a time talk, and convened near Tomachoin, to the north (NH550372). Nearby Lady's Cairn (NH558385) marked the resting place of Lady Grant's coffin on its way to Inverness for burial, but a spurious romantic story had grown up around it of 'an abducted lady, accidentally killed by one of the rescuing party.' In the same area was the mineral Fuaran Dearg, Red Well, a 'cloutie well' where offerings of coloured threads and clothes ('clouts') were hung on the trees and bushes on 1 May, and Creag nan Sithean, hill of the fairies. If you look at Cnoc an Duine, the hill of the man (NH570361) from the right angle you can see the man himself lying on his back.

In *A Garden in the Hills* Mrs Stewart also mentions 'a green place' somewhere south of Balchraggan where a local man who went on to become a minister and army chaplain told her that as a young boy herding the cattle, he met a small group of fairies. When he went home his mother skelped him for telling lies, but he believed in fairies for the rest of his life. 'About the same time, in another place, an old couple had "brownies" living in their outhouse. Every evening they would put a dish of milk out in a hollow stone for their small guests. Every morning it was gone and they were well pleased, for the brownies had to be looked after if they were to be helpful.'

In *Story and Song from Loch Ness-Side*, Alexander MacDonald told the story of a young man, taking the high road in the small hours, who was:

> addressed in good Gaelic by about a dozen little women wearing green caps. They made a circle round him, and remarked that he was very early on the road. Having a loaded gun in his possession, he pointed it at one after another of them; but in every case it refused to fire, and he eventually made off. Later on he tried the gun again, and it fired.

Mollie Hunter, who lived in the area in the 1950s, set *The Kelpie's Pearls* in Abriachan – a tale of an old woman's encounter with a kelpie which lived in a pool beside her house. The writer Richard Frere (*Loch Ness*) set up a sawmill on the steep Abriachan hill, facing the loch, to make fir posts. A strong local demand for hazel products soon became evident. 'Once we had a visit from a whimsical man who needed a stick for his water divining. He searched for many hours and eventually found what he wanted; on leaving with his twisted rod he told us, straight faced, that only certain trees contained the special magic.'

BRACHLA HARBOUR AND THE CLANSMAN HOTEL

Back on the A82 this is the next point of interest travelling south. On the shore just north of the harbour, at NH564331, is a large boulder called Clach Mohr, Big Stone, also known as the Black Rock; it was allegedly thrown by a giant from Dores. The Abriachan giant chucked a white boulder back.

In 1987 the twenty vessels of the Loch Ness Project's 'Operation Deepscan' used Brachla Harbour as their base. They drew a 'sonar curtain' along the loch: three contacts were recorded of a strength less than a 10m monster but stronger than the usual fish echoes...

In 2001, *Nessie's Loch Ness Times* for 10 March reported tailbacks to the laybys here as motorists rushed to view 'what appeared to be the top end of a periscope travelling down the loch.' One witness dismissed it as 'just two ducks.' A plastic plesiosaur is now to be seen in the grounds of the Clansman Hotel, and a purple multi-humped Nessie on the dockside. Boat trips leave from the harbour.

TEMPLE PIER (NH529300)

The last steamers calling here did so before the Second World War. Boat trips leave from the harbour.

On 8 August 1972 an underwater camera took the controversial 'flipper photograph', which supposedly shows a large diamond-shaped flipper. The pictures the public saw were creatively improved by the press; the original is far less impressive. Seven years later, on the 30 July 1979, Alistair and Sue Boyd saw a huge hump from the layby above Temple Pier. It was about the size of a yacht hull.

St Ninian's Well,
Temple Pier.

In 1969 a fake monster was built off the pier for Mirisch Films' *The Private Life of Sherlock Holmes*. On 22 July it developed a leak in a buoyancy tank and sank just east of Urquhart Bay in 650ft (200m) of water. The two-man submarine *Pisces* tried to locate it but the model was never seen again. Is it still there? 'Some say the true beast was so irritated by the way its shape was taken in vain that it sank the model with a single blow from a flipper.' (Richard Frere, *Loch Ness*). In the film, Holmes and Watson are pitted against Germans using midgets to man a submarine disguised as the monster. There is a rumour, reported by Tim Dinsdale, that miniature subs were secretly tested in the loch during the Second World War. Possibly related (as source of the rumour?) is 'The Secret of the Loch', a story in *Detective Weekly* of 25 May 1940, in which Sexton Blake investigates a Nazi submarine that has penetrated the loch.

The name 'Temple' has given rise to the usual vapid speculation about Druids and the Templars. A tour guide told me with complete conviction there was a Druidic temple here. 'Canmore', the website of the Royal Commission on Ancient and Historic Monuments in Scotland, sets the historical record straight. The name actually derives from An Teampull, a common Gaelic word which does literally translate as 'temple' but in practice denotes an early stone church. There are a great many 'An Teampulls' around Scotland, and they are all rather mundane (if early) churches, with not a Templar or Druid in sight. The chapel on this site was in use until at least 1556. The ruins were still here in 1763, and the burial ground, Cill Santninian, lasted until at least 1835. Near the chapel were a rag or cloutie well and two ash trees on which the clouts were hung. Virtually everything was destroyed when the road was built. Only three things remain: a Celtic cross-slab now in St Ninian's Episcopal church (see GLEN URQUHART); a monolith on the north side of the road, presumably placed there in the 1930s, said to mark the site of finds during the road construction; and, a few metres to the east, the well (NH52943002).

Once, people would drink the waters to cure various afflictions and leave shreds of clothing on the bushes nearby. ('A pilgrimage to the holy wells of the Temple and St Columba, and a faithful and proper use of their waters, not only cured the pilgrim of his bodily ailments, but also shielded him from the darts of the Evil One and his agents', as William Mackay put it in *Urquhart and Glenmoriston: Olden Times in a Highland Parish*). Now the well, which still flows, sits largely ignored inside a stone structure.

The chapel was certainly dedicated to St Ninian, who died in around 432, and this has led to suggestions that Ninian actually founded it, but there is no evidence that the saint was ever in this neck of the woods. It appears to have held at least one relic (a crucifix) of St Drostan, which was presumably lost at the Reformation.

'Their evil influence was exercised quietly and in secret and involved the objects of their attentions in misfortune or even death.' Such were the Urquhart witches, who Mackay (*Urquhart and Glenmoriston*) says would congregate on a rock called An Clarsach, The Harp, on the loch shore in the grounds of Tychat. There the Devil sat on the edge of the rock and serenaded them with bagpipes or stringed instruments (hence the name). 'The effect of his music on the old women was marvellous: they danced and flung as no maid of seventeen ever did, and indulged in pranks and cantrips which the lithest athlete could not touch' (Mackay). Tychat is to the northeast of Temple Pier. I have been unable to locate The Harp; it too may well have been destroyed during the road-widening.

In *Project Water Horse*, monster hunter Tim Dinsdale found that the stretch of the loch near the shore here provoked within him 'a curious sensation of unease at night. This was so powerful I had to force myself to overcome it.' A friend, Mrs Cary, a very experienced fishing enthusiast, said she too in her younger days had felt the same unease, and when rowing home she would avoid fishing in the immediate area – 'There was something "unpleasant" about it.' (For more on Mrs Cary, see URQUHART CASTLE.)

Two bronze memorial plaques near Upper Drumbuie (NH51833155) record the scattering here of the ashes of the Celtic artist George Bain and his wife Jessie MacKintosh. There are three cupmarks on a rock outcrop by Wester Achtuie (NH52173133) – although eighty-eight were recorded in 1888 – and more cupmarks on bedrock to the northeast.

5

THE NORTH SHORE OF LOCH NESS II: DRUMNADROCHIT, GLEN URQUHART AND URQUHART CASTLE

Behemoth biggest born of earth upheav'd
His vastness; fleec't the flocks and bleating rose
As plants; ambiguous between sea and land
The river-horse and scaly crocodile

John Milton, *Paradise Lost*, vii, 453

The world's largest kelpie continues to evade capture in Loch Ness and appears
to have developed a positive thirst for publicity.
Newt Scamander (J.K. Rowling), *Fantastic Beasts and Where to Find Them*

DRUMNADROCHIT★★★ ⌁

The centre of the Nessie tourist industry, 'Drum', as it is known locally, is more
than just a monster honey pot, although you have to dig a bit to find the less
obvious sights. Boat trips on the loch can be hired from a number of places.

In around 1880, Mr E.H. Bright and his cousin were walking by the shore
near Drum when they saw a creature emerge from the woods around 100 metres
away. It was dark grey, had a long neck, a snake-like head, and four legs. The animal waddled into the water and quickly submerged, leaving a large wash. Several
three-pronged footprints were later found on the spot. At the time Bright was
about eight years old; his grandfather reluctantly admitted there had been talk of
a strange creature in the past, but 'it was never discussed by the people of the village.' The story is told in a 1962 letter from Mr D.J.A. Briggs of Wimbledon, and
is reproduced in Dinsdale's *The Leviathans*. Mr Briggs also very briefly mentions a
sighting by Bright's friend Jimmy Hossack, possibly as early as the 1860s.

In around 1916, James Cameron, head keeper of the Balmacaan Estate, came
into the bar of the Drumnadrochit Hotel to down a brandy to steady his nerves.
Kenneth Mackay insisted on walking him home; Cameron told him he had been
out fishing when 'an enormous animal' had surfaced, causing him to go dizzy and
fall to the bottom of the boat. He swore Mackay to secrecy; it wasn't until the
fulcrum year of 1933 that the story found its way to Rupert Gould. A few decades
later, in the 1930s, a group of schoolchildren said they had seen a most peculiar
and horrifying animal in the bushy swamp in Urquhart Bay (now designated as a
Site of Special Scientific Interest, although for different reasons).

The Loch Ness
2000 Exhibition.

Between the 1930s and the present day, more sightings than can be easily catalogued here have been reported for the waters of Urquhart Bay. This is possibly due to the sheer number of visitors in the Drumnadrochit area, with the concomitant weight of expectation. Whatever the reason, Urquhart Bay remains 'Nessie Central'.

Loch Ness 2000 Exhibition★★★. If you want to take the mystery of the monster seriously, Loch Ness 2000 is the best place to start. You move through a forty-minute audiovisual tour of six themed spaces which use video, lighting effects and props to explore the biology and geology of the loch and the history of monster sightings and Nessie research. Among the strengths of the exhibition are the candid way it discusses photographic hoaxes while respecting the integrity and sincerity of eyewitnesses. There is also a striking animated 3D tour of the loch floor, and an easy-to-follow explanation of the food pyramid in the loch – basically there isn't enough food to support any large animal, so bad news for leviathan fans, but plenty of thinking – and arguing – material for anyone who wants to seriously engage with the mystery. Even if there are no plesiosaurs here, real-world candidates for the identity of the monster are discussed, including a sturgeon, a truly strange-looking fish with a distinctly 'prehistoric reptile' look. Sturgeons have been caught off the mouth of the River Ness.

Unique to Loch Ness 2000 is the inclusion of some of the actual artefacts – a sonar vessel and a one-man bathysphere – that have been used during Nessie hunts. Like other pursuits that were once thought trivial and ephemeral – such as pop music, *Doctor Who* and comic books – the quest for Nessie has been going long enough now for it to have its own cultural history. Here you can touch the authentic artefacts of that history – a hands-on archaeology of Nessie hunting. The exhibition was designed, scripted and narrated by Adrian Shine of the Loch

One of a pair of carved heads on the entrance to Loch Ness 2000 (the former Drumnadrochit Hotel). Does the crescent imply she is the Queen of the Night?

Ness Project; the Project also runs a field and education centre, hosting scientists from all over the world who are studying Loch Ness, and funding Adrian Shine's research. The exhibition is housed in the former Drumnadrochit Hotel, a grand Victorian pile dated 1882; on either side of the entrance are two carved heads – close inspection reveals that the man is crowned with a star and the woman with a crescent, symbolism of a sun king and a moon queen. To the east of the building a small reed-edged pond supports both a plastic plesiosaur and a live sturgeon, although the latter is rarely seen on the surface except in hot weather.

The Original Loch Ness Visitor Centre★★ nearby is a different beast altogether, with a more traditional film viewed in a small cinema. Presented by Gary Campbell, the programme does an enthusiastic job of covering Nessie sightings but perhaps plays fast and loose with some of the known hoaxes. The cinema and the corridor around it have a number of 'Nessieabilia' images and good photos of places and historic events from the surrounding area. There is a plastic plesiosaur outside. A notice reads: 'Visitors climb on the Monster at their own risk', which is good advice in any circumstances. If you want to characterise the two attractions, you could say 'The Original' is a Loch Ness Monster exhibition (motto: 'we believe'), while Loch Ness 2000 is a Loch Ness visitor centre (which, if it had a motto, would be, 'we investigate').

Careful study of the corridors and walls of the Drumnadrochit Hotel reveals a wealth of Nessieabilia, from photographs and paintings to record sleeves and DVD releases.

South of the exhibition centres, the road bridge over the River Enrick is reputedly the site where MacUian (MacIan) clansmen from Divach and Clunemore ambushed and killed a party of Clan Grant men. They washed the decapitated heads in the pool known today as MacUian's Pool and sent the heads back to the

Grant chief in Strathspey. Also somewhere on the river here is the ford where a pious Presbyterian layman found a boy struggling with the current. He placed the boy on his back and waded across. In mid-channel his load suddenly became very heavy, and on looking round he found that he was carrying 'an Evil Thing of great size, which was trying hard to press him under the water.' The man called upon the Trinity, and instantly the demon vanished. The story is told in William Mackay's 1893 book *Urquhart and Glenmoriston*. The bridge is also a good place to view the ancient shoreline of Loch Ness, dating from an era when the loch was much higher – the ridges to the west, south of the river, are particularly clear. So wherever you are in Drum you're walking through a prehistoric landscape. The village green is home to a floral feature in the shape of Urquhart Castle.

Moving further south, you come to a crossroads, to where the Revd James Doune Smith continued to take his nightly stroll from the Manse for some time after his death (at least according to William Mackay in *Urquhart and Glenmoriston*). The road east takes you to the Manse, now the Benleva Hotel★★, a 300-year-old building that has also been a private home and a college of Celtic culture run by George Bain, the expert on Celtic art. The hotel has a reputation for hauntings. The proprietors Allan and Stephen Crossland related a number of incidents to me. A regular was sitting on the bar stool next to the entrance to the lounge when he felt a distinct, hard push in the back. There was no one there. The hotel dog has been seen several times watching something invisible pass from the bar entrance to the lounge door, and back again. In his room Allan felt a very strong gust of wind, followed by three knocks, repeated twice. Stephen now stays in the room and has experienced nothing out of the ordinary. In one bedroom the chambermaid would close the latch of the wardrobe before cleaning the bathroom, but whenever she returned the wardrobe door was open. A guest was passed on the stairs by an older man dressed in tweeds; he asked the staff who the stranger was, but no one else was staying at the hotel.

One room seems to attract the most attention. A Scottish couple reported someone in the room with them. The next night an Italian man said someone had grabbed his ankle. Much later the male half of an American couple emailed the hotel a year after their stay in the same room, saying he had seen a woman in nineteenth-century costume pointing to the window; he had been too embarrassed to mention it at the time. From 2006, however, the ghosts seem to have calmed down and no recent phenomena have been reported.

The towering, gnarled Spanish sweet chestnut tree at the front of the hotel is reputedly a hanging tree; the large horizontal branch pointing away from the hotel is said to bear the burn mark of the rope. The reputation of the hotel was sufficient to attract an all-night vigil by a ghost investigation team, although as the proceedings were being broadcast live on a radio station, with the concomitant expectations not only of the ghost team but of delivering the entertainment demands of an audience hungry for 'spooky thrills from Loch Ness', the results were, perhaps inevitably, due more to imagination and over-interpretation of the mundane, rather than anything authentically supernatural.

Nessie simulacrum,
Old Kilmore
graveyard.

Past the hotel is Old Kilmore churchyard★ (NH51522958), with carved grave-stones and a nineteenth-century 'anti-grave-robbing watch house'. A tradition circulates that several of the old earthfast grave slabs were intended to protect the occupants from the depredations of wolves, although this story is told elsewhere and I have been unable to disentangle folklore from fact. The current ivy-covered ruins have a carved stone with the words *Domus Dei* (house of God), 'AG', and the date 1630, and are from the seventeenth-century church built by the Revd Alexander Grant. Before the Reformation there was a twelfth-century church dedicated to St Mary, Cill Mhoire (= Kilmore). Prior to that... Well, in Book III chapter 14 of his *Life of St Columba*, St Adomnan describes how Columba was 'beside the lake of the River Ness' when he suddenly announced that he must go quickly to baptise a virtuous pagan, who was near death. He baptised the man, Emchat or Emchattus, his son Virolecus, and their household at a place Adomnan called Airchartdan. Scholars have been arguing ever since where Airchartdan was. Isabel Henderson, in 'Inverness, A Pictish Capital' (Field Club), says that Airchartdan 'is a complete transmutation of a British name into Irish and, on this basis, it has been suggested that there was a Columban monastery in Urquhart in Adomnan's time.' In other words, Kilmore may be the site of a church founded by St Columba in around AD 565. Alas, this is really just academic speculation, as we will never really know. The Pictish St Drostan is also mentioned as a founder, as are of course the inevitable Druids.

The graveyard has several magnificent old yew trees. In a fascinating lit-tle book, *The Churchyard Yew and Immortality*, Vaughan Cornish says that yews, a pre-Christian symbol of immortality, were planted on pagan religious sites, and somehow survived the advent of Christianity, becoming the accepted tree for graveyards. Vaughan also quotes Walter Johnson's *Byways of British Archaeology* (1912): 'in the north of Scotland the yew was credited with a peculiar property. A

Drumnadrochit parish church, gravestone.

branch of graveyard yew would enable one chief to denounce another in such a manner that, while the clansmen standing by could hear the threats, the intended victim could not hear a word.' The yew had to be grasped in the left hand. Back in the village, the current parish church (NH509295) has more modern gravestones, including a poignant one depicting a young lad in a Scout's uniform. To the west, on a terrace above the games park (NH505293) is the small burial ground of the Grants of Balmacaan.

'UFO Sightings at Loch Ness' – I don't think you can get a better attention-grabbing headline than that, which was the lead story in *Nessie's Loch Ness Times* on 15 February 2003. Lights were seen over the village during successive nights, and a video taken by Ian and Liz Gresham of Drumnadrochit was shown on BBC Scotland and the Fox network in the USA. The best guess is that it was an example of the phenomenon called 'Earthlights' by researcher Paul Devereaux. Earthlights are an electromagnetic discharge caused by the geological stresses of fault lines in the earth's crust. Local scientist John Dijkslag, from Croy, agreed, and was quoted as saying: 'It's a light show by Mother Earth… the lights originate in the fault line in the middle of the loch.' Similar lights were seen above the Kessock Bridge in December 1990.

Part of the local path network (pick up the leaflet from the tourist office) takes you to the site of the former Balmacaan House in the southwest of the village (NH497284), once a titanic mansion lording over an equally extensive estate. The American millionaire Bradley Martin took over the estate in 1884. Given that

Bradley was already on record for throwing the most expensive party ever, it was no surprise that he lived it up as a laird, not only entertaining extravagantly but also paying his staff well. Richard Frere, in *Loch Ness*, tells the story of F.S. Spencer, Bradley's American butler, who, having embezzled household funds to fund his alcohol and gambling habit, got drunk on whisky and, just as a large party was starting, ostentatiously shot himself on the staircase. The house was demolished in 1972: 'As the explosive charges rocked the great walls it is said that ghostly faces were seen peering through some upper windows' (Frere).

Taking one of the uphill paths through Balmacaan Woods brings you to Craig Mony (or Craigmonie) hill fort (NH50029), with spectacular views. The legend is that this is the scene of the last stand made by a Viking army. Monie (or Moni), son of the king of Scandinavia, landed in Crinan, Argyll and laid waste to the country. A counterattack cut off his ships so he retreated north through the Great Glen. The Vikings were defeated on the plain around Drumnadrochit and Moni was killed at CORRIMONY. Meanwhile the princess, his sister, hid in a crevice called Leabaidh-Nighean-an-Righ, 'the Bed of the King's Daughter'. The Highlanders found her and let her live among them for many years. Like I said, it's a legend.

Another walking route and minor road takes you up the steep hill to Divach Falls. Where the road crosses the River Coilty (NH497281) is the site of a life-saving leap across the gorge by a Grant rent-collector fleeing from MacIan pursuers. The gorge is spectacular; repeating the Grant's exploit is not recommended. Divach Lodge (NH494273), now a private house, was once a summer destination for Edwardian high society – its position perched on the edge of an abyss, overlooking Divach Falls, attracted Lily Langtry, Ellen Terry, Anthony Trollope, Edward VII (and mistresses) and Sir James Barrie, the latter of whom conceived the idea for Mary Rose here. Immediately outside the lodge on the roadside is a peculiar chair-like structure roughly constructed of large stones. The back of the 'seat' is incised with two irregular ovals and what may be the letters:

I B (P?) O
X

followed by a regular oval below. Ruth and Frank Morris, in *Scottish Healing Wells*, identify this as the covering for a well, built over because of a drowning.

BUNLOIT AND GROTAIG

A narrow, steep 5km road winds south of Drum to Grotaig, home to the Goshem pottery (open to visitors) and commune (NH490237). Here also resides Neil Oram, one of the more extraordinary characters associated with Loch Ness. His main claim to fame is that he wrote *The Warp*, the longest play in the world (performances vary between eighteen and twenty-six hours, depending on how much the cast are able to get a move on). Its rare productions have taken on a semi-legendary character. The central character, Phil Masters, is a kind of every-hippie, constantly following one promised route to nirvana after another, to end up only with the search and not what is sought. Other characters include St Michael of the Cross, Cynthia the Laser Christ Woman, a prophet called Bob God, and Arthur the Cosmic Grocer. From descriptions, it's a very 'sixties' piece, taking in Stonehenge, alien abduction, robots, telepathy, sex, drugs, Scientology, open relationships, past lives, the Age of Aquarius, time travel and 'vibrations'. And lots and lots of New Age psycho-political theorising. The most graspable reference point might be to imagine the parallel-universe logorrhoeac offspring of *The Archers* and the original *Hitch-Hiker's Guide to the Galaxy*, but with two hour-long meal breaks and an interval for beer, sausages and coffee. One actor described his minor part in *The Warp* to me as 'the most extraordinary, strange and memorable experience of my career', but I suspect it is more fun to appear in or read about than to actually sit through the full twenty-four-hour experience. If you are keen to check it out, the entire 1979 ICA production (directed by the doyen of alternative theatre, the great beetle-browed eccentric and Fortean *agent provocateur* Ken Campbell, and starring a then-unknown Bill Nighy and Jim Broadbent) is available on six three-hour videotapes from Neil's site www.warp-experience.com, from where you can also download the full script. But don't say I didn't warn you.

In 2000 a youth hanged himself in the woods by Goshem. As reported in the *Sunday Mirror* of 4 June, an anonymous hacker then posted messages on the website of the commune's organic farm, accusing Neil Oram of running a cult encouraging suicide and of being involved in black magic. Local people, it was claimed, lived in fear of 'sinister goings-on' at the farm. The whole thing was not only bunkum (the police had already stated there were no suspicious circumstances surrounding the death, and the people at Goshem tend to be on the gentler side of humanity) but also disrespectful to the dead boy. And to cap the ludicrousness, Neil was accused of being linked to – you've guessed it – everyone's favourite bogeyman-of-convenience, Aleister Crowley.

Mackay's *Urquhart and Glenmoriston* gives details of the fearsome cailleach or supernatural hag who lurked in the mountains hereabouts. The Cailleach Allt-an-Dunain lived in Allt-an-Dunain, a burn which runs into the Coilty, near the Clunebeg bridge, at NH503205; 'Many a man did she waylay and destroy on his way across the bleak Monadh Leumnach.' She had a particular animus against Macdougalls and Macdonalds, and her favourite killing ground was the Bunloit road, there disposing of Somerled Macdonald in the 1790s, Dugald Macdougall about a decade later, and then his son, young Dugald. She was last seen in the 1850s by Mary Macdonald of Grotaig, who, despite being a Macdonald, survived to tell the tale, only dying in 1902. The Cailleach Allt-Saigh, who lived near the Alltsigh burn, protected people from the malice of Cailleach Allt-an-Dunain by warning them of her murderous plans.

GLEN URQUHART★★

This attractive glen runs west from Drum and is easy to explore. Old records give us traces of witchcraft, folk magic and apotropaic rituals, and again many of the details come from Mackay's *Urquhart and Glenmoriston*, written in 1893. Crops were given protection by marching through and around them carrying blazing torches on the eve of St John the Baptist. 'Lambs were buried at the threshold of dwelling-houses and cow-huts, as a protection from the demons that sought admission.' Michael Kynoch buried a young ox alive, clearly a propitiatory act as Kynoch's cattle were dying and he was trying to influence some kind of supernatural agency. (Was this the fairies? Some kind of spirit of the earth or the hills? A cattle-related Christian saint like Maelrubha, to whom bulls were still being sacrificed in Loch Maree? We'll never know.) To the Kirk Session of Urquhart it was 'a sacrifice to Satan' and on 10 October 1658 Kynoch underwent a penance and punishment (two centuries later a live cock was buried at Lewistown [Lewiston] 'as a peace offering to the spirit of epilepsy'). The Kirk Session also admonished Marjorie Gray for cursing David Innes; she had done so on her bare knees, which, by imitating the posture of prayer, added power to the curse. A clay figure was found near the front door of the house of an Army officer in the glen. The workmen who found it were horrified and threw it away but the major collected the corp crèadha of himself and presented it to the Pitt Rivers Museum in Oxford, where it still resides although it is not on display.

Fairy lore was universal, as was the rowan tree to keep them away. The Bible or a bar of iron was placed in the bed or the cradle, to protect the mother (who could be abducted to act as a wet-nurse for elvish imps) or the infant: in the 1830s 'a child was taken out of a Glen-Urquhart cradle, and a changeling put in its place which soon withered away and died.' Offerings of milk were poured on the fairy-knowes at Tornashee and Lochletter to persuade their inhabitants to refrain from milking the cows or taking the substance out of the milk in the dairies.

Up to the 1820s an ancient hand bell was rung in front of the coffin at funerals, to protect the corpse from demons who would claim the departed soul. An Clagan Beag, 'The Little Bell', was carried by the beadle, who was paid a small fee, the last incumbent being Ewen Koy Macfie. Despite local opposition, the spirit of evangelical Protestantism swept away the custom and the bell disappeared with it.

Marian McNeill in *The Silver Bough* identifies Creag Neimhidh in the glen as 'the rock of the Nemet', from 'nevay', a Druidic sacred site. I have been unable to locate it.

GLEN URQUHART – MILTON

Off the steep A833 north of Milton there are several prehistoric sites. Clachmhor Cupmarked Stone★ (NH49923109), with at least ninety cupmarks, is in a field northeast of Culnakirk farm. A possible surrounding ring of stones reported in

Victorian times has vanished, if it was ever there. Another two cupmarks can be seen on an earthfast boulder about 50 yards (45m) to the west (NH49873107). Carn Daley Chambered Cairn★ (NH49453145) is a Clava passage grave in the croft of Easter Balnagrantach. Damaged, but still worthwhile, if only to visit the supposed home base of Daley the Druid. The story is well-worn. Many years ago, there was no loch in the Great Glen. A magical spring was guarded by the Druid Daley (or Daly), who placed a taboo upon it: anyone was allowed to use the waters for healing or other beneficent purpose, but they must always replace the cover, else a great disaster would befall the area. One day a woman was collecting water when she heard her infant cry out (the source of the pain being fire, scalding liquid or an adder – versions vary). She forgot the Druid's instruction and the well overflowed and flooded the valley, taking the low-lying farms with it.

This is a common creation myth for a number of lochs, but here it has given rise to one of the most ludicrous examples of fantasy place-name etymology in Scotland. On seeing the flood, the locals are said to have exclaimed, 'Tha loch nis ann' (There is a loch there now), and 'loch nis ann' became 'Loch Ness'.

Mackay reports that Peter Fraser, a farmer from Culnakirk saw the phantom battle of Blar-an-Aonaich behind Culnakirk, with 'spectre armies engaged in a sanguinary struggle, foreboding, it is feared, a conflict and carnage the like of which our Parish has not yet seen.' Fraser died in 1913. Mackay's account, written in 1893, implies that others had seen the battle in the past. Mackay also noted that, 'Alexander Mackay, the laird who sold Achmonie, for years after his death continued his old earthly custom of visiting his stables.' Achmonie (Achmony) is at NH503308, east of Culnakirk.

POLMALLY

R. Macdonald Robertson, in *Selected Highland Folktales* (1961) relates an experience recounted to him by the late Alexander Gunn, shepherd, formerly of Balchrick, Sutherland. When he was hired by Mr Grant, laird of Polmaily, Gunn was asked where he wanted to live. The shepherd pointed to a house opposite the farm, but the laird refused straight away, because it was haunted. Gunn scoffed at this, and set up home. The first night he slept well. 'You're a brave man, Sandy,' said the laird the next day and gave him a dram. The second night passed equally peacefully. On the third night Gunn was woken at midnight by a terrible noise, as if all windows and doors were being smashed in. The building shook as if in a storm. Overhead in the attic came a noise like a horse trampling and wallowing. Gunn lit a candle by his bedside and sensed the presence of evil. Grabbing hold of his Bible he hid under bedclothes until the storm subsided some five or six minutes later. Everything loose in the house had moved and doors had crashed open, but Gunn saw nothing. Next morning he told the gardener, who said he too had spent a night in it and it was a droch àite, an evil place. Gunn stayed for weeks with the Bible under his pillow. The noises only occurred every third night.

Cairn erected in memory of Pamela C.D. Ross, killed by lightning here on 2 August 1950.

St Ninian's church, Glen Urquhart. Anti-grave-robbing mortsafe.

GLEN URQUHART – UPPERTOWN

High on the moors to the north of Balbeg is a small cairn of stones★ (NH45233242), now in poor condition, on which can just about be seen the words: IN MEMORY OF PAMELA C.D. ROSS KILLED BY LIGHTNING HERE ON 2 AUGUST 1950. Pamela Ross had connections with the glen, and the family came and built the cairn some time after her death. Arriving at this sad memorial hidden away on a desolate moor, I found my head filled with Joy Division's mournful 'In A Lonely Place'. Directions: take the minor road north from the A831 through Marchfield to Uppertown (no cars after the gates). Follow the track onto the moors past Achratagan croft, then a former quarry (on the right) and a wind turbine (on the left). Follow the rough track northeast; at the first fork turn right, then ford the Allt a' Bhaile Uachdaraich and at the second fork (which is not obvious) turn left. The cairn is some 100 yards (91m) north, hidden behind a slight rise.

Corrimony
Chambered Cairn,
looking from the
cairn and passage
to the outer ring
of standing stones.

GLEN URQUHART – ST NINIAN'S EPISCOPAL CHURCH★

Situated in a lovely spot on the north shore of Loch Meiklie (NH43123042) this small, pleasant church has an attractive graveyard with a metal mortsafe (used to prevent fresh corpses being bodysnatched). Incorporated into the altar is a medieval sculptured sandstone cross which was formerly in the chapel at TEMPLE before being taken to Corrimony House. When the latter burned down it found its way here. Earlier accounts call it 'St Ninian's Stone' or 'The Templar's Stone'. Around the edge reads the inaccurate legend, 'From the Knights Templar Temple house'.

GLEN URQUHART – BALMACAAN FOREST

Carn Mharbh Dhaoine, the Rock of the Dead Men, marks the site of the 1691 Battle of Corriebuy (Coire Buidhe). A party of Urquhart men confronted some cattle-thieves from Lochaber. After arbitration the reivers agreed to hand over the plunder and all seemed well – until a hare appeared. Believing it was a well-known local witch in disguise, one of the Urquhart men shot at it. The Lochaber men thought themselves under attack. In the resulting mêlée most of the Glen Urquhart men were killed, and small cairns were raised where they fell. The cairns are still there at NH42002596, but hard to find in this trackless area several kilometres south of Shewglie, so in 1996 a new, single cairn was raised by the Glen Urquhart Heritage Group. One of the topping-out stones was brought from Iona.

CORRIMONY★★★

A signpost on the A831 takes you along a minor road to the wonderful Corrimony Chambered Cairn★★★ (NH38303030), easily the best Clava cairn outside the

Corrimony. Victorian mason's
mark on one of the standing
stones.

eponymous monuments themselves. It consists of a large central burial cairn surrounded by a circle of eleven substantial standing stones. Part of the low entrance
passage in the cairn is still complete so you can crawl along it into the central
chamber, where the stain of a single female occupant in a crouched position was
found. The chamber is roofless – a large, flat, cupmarked stone, thought to have
been the cap-stone of the chamber, lies on the body of the cairn. One of the
stones on the northwest is reputed to have cupmarks but I couldn't find them.

The 1952 excavation by Stuart Piggott revealed a number of surprises – such as
pottery decorated with Willow Pattern. Yes, the Victorians had been here already,
and had not only removed the body but also reconfigured the site for their own
purposes – of the eleven stones forming the outer ring, four are replacements. The
original builders had also scattered white quartz pebbles around the cairn. Quartz
scatters are so common at ritual and funerary prehistoric sites that archaeologists
have taken to calling named them 'godstones'. Their exact purpose is unknown,
but we have to conclude they had a ritual or symbolic value, possibly connected
to the apparent magical property of white quartz – rub two pieces together and
each will glow with light called picoelectricity.

Following the road past the cairn takes you to a cemetery named after St
Curadan (also known as Curitan or Urabon, active AD 700-750), filled with
Victorian gravestones (NH37673006). The church is long gone, as is St Uradan's
Well; the original site was probably an ancient Celtic foundation. Built into the

northeast wall is a triangular basin-stone, probably a font connected with the chapel; for years it was used as a gravestone by a family of McDougals. A modern version of the damaged plaque above the stone reads in Gaelic and English, 'Memorial to Warriors. This Wall was erected with the generous help of Natives and Foreign Friends in the year 1890.'

Close to here stood Corrimony House, which burned down in the 1950s. In *A History of the County of Inverness*, J. Cameron Lees tells us about one of the house's distinguished owners, James Grant (1743-1835). Grant was an advocate and moved in political and literary circles in Edinburgh. Like many men of his period he was interested in the origins of things. He consequently wrote the comprehensively-titled *On the Origin of Society, Language, Property, Government, Jurisdiction, Contracts and Marriage*, as well as *On the Origin and Descent of the Gael, with an Account of the Picts and Scots, and Observations Relative to the Authenticity of the Poems of Ossian*. In the latter he claimed that both Greek and Latin were descended from Gaelic, and the Scottish origin of Roman and Greek civilisations could be deduced from 'their stature and complexion, their manners and customs, their modes of living, their dress, their weapons, their religion and their language.'

CORRIMONY FALLS★★★

From Corrimony you can walk to the nearby signposted nature reserve (highly recommended). The first part of the walk passes through an avenue of trees; on the left is a single 5ft (1.5m) high standing stone, Mony's Stone, Cnoc Mhònaidh (NH371300). 'Tradition', that old fallback, says this is where the Viking prince Mony was killed after the defeat at Craig Mony (see DRUMNADROCHIT), although as usual the stone pre-dates the story by at least two thousand years. The stone may be a part of a larger, destroyed prehistoric monument.

Once the track hits the main forest don't follow the waymarked route but bear left along a small path – you'll know you're going in the right direction if the noise of the waterfall is getting louder as you descend. Eventually you reach the foot of the Corrimony Falls★★★. There's nothing particularly mysterious about the site but it is so beautiful I had to include it, and sitting near the bottom of the falls, feet in the water, watching the torrent fly off the rocks above, is definitely a numinous experience. Nearby a tiny disused hydro-generation shed holds rusting relics of a bygone era. Next to it is a structure across the river marked as 'footbridge' on the Ordnance Survey map, although as it consists of nothing but a former water supply pipe, now almost rusted away – you'd need to be being chased by bloodthirsty clansmen before you'd trust yourself to it. Yomping through the pathless undergrowth on the edge of the gorge takes you to a view of the top of the falls, with a skein of more rusting pipes from the abandoned bijou hydroelectric scheme. The *NSA* claims that after Culloden several senior Jacobites hid in Mony's Cave near here, and that it was big enough to hold sixteen-twenty men. As is usually the case with alleged Jacobite-harbouring caves, I failed to find it.

Urquhart Castle.

URQUHART CASTLE★★★ ᴌᴼᴿ

This extensive medieval ruin is two miles south of Drum; the distance can be safely walked by roadside pavement. On 29 July 1955, Peter Macnab was about to take a picture of the castle when he saw a huge animal on the surface of the water. He did not release the picture (which shows a couple of humps, probably boat wakes) until 1958 for fear of ridicule. Although the monster is not clearly visible in the photograph, the castle is. As a result, Urquhart Castle has achieved iconic status through association with Nessie, an association that has grown as all forms of media, from logos to adverts, visually pair the prehistoric monster with the historic monument. The site is worth visiting for its own pleasures, but I suspect many visitors hope to join the extensive ranks of those who have witnessed 'something' from the battlements.

On the 21 May 1977, Tony 'Doc' Shiels was at the base of the tower of the castle when:

> Quite suddenly, a small dark head on the end of a long sinuous neck broke the surface of the water, about a hundred yards away... Its neck was four or five feet long, greenish brown, with a yellowish underside. Its open mouthed head was tiny in relation to the muscular neck... I stood there mesmerised by the brief dreamlike vision. My heart beating rapidly, hands shaking as I lowered the camera, whispering expletives, ecstatic.

The resulting two photos, now famous, clearly show what appears to be a reptilian head atop a long neck. There even seems to be a gleam in the monster's eye. This is a fascinating sighting not only because of the quality of the image but because of the nature and ambiguous reaction of the witness. Many accounts of monster sightings take great pains to emphasise the reliable, solid nature of the eyewitness, in an attempt to assure us that what we are being told is not a result of intoxication, imagination or incapacity.

Now Doc Shiels is, among other things, a wizard and showman, and his spirited, surrealist engagement with Fortean topics has added greatly to the gaiety of nations. At the time of the sighting he was engaged in 'Monstermind', a typical Doc project in which seven psychics from around the world were to coordinate their efforts in an attempt to manifest monsters in the physical world. By Doc's account (given in full in his book, *Monstrum! A Wizard's Tale*) the results were spectacular, with 1977 bringing a record number of sightings of water monsters from around the world. On the day before his sighting Doc had performed a ritual to invoke Nessie using the Niddnidiogram, his personal sigil for raising monsters; it looks like an eye with a trident. (Many modern magical practitioners prefer to create their own sigils – magical symbols – rather than just use off-the-shelf symbols from the latest DIY spell book; this way, the sigil is an intensely personal expression of the individual's magical desire, and may not make sense to anyone else. In other words, the Niddnidiogram is Doc's unique way of accessing aquatic dragons; if you want to invoke Nessie, use your own sigil.)

The invocation was apparently successful: the next morning Doc and four friends were in the car park of Inchnacardoch Lodge near Fort Augustus when they all saw three humps gliding through the water. None of them had a camera, but later that day, at 4 p.m. in Urquhart Castle, Doc was better prepared. But there remains a question mark in Doc's mind – if the Monstermind experiment had indeed summoned Nessie, was the monster he photographed a real flesh and blood animal or a temporary manifestation from Another Place? (For some, of course, Doc's performer persona and the idea of monster-raising by telepathy have irredeemably tainted the photographs, and Stuart Campbell (*The Loch Ness Monster: The Evidence*) states that they are unequivocally fakes, and provides a detailed analysis to back this up.) *Monstrum!* also explores Doc's theory that Nessie is a malevolent supernatural entity, and that those involved in summoning the creature suffered a psychic backlash – in the months following Monstermind, several of the psychics involved fell ill or vanished, and Doc endured an endless catalogue of personal setbacks and disasters. This echoes not only the way earlier generations of Highlanders refused to talk about or even acknowledge the beast, for to do so was to invite ill-fortune, but also Ted Holiday's theories and experiences (see LOCHEND and below).

E.D. Baumann (*The Loch Ness Monster*) relates a variant of the widespread 'going fishing for great serpents ends in disaster' motif. A farmer had a huge hook made and baited it with a dead sheep, but weeks of effort produced not a nibble of Nessie, so he switched to night-time fishing. The following morning his empty boat was found, floating in front of Urquhart Castle. 'And Leviathan, do you fish for him with a hook, or with a line, or do you restrain his tongue?' (Job 41:1).

The Historic Scotland visitor centre has extensive interpretation, including a dramatised film telling the castle's history, and there are several different levels of guidebook available, so here I'll concentrate on some of the less-explored parts of the castle's heritage. Archaeological investigations have found evidence of a prehistoric dun and Pictish occupation on the site, although this is all buried beneath the medieval castle. As a result, Urquhart is one of several candidates for the fort where King Brude of the Northern Picts met St Columba (see CRAIG PHADRIG FORT). The reception area, meanwhile, has a replica of the Garbeg Pictish Stone★, which was found in the hills north of Drum (the original is in the National Museums of Scotland in Edinburgh). There are two clear carvings, a V-rod and crescent, and the mysterious 'Pictish beast', which some have seriously considered as a representation of Nessie.

Katharine Stewart in *The Story of Loch Ness* quotes an unnamed source: 'It is believed in the Parish that there are two secret chambers underneath the ruins of the Castle – the one filled with gold and the other with the plague. On account of the letting loose of the pestilence, no attempt has ever been made to discover the treasure.'

Richard Frere tells us about Big Dog, An Cu Mor, a hunting hound owned by the Irish mercenary knight Conachar Mor Mac Aoidh, who acquired the castle around 1160 as reward for military service to David I. Conachar wanted to get rid of Big Dog because he was old and sick, but an old woman with second sight said, 'let the dog live, his own day awaits him.' That day came when Conachar, out hunting, was wounded by a huge savage boar – Big Dog leapt at and killed the boar, saving his master with his last breath. Versions of this story are told right across Scotland: they all share the 'his own day awaits him' motif. A local variation from Glenmoriston, 'The Story of the Four Hunters and the Glastigs', is recorded in Alexander MacDonald's *Story and Song from Loch Ness-Side*. A man had a black dog who could never be got to work: when criticised about this he always said, 'His own day is before him.' One day he met an uncanny being, in some versions a witch disguised as a beautiful woman and in others a demon of the forest transformed as a white fawn. The man was saved from death by the dog, who left the fight hairless and almost mauled to death.

Back at Urquhart, Conachar went on to father the clans of the Mackays, Forbes and Urquharts, all of whom have a boar's head on their arms. After many years Conachar died and was buried with his sword beneath the big Clach Ochonachair, Conachar's Stone. But as Frere so aptly puts it, 'Nobody knows where Big Dog is buried.'

STRONE POINT

Strone was home to Wing Commander and Mrs Cary, with whom F.W. (Ted) Holiday stayed during the time of the exorcism of Loch Ness (see LOCHEND). The final of the four land-based exorcism points was at Strone. What happened next was recounted by Holiday in an article for *Flying Saucer Review* (Vol. 19, No. 5 September-October 1973) and in his book *The Goblin Universe*. After the exorcism Holiday was keen to visit the site of an alleged UFO landing but was cautioned against this by Dr Omand, who thought there was something sinister about UFOs. That evening Holiday discussed the matter with the Carys. Mrs Cary twice advised him not to visit the UFO site, on the grounds that there was the danger of abduction. Faced with this opposition, and perhaps in a sensitised state after the exorcism, Holiday decided not to go.

> At that precise moment there was a tremendous rushing sound outside the window and what looked like a whirling mass of dark smoke appeared. A series of heavy thuds shook the wall and door and for an instant I thought that the corner of the house was collapsing. A rosebush outside the window seemed to be trying to tear itself out of the ground. An initial wave of terror, during which I stared fixedly at the window, was soon replaced by calm. The episode lasted about 15 seconds. Mrs Cary was greatly alarmed; yet the Wing Commander, standing only a few feet away, neither saw nor heard a thing.

The next morning Holiday asked Mrs Cary to relate her experience; mostly it was the same as his own, but she added:

> looking at Ted, I saw a beam of white light that shot across the room from the window on my left. I saw a white circle of light on Ted Holiday's forehead. It was white light... not like electric light... and the circle was about three or four inches in diameter... The light stayed on only for perhaps a second but I definitely saw it.

Holiday had seen no light. The spot on his forehead where the light hit was where the holy water had been applied during the protective rite before the exorcism. For the experience at the alleged UFO landing site, see FOYERS.

6

THE NORTH SHORE OF LOCH NESS III: DRUMNADROCHIT TO FORT AUGUSTUS

Now the serpent was more subtle than any beast of the field which the Lord God made.

Genesis 3:1

SOUTH OF URQUHART CASTLE 🐍

A beehive cairn on the side of road at Lenie (NH518269), 2km from Urquhart Castle, marks the death of John Cobb, whose boat *Crusader* disintegrated on 29 September 1952 in an attempt to break the world water speed record. Some newspapers tried to suggest Nessie was to blame, which unnecessarily trivialised an event made even more tragic by the fact that the actual cause of the crash was the wakes created by Cobb's own support boats.

Further south, Achnahannet ('Field of the Holy Place', NH513262) was the base camp of the Loch Ness Phenomenon Investigation Bureau from 1962-1972.

From their house in Foyers, on the other side of the loch, John and Ann Forsyth noticed on occasion a thick patch of white smoke above a clearing at Lon na Fola (NH476221) on the Great Glen Way, which in this area runs parallel to the A82. At first they thought it was caused by campfires, which are banned in the dense forestry plantations through which the Way runs; but the Forestry Commission staff found no evidence of either camping or fires, and the area is uninhabited. Nevertheless the phenomenon persisted. Eventually John identified the cause – under certain atmospheric conditions, a clearing in a forestry plantation will produce a temporary patch of thick mist which from a distance looks like smoke. The patch of mist, known as a katabatic mist, only lasts for a few minutes, and then disperses. This is a classic case of observation and investigation in pursuit of understanding a strange phenomenon. There is also the potential for the creation of a new piece of folklore. Lon na Fala means 'the Meadow of Blood', for it was here in 1603 that a bloody clan battle took place between the Mackenzies and the MacDonalds of Glengarry, with the former victorious. If the mist phenomenon persists, expect to hear tour guides start talking about 'the white spirit of Lon na Fola', and how the ghosts of the dead men return in a white cloud.

ALLTSIGH

On 22 September 1933, the Revd W.E. Forbes was surprised to find the Half-Way House tea-room (now the excellent Alltsigh hostel run by the Scottish Youth Hostel Association) apparently deserted. In response to a call, a voice from upstairs replied, 'We can't come down yet – we are looking at the Monster.' So six people, staff and visitors alike, stood on the balcony and for ten minutes watched a long-necked animal with a snake-like head, two humps and a tail move across the loch. The proprietor, Miss Janet Fraser, was blasé about the sighting – after all, she had seen the creature three times before.

The building is reputedly haunted by a young woman who was murdered by a jealous suitor: Malcolm MacDonnell killed both his brother Alasdair and the object of their mutual affection, Annie Fraser. The latter's body was concealed under the floorboards, and her footsteps have been heard crossing and re-crossing the floor, even though the present building was only completed in 1930. Her ghost has also apparently been seen in the hostel and in the area. Malcolm fled the scene, but drowned crossing the loch in a storm. Some months later the bag of gold he was carrying was washed up near the scene.

Meall na Sroine (NH445185), the summit above the hostel, has a rocking stone weighing several tons (to the west of the burn); a slight effort will set it moving in its natural cradle. To the north is the mountain of Mealfourvonie or Meall Fuar-mhonaidh. The *NSA* of 1845 relates the legend of a bottomless 'small circular lake' which was linked by underground channels to Loch Ness. The most likely candidate is Loch a' Chaise (NH453216). Alexander MacDonald elaborates the tale further in *Story and Song from Loch Ness-Side*: a herd-boy threw his *glocan*, a piece of stick with a stone fixed into a split at one end, at a cow on the top of Mealfourvonie. The stick missed, fell into a well, and much later was found at Bona on the loch's north shore. Clearly this is how Nessie enters and exits the loch.

INVERMORISTON★

Between 1900 and 1907, John MacLeod was fishing from a rocky ledge above a pool in the mouth of the River Moriston when he saw a creature 30 to 40ft long with a head like an eel and a long tapering tail. He cast his line in its direction and it moved away. Although first reported in 1934, MacLeod was entertaining visitors with this 'fisherman's story' before the First World War.

South of the road as you enter the hamlet from the north is the old grave-yard, Clachan an Imbhir★ (NH42211664), in a beautiful leafy setting. Like many Christian sites in the Great Glen, the original church here was supposedly founded by St Columba, for which there is no evidence beyond local tradition. The grave-yard gate is guarded by two pairs of impressive monoliths in the style of tall standing stones; this is obviously a local fashion – another striking monolith (with a mason's

Above left: Invermoriston – monolith at graveyard entrance.

Above right: Invermoriston – modern roadside monolith.

Invermoriston – graveyard gate monoliths.

Invermoriston – water-worn stones, Clachan an Imbhir graveyard.

mark) sits in the wall by the entrance from the road to Invermoriston House, and others mark field and house gateways elsewhere in the glen. The burial ground itself has a number of striking Victorian monuments. Several Macleod gravestones have been set into a stand-alone gabled wall, along with two fantastically-shaped water-worn stones of the kind that usually provide apotropaic protection at the entrances to houses, churches and graveyards in Glen Lyon, Perthshire. These are the only stones of this type that I know of in the Loch Ness area.

A story is told of Alexander Grant of Achnaconeran who returned home after many years as a soldier. Almost immediately he became very ill and died of 'strong colic' and was buried here. His fiancée arrived a day after the burial – and heard groans from beneath the earth. She told others, who opened the grave – to find the body had turned in the coffin and was laying face downwards. (Source: MacDonald, *Story and Song from Loch Ness-Side*.)

Just south of the A82/A887 junction is St Columba's Well★. This is where tradition insists Columba blessed a cursed well and left it not merely wholesome but actually curative, its specialities being rheumatism and hangovers. Christine Macdonald, a lifetime resident of Achnaconeran, remembers that as late as the 1960s the well water was specifically collected for the flasks on the dining room tables of the Glenmoriston Arms hotel. Columba's well-cleansing is described in Adomnan's *Life of St Columba*, although the actual location is not named. Long derelict, in 2006 the well was cleaned up and a new viewing platform installed, along with a plaque stating that, pre-Columba, the water caused boils and ulcers to appear if splashed on skin.

On the other side of the road to the well, a woodland path leads to a riverside gazebo, a recently restored nineteenth-century folly, with good views of the current and former bridges upstream. Kenneth MacRae in *Highland Ways and Byways* says that when the oak trees, known as the Seven Maidens of Port Clair, were planted in 1600, a curse was placed on anyone who cut them down. By the time MacRae was

Monster simulacrum,
Invermoriston.

writing (1953) three of the trees had already been felled, but no supernatural comeback had been recorded. I've been unable to identify the location of the trees.

A minor road (and the route of the Great Glen Way) runs west to Dalcataig.
Halfway along is Tom-na-h-Aorainn, a small tree-covered mound, where the cries
of the Bodach, a grumpy male spirit, have often been heard. Another road leads
steeply north up to the Achnaconeran hill, site of Creagan-na-h-Uamhach, The
Rock of the Cave, once inhabited by a giant; Na Sìtheanan, the fairy knowes; and
Tom-an-t-Seòmair, The Chamber Knoll, whereon was situated Seòmar Rìgh, a
king's chamber or palace. I have not been able to find any of these.

GLENMORISTON

Alexander MacDonald's 1914 book *Story and Song from Loch Ness-Side* is a treasure
trove of apotropaic customs and folklore from the glen: if a word of the baptismal
service was mumbled or missed out the child would be a sleepwalker in later
life; if a girl and boy were baptised at same time and had their names accidentally transposed the girl would have a beard and the boy an effeminate look; the
Bathing Blessing was repeated during the baptism to counter the Evil Eye:

> A palmful of water for your years,
> A palmful of water for your growth,
> And for your taking of your food;
> And may the part of you which grows not during the night
> Grow during the day:
> Three palmfuls of the Holy Trinity,
> To protect and guard you
> From the effects of the Evil Eye,
> And from the jealous lust of sinners.

Another charm against the Evil Eye invoked St Peter while filling a bottle noisily with water, and was effective against 'swelling of neck and stoppage of bowels/against nine conair and nine connachair/and nine slender fairies/against a bachelor's eye, and an old maid's eye'. According to *Carmina Gadelica*, Vol. 2, 'nine conair and nine connachair' translates as 'nine paths and nine shouts (or uproars)'. Nine is a very significant number in Gaelic folklore, although what the significance of the 'nine paths' was eludes me.

As a child, MacDonald witnessed a ritual to counter the Evil Eye. A woman part-filled a wooden milking pail with water over which the dead and the living had passed (that is, from under a bridge on a coffin road or route to the graveyard) and dropped in a silver sixpence while chanting. If the charm worked the coin would stick by its rim to the vessel when it was emptied. If the silver fell out with the water, a more powerful charm was needed. Sometimes this was requested from someone further up the magical food chain, such as the famous Willox the Warlock from Gaulrig near Tomintoul. Macdonald mentions one case where Willox cured a child who suffered convulsions with a charm which was sewn into a piece of cotton placed over the heart.

The Chastening Charm was chanted to counter various diseases while counting the rosary beads (which means that this ritual dates from before the Reformation), repeating a line of the charm as each bead was passed:

Bead number one (Paternoster)
Bead number two, three, four, five, six,
Bead number seven;
And may the strength of the seven beads
Cast out your disease
Amidst the grey stones over by.

Other traditions included the following:

Dreams could be predictive: an old man dreamed the exact day of his wife's death; another man dreamt that a long-dead woman spoke to him saying she had come for his mother, and the old woman died soon after.

The identity of the first footer on New Year was important: the most favoured visitor was a dark-haired man; flat feet were bad, and a badly dressed red-headed woman with no hat was the worst.

Certain people were lucky or unlucky to meet on the road, especially when starting a journey or nearing home.

Hair and nail cutting should not be done on Sunday, Tuesday, Friday or the first Monday of the quarter.

For good luck, you should view face foremost the first calf, lamb or other young animal seen of the year; the first snail of the year should be seen on grass rather than on bare ground or stone.

You should not hear the first cuckoo without having eaten that day. Finding a cuckoo's nest was an ill omen.

The last to join a funeral procession would be the next to be carried.

To measure a shroud for a living person was to ensure their early death.

Do nothing else between sitting down to eat and finishing.

Always bless a child, a bride and young animals seen for the first time.

A cat passing between a newly married couple meant unhappiness, while a cat jumping over a corpse was a very bad omen.

A tooth must be thrown on the fire. If the mice got it no new tooth would grow.

A common saying was, 'No evil can come out of fire.'

Anything touched by a spider would be replaced soon.

Putting on clothing inside out brought bad luck but new clothes at Easter meant good luck.

Gifts of money to a child should never be just a single coin.

Turning back after leaving the house was a sign of an unsuccessful journey.

Deep-sunk eyes were signs of envy, cunning and the Evil Eye.

The charm for sprains and dislocations involved drawing a knotted thread of common yarn through the fingers of both hands while whispering, as the knots came into contact with the fingers: 'Christ rode a brown horse/And the brown horse broke its leg/Christ put marrow to marrow/Bone to bone, flesh to flesh/And the brown horse's leg was healed.'

Certain families had the power to stop bleeding from a great distance.

'Dislocation of the heart' was cured by pouring melted lead into water in a wooden vessel placed on the patient's head. A piece of lead resembling the heart was found in the water and turned around. At the same time the dislocated heart went back into place and the piece of lead was then used as an amulet against recurrence of the problem.

Married women carried charms and amulets in the shape of the silver heart, a silver pin or a piece of iron. One woman was surrounded by nine shadowy female entities intent on abducting her as she lay in bed, speechless and weighed down by a great power. 'Ah, we cannot touch her,' said one, 'she has a silver heart in her breast-cloth.'

William Mackay's *Urquhart and Glenmoriston* gives us the 'well authenticated' story of Eobhan Ban a Bhocain, Fair Ewen of the Goblin, who lived in Glenmoriston somewhere at the start of the nineteenth century. Under the terms of his pact with Satan, Ewen had to deliver a report of his daily activities in person each night. Like any job, it palled after a while and Ewen tried to skive off, but 'no matter where he was when the hour of meeting arrived, something within him forced him to keep the appointment.' He even emigrated to America, but the Devil followed him across the ocean and forced him to return. Eventually he had his neighbours sit up one night to stop him. At the appointed hour he fought so hard to leave they were forced to tie him up, but 'a high, shrieking wind shook the house to its foundations, and strange sounds and noises were heard.' Ewen was released, went to his appointment, and was found dead next morning.

GLENMORISTON – INVERMORISTON TO TORGYLE BRIDGE

Most of the traditions in this section come from Alexander MacDonald's invaluable *Story and Song from Loch Ness-Side*. Somewhere near Levishie (NH405177) is the Feithe-Shalach, The Filthy Bog, where 'an uncanny animal caused fear and trembling to many a late wayfarer.' To the west are two conical mounds on opposite sides of the river, An Tùr (NH398176) and An Dùnan (NH400172), each home to a hag or cailleach who hated each other. Bhlàiridh (NH383167) was the supposed graveyard for the warriors killed in a battle between the locals and a Viking army led by a king called Eric. There is no other documentary evidence for the presence of Scandinavians in the glen, and there is nothing on the ground to support the idea of a graveyard.

There are several stories around the Dundreggan area of an unnamed woman who had a reputation of being, if not a witch, then at least a bad egg. She assured a band of cattle thieves on the other side of the frozen river that the ice was safe to cross. They all drowned in what is now the Pool of the Twenty Men. There are only two burial grounds in the glen. When the woman died the residents of both Invermoriston and Dalchriechart opposed burial in their respective graveyards and an inconclusive fight broke out in the centre of the glen. The solution was to bury her on the site of the punch-up. The grave is marked by an unremarkable plain stone on the north side of the road a little east of the Dundreggan dam. The locally available booklet *Glen Moriston: A Heritage Guide* (try the café at Redburn) says the stone stands in a north-south orientation, consistent with the conventions of witch burial.

Striking north from the dam through the forestry plantation brings you to Loch A'Bhainne. A standing stone, unmarked on the Ordnance Survey map, is at NH36301688, while close by (NH36831729) is a strange structure of no obvious purpose, made of drainage pipes, iron rods and concrete. Is it some kind of memorial?

Dundreggan township was notorious for fairies, who were constantly trying to kidnap women who had recently given birth, to act as nannies for their own fairy children. Mackay, writing in 1893, said: 'their last attempt to steal a newly made mother has not yet been forgotten.' Ewen Macdonald was out one night working when overhead he heard a rushing sound and his wife's voice. He said the name of the Trinity and threw his knife into the air – and the fairies, unable to bear holy words or iron, dropped his wife down beside him. The burn he was crossing at the time was thereafter called Caochan na Sgine, the Streamlet of the Knife.

Mackay has further stories from Dundreggan. Two men were reaping on a hot day. One said out loud he would like a drink of buttermilk. Instantly a small woman appeared and offered him some. He wisely declined, but his companion

The Glen Moriston
Footprints.

drank, and died within a year and a day. Exactly the same story is told of LOCH
DUNTELCHAIG on the other side of Loch Ness. A farmer, asleep on Sidhean
Buidhe, the Yellow Fairy-knowe, woke to a child's cries. Underneath the earth
he could hear a voice hushing the child with a promise that food was coming, as the white cow would soon spill her milk. The white cow was of course
the farmer's own, and no matter what precautions he and his wife took during
that evening's milking, it kicked the pail, and the milk seeped into the ground. I
have been unable to locate Sidhean Buidhe, but there is the 10m high Sidhean
Mullach, fairy knoll, north of the road (NH32941461). Somewhere near here was
Tomnachroich, the gibbet knoll.

One kilometre west of the tearoom, at the second passing place, there is a
metal gate with a rights-of-way signpost. A short path leads to the Glenmoriston
Footprints★, behind a rough cairn. In 1827 a travelling preacher, Finlay Munro,
was heckled by two young men, who called him a cheat and a liar. He replied that
the ground on which he stood would bear witness to the truth of his words until
the final Day of Judgment. Two parallel marks in the ground are said to be his
footprints, wherein no grass grows. The marks are, it must be said, less impressive
than other religious footprints elsewhere.

Slightly further west (NH308133) on the north side of the road is the former
Torgyle Catholic Chapel, built in 1841. Although architecturally undistinguished,
and lacking a graveyard, its arboreal location and general air of rural dilapidation
means that, in the right conditions, it has what I call 'the Stephen King look'.

Kenneth MacRae tells a story connected to Torgyle Croft, formerly an inn. A
piper retreating from Culloden was approaching the inn when he heard hooves
behind him: he ambushed and decapitated the redcoat who was chasing him. The
piper wanted the soldier's boots but they would not come off, so out came the
sword once more and he cut off both legs and carried them with him to the inn,
where he slept in the byre. Next morning the dairymaid saw the boots and legs

Glen Moriston
– gargoyle.

Glen Moriston – face
in cairn supporting
gargoyle.

and fled into the inn saying the cow had eaten the traveller. Before the true facts
were known the cow was shot and buried. MacRae also says the crosses on the
pillars of the 1826 Torgyle Bridge were put there at the request of a local keeper,
although we are not told what they were intended to counter (fairies and/or
witches would be a good bet).

GLENMORISTON – DALCHREICHART

A minor road runs west from Torgyle Bridge. After 2km, just after the school, is a
small forestry plantation. Within, and next to the road, can be found the small tarn of
Lochan a' Chrois, the Lochlet of the Cross (NH286127). Although there is nothing
to see now, an island in the lochan was once the site of a sanctuary, An Abait, 'The
Abbey', although it is unlikely there was any substantial building here. The right of

sanctuary prevailed probably until the fourteenth century, and the area of the sanctuary, once marked by crosses, stretched from Tomchraskie (NH2512) to Tomnacroich and from Mam-a'Chrois (NH2607) to Ruigh-a'Chrois. There may once have been a cross on Lochan a'Chrois. A little further west a track leads off south to Dalchreichart graveyard★ (NH279127), also known as Clachan Mheircheard. The oldest gravestones are mid-nineteenth century, but the site goes back much earlier.

The founding legend has St Merchard, the future patron saint of Glen Moriston, touring Strathglass with two missionaries when he spotted a white cow standing under a certain tree every day. It never ate but was always well-fed. Merchard dug into the roots and found three new bells, the spot now being called Crineglack of Erchless (Croabh nan Clag – the Tree of the Bells). Each holy man took one bell and founded a church on the site where his bell rang for the third time. One saint founded the church at GLEN CONVINTH. A second went to Broadford in Skye. Merchard went south. His bell rang for the first time at Suidhe Mhercheird (Merchard's Seat), the second time at Merchard's Well and the final time at the side of River Moriston, where he built a church.

The well is lost and there is no trace of the church. For many years, however, the bell hung on a stone on the wall encircling the graveyard. Despite Merchard placing a curse against removing the bell, a Miss Grant had it brought to Invermoriston House, and placed in one of the large old trees of the mansion. It began 'to make its presence known in ways not conducive to the comfort of the family' (MacDonald, *Story and Song from Loch Ness-Side*) and her father asked her to return it. Before funerals it often rang out in Gaelic: 'Come home! Come home! To your lasting rest!' Stuart McHardy in *Scotland: Myth, Legend & Folklore* adds other details: if the bell was removed, it would fly back to its original site; the bell rang out one night to alert the local people to a murder being committed just that moment in the kirkyard – the murderer was found nearby and hanged; and St Merchard appeared in a terrifying dream to a laird's law-officer, warning him not to oppress a poor widow, who had prayed to the saint. At the end of the nineteenth century the bell was stolen by some labourers working in the area and lost forever. Also now gone is the former baptismal font, which never dried up.

According to MacDonald, three brothers agreed to be buried side by side in the northwest of the cemetery, facing west to their beloved Coire-Dho. This was a reversal of the usual Christian practice, where graves are aligned to the east to greet the rising sun on the Day of Judgement. The graves are now lost and all surviving headstones face east.

The Glenmoriston Heritage Group's booklet *Glen Moriston: A Heritage Guide* traces a now-vanished coffin road from Glen Garry to Dalchreichart; it was in use up to the early part of the twentieth century. It entered the glen near the summit of Ceann a Mhaim (NH276089) and skirted the east shoulder of the hill down to Achlain (NH278126), where the party forded the river. Once, an argument over precedence – essentially, who should be chief mourner – broke out when the coffin of a Glenmoriston native was taken outside the house. Just as the fight was about to start a man looking out the window saw Satan going about, laying his black finger on a shoulder here and there. Fortunately things calmed down and the funeral proceeded peacefully.

At the start of the eighteenth century Alasdair MacLain, of Balintombuie, close to the graveyard, was a noted practitioner of the divination magic known as the Taghairm nan Daoine (the Taghairm of Men). He sat inside a large cauldron just outside the entrance of the cemetery and summoned the dead, who filed in front of him until one could relate the desired information about the future. On one occasion three thousand of the dead passed by, crowding the surrounding fields, before finally his own niece appeared, and 'revealed to him the evils that were to befall himself' (Mackay). He gave up magic, but in due course the prophecy came to pass when he was shot in a confrontation with a party of Lochaber cattle thieves. He fell three times before he died, and each place was marked by a cairn. The Heritage Guide suggests one of the cairns may be the one at NH274141 in the forestry behind Balnacarn, as it is a 'singularly tall structure for its width, having the general proportions of a large man.'

GLENMORISTON – MACKENZIE'S CAIRN

Back on the A887, and about four miles/seven kilometres further west, on the south side of the road, is the noticeable Mackenzie's Cairn (NH23581122). Roderick Mackenzie was a decoy, his close physical resemblance to Bonnie Prince Charlie having been used several times to fool the Hanoverians. On this spot he was shot by an Army patrol. As he lay dying, Mackenzie exclaimed, 'You have murdered your Prince.' The delighted soldiers cut off his head and took it in triumph to Fort Augustus, expecting to receive the £30,000 reward. For a vital interval before the truth was learnt the hunt was scaled back, allowing BPC to eventually escape to France. A cross marking Mackenzie's grave (body, *sans* head) is nearby.

GLENMORISTON – COIRE-DHO

This mountainous wilderness stretches to the northwest, around the valley of the River Doe. It was in this area that BPC was sheltered by the Seven Men of Moriston. Charlie could have done with the aid of Daibhidh (David) and Mor (Marion), described as goblins but probably the hairy anthropoid spirits known as urisks. They were generally peaceful but objected to Glen Urquhart tenants grazing their cattle in the area, and once chased the farmers away with a huge uprooted fir tree. Alexander MacDonald relates a tradition that one year Coire-Dho produced a spectacular grass crop: because of the mild winter the grass was not needed until early summer, much later than usual. When the time came the barn door was found to be blocked inside by fallen grass. One man entered through the roof and screamed out: 'Save yourselves and set fire to the barn; inside here is all alive with serpents.' Some of the snakes were seen jumping several feet above the burning building, hissing with terrible ferocity as they fell back into the flames. The man's charred body was found in the ruins.

Lar Bhan Coire-Dho, the White Mare of Corrie-Dho, was a supernatural creature who enticed the farmers' horses and rendered them useless. At last the people of Glenmoriston and Glen Urquhart decided to get rid of her. They surrounded her in an ever-decreasing circle, until Alasdair Cutach, Alasdair the Short, the fastest runner in the area and a famous hunter, grabbed her tail – and found he could not let go. She took off at once, dragging Alasdair behind her, and fled to the remote area around An Sloch Dubh to the north (NH396202). Next day his mangled corpse was found, but the White Mare was never seen again. This whole wild, mountainous region between glens Urquhart and Moriston is known as An Craach, The Craach. It was home to a malevolent witch, the Cailleach a' Chrathaich, who lived beside Loch a' Chrathaich (NH3621). She had an especial hatred for Clan MacMillan. She would waylay an unsuspecting traveller and steal his bonnet, upon which she would dance until a hole was worn in it – at which point the man would drop dead. 'In this way fell at least five Macmillans within the last 125 years and all were found in the heather without a mark of violence.' (Mackay, writing in 1893.) One Glenmoriston man escaped her only with the help of his dog, who ended up almost flayed alive. The man himself was ill in bed for months. Donald Macmillan of Balmacaan managed to wrest his bonnet back before the Cailleach had rubbed it through. As he fled she predicted that he would die at nine o'clock on a certain date. When the evening arrived, his family and neighbours gathered around him, and prayed and read the Scriptures, but as the clock struck nine, he fell back in his chair and breathed his last. Mackay says the Cailleach was last seen by a member of the Clan Macdougall whose son still lived in the area in 1893.

FORT AUGUSTUS★★ ₪

Easily visible from the road as you approach Fort Augustus is Cherry Island★, an artificial tree-covered crannog in the shallow Inchnacardoch Bay (NH38601025). Its original name was Eilean Muireach, Murdoch's Island. When the island was explored by diving suit in 1908 by a pioneering monk from the Abbey (possibly the first underwater archaeological investigation in the country), a causeway was traced from the northwest corner towards the mainland. A castle, possibly a hunting seat, is known to have existed on the island in the fifteenth century. About 150 yards (140m) northeast, and now submerged and only marked by a post, is Eilean nan Con, Island of Dogs (NH38751040), possibly used as kennels for the hunting dogs. The surface area of Cherry Island has been greatly reduced since the construction of the Caledonian Canal raised the water level of the loch. Richard Frere in Loch Ness quotes one of Cromwell's troopers: 'here was an island (that) swims in the midst of the ocean… it floats from one part of the Lough to

Looking north up Loch Ness from Fort Augustus.

Fort Augustus: the locks of the Caledonian Canal, with Nessie.

the other', a description that Peter Costello (*In Search of Lake Monsters*) wonders might not be an early description of Nessie instead.

On 5 August 1933, Commander Meiklem and his wife observed through binoculars a huge humped animal with very rough skin in the water near the island.

In 1977, on the 21 May, the day after his magical summoning of Nessie, Tony 'Doc' Shiels and several others in the car park of the Inchnacardoch Lodge Hotel saw humps in the water (see URQUHART CASTLE for more details). Dom Cyril Dieckhoff, in 'Mythological Beings in Gaelic Folklore' (*TGSI*), states that Inchnacardoch House had a brownie, but I can find nothing more on this.

The minor road west through Jenkins Park eventually comes to Auchterawe burial ground★ (NH34780741, also known as Allt na Cille, Burn of the church, although any church has long gone), with carved gravestones.

Fort Augustus used to be known as Kil Chumein, the church of Cumein, until 1730, when General Wade named the newly completed fort after the youngest son

Above and right:
Fort Augustus
Abbey.

of George II – William Augustus, Duke of Cumberland (later of Culloden infamy). In 1746 the first shot from the Jacobite artillery on the hill behind the fort exploded the powder room and the Hanoverians surrendered. After Culloden, Cumberland set up a base here, and was presented with the head of Roderick Mackenzie, the decoy for BPC (see GLENMORISTON). In the nineteenth century the fort was sold to Lord Lovat, who in the 1870s gifted it to the Benedictine Order for use as a monastery. In 1880 *The Antiquary* reported: 'Twenty-seven skulls, and a corresponding quantity of vertebrae, and other bones, have been discovered during the past month by workmen in levelling some earthworks at Fort Augustus…They were at regular distances from each other, but with no traces of coffins. If the earthworks are coeval with the fort, the bones must be at least 150 years old.'

The military buildings were rebuilt as St Benedict's Abbey★★, a magnificent Victorian edifice replete with towers, spires, statues in niches, gargoyles, inscriptions and other neo-Gothic elements: Hogwarts-by-the-Loch. One of the former guardrooms was converted into the Chapel of Holy Relics, decorated with mural paintings in the style of Roman catacombs. The architect, Peter Paul Pugin, also designed the chairs and refectory tables and the study desks in the monks' quarters. In the former armoury 'Pax' (Peace, the Order's motto) was inscribed on the fireplace beneath a statue of St Benedict. The library held 40,000 books including some manuscripts from the eleventh century. Seton Gordon, in *The Highlands of Scotland,* notes that the tradition that a particular tree in the grounds was used to hang Jacobite prisoners is unfounded; the prisoners were actually shot on what became the cricket pitch, and the tree was merely planted in memory of Culloden. In 1998, after various vicissitudes, the Abbey closed, and became prey to dry rot and neglect. At the time of my visit it was closed for conversion into flats; hopefully a footpath will be instituted which will allow visitors to be able to appreciate the restored architectural treasures (such as a Roman altar-stone with carvings of three mother-goddesses, brought from near Edinburgh and placed over a doorway, a strangely pagan preservation in a Christian setting). I recommend binoculars to help you study the exterior features. The weathervane on the tall mock-battlemented tower has a bird with wings aloft holding something circular in its mouth; I am tempted to think it is the Host.

In the early 1730s the father of Hugh Fraser of Balnain was playing cards in an inn at Fort Augustus when a servant girl bringing in a basket of peats suddenly dropped it and cried out, 'Hugh! I see Hugh in the hands of the redcoats!' Hugh was a smuggler, and had at that moment been killed in a struggle with two soldiers on a Customs House Boat near Inverness.

In 1933, 'MYSTERY FISH IN SCOTTISH LOCH – Monster Reported at Fort Augustus' was the headline of a minor news item in the *Scottish Daily Express* on 9 June, the first time the story was reported outside Inverness newspapers, and the modest beginning of Nessie's soon-to-come worldwide fame. The piece read, 'A monster fish which for years has been somewhat of a mystery in Loch Ness was reported to have been seen yesterday at Fort Augustus.' Note the report is of a monster fish – Nessie the prehistoric monster was still to come.

The *Scotsman* of 17 October of the same year reported that a local man had seen a long-necked creature near Fort Augustus. For the first time, the 'plesiosaurus' word was used, and the archetype was created. Shortly after, the identity of the man was revealed as Alex Campbell, a water bailiff in the employ of the Ness Fisheries Board. Campbell remains both an inspirational (to monster hunters) and controversial (to sceptics) figure to this day: over the following years and decades he became Nessie's chief cheerleader, reporting a record number of sightings, the details of which changed in various interviews and self-penned articles. At one point he withdrew the original sighting, claiming it was caused by cormorants distorted by mirage. Some of the claimed earlier sightings from elsewhere may also have had their origin with Campbell, possibly as part of a campaign to retrospectively create a tradition of monster sightings before the *annus mirabilis* of 1933 (see,

Kilcumein churchyard, Fort Augustus.

for example, ABRIACHAN). Michel Meurger (*Lake Monster Traditions*) describes him as 'a mediator between country belief and modern sensationalism.' It's safe to say that without Alex Campbell there would be no Loch Ness Monster industry.

In 1971, on the 14 October, a ten-foot high neck was seen in a disturbance in the waters of the bay off the Abbey. The witnesses were a monk, Father Gregory Brusey, and Roger Pugh.

At the end of the nineteenth century, another of the stories that had been passed down in Karen Wood's family (recorded in *The Folklore of South Loch Ness-Side*) tells of young apprentice engineer who worked on the canal at Fort Augustus, opening and closing the lock gates. One day, after letting a boat pass, the gate jammed. The water was drained from that part of the canal and revealed a huge, dead sea serpent stuck in the half-closed gates. They lifted it out with ropes and left it on the town dump, where locals went to have a look at it as it decomposed. Wood's report was a private document; as far as I know this story has never been published before.

In the present day, there is a floral Nessie family by the bridge over the Caledonian Canal. Donations can be deposited in the mouth of the baby Nessie. Inveroich House (private), on the tip of the spit of land between the canal and river, has a step at the back door inscribed with an arrow and 'WD 1857'. It formerly belonged to War Department and is the oldest house in Fort Augustus.

Thomas Pennant, in *A Tour of Scotland and a Voyage to the Hebrides* (1772) reports that during the earthquake of Lisbon (1 November 1755) the waters of Loch Ness were 'affected in a very extraordinary manner.'

They rose and flowed up the lake from east to west with vast impetuosity, and were carried above 200 yards [183m] up the River Oich, breaking on its banks in a wave near 3 feet [1m] high, then continuing ebbing and flowing for the space of

Cullachie Lodge, built on the site of brownie-haunted Old Culachy House.

an hour; but at eleven o'clock a wave greater than any of the rest came up the river, broke on the north side, and overflowed the bank for the extent of 30 feet [9m].

Alexander MacDonald, in *Story and Song from Loch Ness-Side*, noted: 'The old people used to say there was a connection between the loch and the volcanoes of southern Europe.'

One of the best views of the loch can be obtained by walking down to the shore at Borlum Bay★, to the east of the village. On a good day you can see the entire length of the loch, which can lead to a phenomenon perhaps unique to Loch Ness. The best description is from Richard Frere in *Loch Ness*:

> Due to the length and straightness of the Great Glen fault, it is possible... to see sky and water join. The Earth's curvature has drawn the low ground in the Ness Valley below the visible horizon. Though it is commonplace to watch a ship climbing out of the sea, the same effect here is quite startling; at first glance it looks as though the Loch extends to infinity.

Mirages are common here. Borlum Bay was third of the points for the exorcism of Loch Ness (see LOCHEND).

Just past the campsite on the A82 south of the village, a tarmac track leads east to Kilcumein churchyard★, possibly the site of the original foundation of Kilcumein and the ancient parish chapel, although no trace of a church survives. St Cumine's Bell, with healing powers, was kept at the graveyard. John Anderson, hero of a Burns' poem, is buried here. Kenneth MacRae, in *Highland Ways and Byways*, writes that just outside the wall is buried the son and heir of Archibald Fraser of Abertarff. Having lost his only son, the embittered father had the boy buried outside the graveyard to spite the Almighty. I could not locate any grave marker to back this up.

Leaving the cemetery by the stone stile and following a track brings you to a minor road; turn right here to get to the start of the Corrieveckie mountain path, an old military road. A kilometre or so along this route can be seen the pink-washed walls of Cullachie Lodge (private), a grand modern building in neo-baronial style which stands on the site of Old Culachy House. In 'Mythological Beings in Gaelic Folklore', Dom Cyril Dieckhoff described its resident brownie, which would noisily move furniture at night, although in the morning everything was normal. Dieckhoff was told this by 'an old native of Fort Augustus who, with her father, was present at the time, and who believes that the Brownie objected to their coming to the house.' When the old house went, so did the brownie.

Back on the minor road, in the direction of Fort Augustus, the road passes Ardachy (private); somewhere near here was the now-demolished Ardachie Lodge, site of an unusual haunting. In 1952 Peter McEwan and his wife moved into the nineteenth-century lodge, hoping to raise pigs. The couple hired a Mr and Mrs MacDonald as housekeepers to look after their small children. Mr MacDonald had been a London postman and gave up his job for the pleasure of moving back to Scotland; neither he nor his wife had ever been to Fort Augustus before and knew no one there. On their first night the MacDonalds were disturbed in their beds by the sound of footsteps outside their room though no one was there. Later, Mrs MacDonald saw an old woman beckoning her. They moved to another room, only to be kept awake by loud knocking on the wall, which woke the McEwans; the house was now roused – something was going on. The climax came when Mrs MacDonald saw an old woman, candle in hand, crawling down the corridor outside their bedroom. This rattled the McEwans, because Mrs Brewin, the wife of the previous owner, had been obsessed with the notion that the servants were stealing and hiding items; crippled by arthritis, she had crawled around at night with a candle trying to catch them.

The Society for Psychical Research sent two investigators to question Mrs MacDonald. They heard loud knocks from the wall, after which Mrs MacDonald rose, white-faced, claiming to see the spirit of Mrs McEwan, her employer, in a doorway. Later, following more knocks, Mrs MacDonald entered some kind of semi-trance state and stated that the trouble stemmed from the ghost's distress that a favourite rose tree had been allowed to die. The gardener confirmed the death of the tree. The McEwans had had enough and left, and the MacDonalds also returned to London. These details are taken from Colin Wilson's books *Poltergeist!* and *Mysteries*. Wilson concentrated on Mrs MacDonald's character – 'rather tense, highly strung', with no previous psychic experience – and suggested that some quality present in the house somehow amplified her latent psychic abilities (her first comment on arriving at the lodge was that there was 'something wrong with the place'). Unfortunately the entire case is now a dead end as the house, which had remained empty since the haunting, was demolished in 1968. As 'The Ghost of Ardachie Lodge', the case was dramatised for television in the 1977 BBC series *Leap in the Dark*.

7

THE SOUTH SHORE OF LOCH NESS I: FROM FORT AUGUSTUS TO DORES AND INVERNESS

Persons who busy themselves about the subject of Satanism and Black Magic are rarely to be depended upon for accuracy of statement.

M.R. James, letter to *The Times*, 21 January 1932

This chapter follows the road along the shore of South Loch Ness. The alternative upland route, through the hills and the 'lake district', is covered in the next chapter. Note – walkers and cyclists who want to avoid the steep slog over the B862 to Whitebridge can take the Loch Ness Express from Fort Augustus to Foyers (it also stops at Urquhart Castle and Inverness).

GLENDOEBEG

Somewhere near here (NH416091) is the site of an odd episode in Jacobite legend. After Culloden, a man called Corrie or Gorrie, a thief and highway robber known to his mum as Alexander Macdonald, took up a position on the road here to assassinate the Duke of Cumberland. The details of what happened next vary depending on which version of the story you read – he fired a musket stolen from Fort Augustus and missed, he fired a blunderbuss filled with lead, rusty nails and scrap iron and missed, or he simply lost his nerve and ran away – but all agree on the key detail that he fled to a cave. The troopers stood guard outside for several days but he refused to come out – in some versions he lived in the cave for many years until at last, an old, bent man, he was persuaded by his wife to return to the open air before dying. An alternative, or possibly parallel, tradition is that fourteen boys hid for thirteen weeks in the cave, sheltering from the redcoats who had taken or killed all the family's livestock even though they had not followed the Jacobite cause. A narrow corridor leads to the utter darkness of the inner cave. Corrie's Cave is on Craig Corrie, on the lochside at approximately NH405105. Very close is the memorial to Mary Hambro, a banker's wife drowned in a speedboat accident; her body, along with a diamond necklace, was never recovered, and divers were said to return from the search with their hair turned white – both classic examples of 'The Lake That Does Not Give Up Its Dead' and 'The Terrified Divers' motifs (see INTRODUCTION). Further north up the shore is Horseshoe Craig, a huge semicircular landslip.

Horseshoe Craig,
south Loch Ness side.

SUIDHE CHUIMEIN (ST CUMMEIN'S SEAT)

This is the highest point on the road, with spectacular views on a good day (NH449105). The *NSA* says the cairn here marks the spot where the chief of Clan Cummin died, although usually the place name is ascribed to St Cummein, Abbot of Iona. A far-fetched story is told about a lady in a crinoline blown from here to Loch nan Lann (NH440130), a distance of about 1.25 miles (2km).

FOYERS★

Foyers is a split-level village in the Alpine style, with the road and a network of attractive if steep paths connecting the two parts. Paths lead from the post office and café (which has a live webcam focused on the nearby red squirrels) in Upper Foyers to the Lower Falls★, a sublime sight. The Upper Falls, less striking but attractively viewable only in glimpses, are reached by taking the short road at the very south end of the village, towards the hydro intake. There was once a log bridge over the falls. The *NSA* relates the case of a drunk man who one moonlit night happily crossed the log bridge over the falls. When he returned to the spot, he was so horror-struck at the abyss over which he had blithely passed that he took to his bed and soon died. This is a tale told of other waterfalls, and has all the hallmarks of a tall story told to impress tourists. The bridge may be the site of an unlikely episode in Polson's *Scottish Witchcraft Lore*. On their way to a mill to steal meal, six witches crossed a narrow wooden bridge over a deep ravine. Several youths took planks out of the middle of the bridge and set fire to whin bushes near to their cottages – the witches thought their houses were on fire, ran back, and fell through the gap into the deep waters.

Following Culloden, Hugh Fraser of Foyers hid in a cave for seven years, his secret kept safe by the loyal locals who referred to him in code as Bonaid Odhair

Lower Foyers,
cypress tree with
branches rooting in
the ground.

(Dun Bonnet). Supposedly the cave is the one called Bonagour's Cave, on Carn Dearg (NH489189); it is difficult to find, very, very small and very dull. A girl bringing food to the cave was followed by a redcoat – Hugh killed the spy and buried him where he fell. Then a boy carrying a cask of beer for him was met by troopers just above the falls. He refused to give Hugh up so they cut off his hand and the cask tumbled into the chasm. A shoemaker's wife from Fort Augustus who sold groceries from a small cart was robbed and killed somewhere in the area. Various people were seen wearing vests made from her cloak. Her pony wandered close to Hugh's cave: he ordered its feet to be tied together and had it thrown into Lochan Torr an tuill (NH521228).

Lower Foyers has several points of interest, as well as superb views of the loch. The branches of the massive cypress tree just west of the old bridge reach back down to root in the ground. In the dusk it has a distinctive atmosphere. A path from here leads west to a modern burial ground, on the other side of which is a memorial to Jane, wife of Thomas Fraser of Balnain, (d. 1817), decorated with heraldic and symbolic figures★. South of here the little-visited woods and pebble beaches are home to feral goats. The small inlet by the monument (NH490210) is Camus Mharbh Dhaoine, The Bay of the Dead Men. *The Hub of the Highlands* gives the origin of the name: in the early fifteenth century the young bride of Gruer Mor from Portclair (now Invermoriston) was making her rounds of the loch for the traditional receipt of wedding presents, when she was grossly insulted by Lawrence Grant in Foyers. Gruer sailed his galleys across the loch and defeated Grant's men here on the water. Grant made it to the north shore but was killed in the woods above Ruiskich, at Ruigh Laurais (Laurence's Slope, NH480217, north of Invermoriston). Gruer then seized Foyers.

Huisdean Frangach, French Hugh, the founder of the Frasers of Foyers family, had a heroic career which became elaborated with common legendary tales of

Lower Foyers, Jane Fraser
memorial.

adventure. A brave, handsome fellow, he sailed away to foreign lands, freed a cap-
tive maiden in Turkey using a magic knife taken from a wicked crone, overcame
the hag's spells and magical net and escaped on his ship. In another tale he was
spending the night in a lonely inn in France when he heard a nurse singing a
child to sleep with a lullaby whose verses warned that Hugh was about to be
murdered. Our hero escaped in the nick of time, killed the pursuing hounds with
his bare hands, and escaped with the woman via a rope made of blankets, eventually bringing her to Stratherrick as his bride. These details are given in 'Places,
People and Poetry of Dores in Other Days' (*TGSI*) by Revd Thomas Sinton.

On 12 November 1933, on the shore at Foyers, Hugh Grey took the first
'monster' photograph. It is a deeply ambiguous image – my favourite suggestion
(because it is so gloriously mundane) is that it shows a Labrador in the water
shaking a stick.

In 1934, with Nessie fever in full swing, the *Daily Mail* hired a big-game hunter,
the almost comically flamboyant Marmaduke Wetherell, to track down the beast.
The 'discovery' on 4 January of strange footprints at Foyers led to an embarrassing climbdown when plaster casts of the prints were identified by the British
Museum as being from a hippopotamus. Wetherell had used one of his hunting
trophies, a hippo foot ashtray.

Wrecked boat,
Foyers beach.

On 23 April 1960 at Foyers Tim Dinsdale, possibly the most noted of the monster hunters, took his famous film of something moving in the loch. For many
years it was the most talked-about moving image of Nessie; recent analysis has
shown it to be of something much more mundane – a boat. Even so, the Dinsdale
film is one of the key documents in the evolution of the Nessie story.

Between 1969 and 1983, the road past the old aluminium factory, which
leads to the pier, was where the late Frank Searle had his caravan and Monster
Exhibition. Searle spent years living a frugal existence on the lochside, hoping
to get photographic proof of Nessie's existence. His earlier pictures intrigued
and even convinced some other monster hunters, but he soon started trying to
flog obvious hoaxes. Over time something of a feud developed between him and
other members of the Nessie fraternity, and a sigh of relief went up when he quit
the loch in 1983. His book *Seven Years With Nessie* can be read as a prime example
of the genre of self-serving literature. When he died in 2007 at least one obituary
described him as 'colourful'; rival monster hunters from the Searle years probably
had other words in mind, like 'dodgy', 'duplicitous' and 'dangerous'.

Further on is the Foyers pumped hydroelectric power station. During the day
water from Loch Mhor high in the hills drives the turbines; at night the water is
pumped back up again, to return the next day. There is an unconfirmed story of a
large eel being trapped in one of the water inlets.

In the magazine *Flying Saucer Review* (Vol. 19, No. 5 September-October 1973)
Ted Holiday reported the sighting of a UFO by his friend Graham Snape and
other witnesses on 13 August 1971. Snape's object was luminous and fast and
travelled down the loch southwards, about level with the tops of the hills in
the background. It was 'irregular in shape although roughly circular. The most
impressive feature was the colour which was a white core with a purple/vio-

let annulus around it.' The main part of Holiday's article was taken up with the alleged sighting three days later of an alien spaceship in a forest clearing near Foyers. The witness was Jan-Ove Sundberg, a Swede, who claimed to have seen three humanoid figures in diving suit-type clothing enter a cigar-shaped craft which rose vertically without any sound and which then moved rapidly over the hill in the direction of Loch Mhor. Sundberg took one photograph of one of the aliens stepping into the craft.

Some years later, Stuart Campbell subjected the report and the photograph to analysis (*Flying Saucer Review,* Vol. 26 No. 6 March 1981). According to Campbell, Sundberg told him that after his return to Sweden, he was visited by 'mysterious men', and 'telephone callers told him to forget all that he had seen at Loch Ness, a "black figure" walked at night in his garden leaving strange dumb-bell-shaped footprints, poltergeists plagued the house, and he had experienced "bad dreams" about flying saucers' – all classic *Men In Black* post-UFO sighting experiences. After some effort Campbell located the exact place from where Sundberg's picture had been taken – it was from the road to Lower Foyers, southwest of the Foyers Hotel, looking west down a slope towards the shore – and took his own photo of the scene from the same perspective. There was no clearing within or around the plantation. The blobs of light in the original photograph turned out to be daylight coming through the tree cover. Campbell concluded that [Sundberg] 'photographed a perfectly normal Scottish pine forest... It may be concluded that the report is due to either a hoax or a hallucination.'

BOLESKINE HOUSE AND ALEISTER CROWLEY

In 2007 Frank and Katie Ellam of Easter Boleskine, a private dwelling which lies on a separate stretch of land to the north of, and unconnected to, Boleskine House, told me that when they moved in, the removal firm had been unable to find locally-sourced helpers, as they had been frightened off by the name (on the second day of the move, once it was clear that the address was not Boleskine House, there was no problem with local labour). And when writing out the farm's address for business and deliveries, many people in Inverness were still taken aback by the name. Such is the still-thriving power of the word 'Boleskine'.

'The folk of the district still remember with a mixture of horror and amusement the antics of [Crowley]... Many are the stories told about him.' (Kenneth MacRae, *Highland Ways and Byways*). Many indeed. Trying to entirely separate fact from fiction at Boleskine House is probably now an entirely futile task, partly because the myth has grown and mutated to a grotesque degree, and partly because the source of many of the stories comes from the writings of the man himself – and he was hardly the most reliable of narrators.

I should make it clear from the start that Boleskine House and its well-fenced grounds are private property; please do not disturb either the owners or the people living in the lodge at the foot of the drive.

Boleskine graveyard, opposite Boleskine House.

Footpath signpost. Note 'Boleskine' refers to Easter Boleskine, not Boleskine House.

A notice in the *Inverness Journal* of 1 December 1809 says the '"Cottage of Boleskin", property of the Honourable Archibald Fraser, was finished with Masonic honours on St Andrew's Eve (29 November).' If you're expecting something grand and overpowering, scale back your expectations: it was then, and is now, a handsome, relatively modest Georgian villa (at least by the standard of Scottish country houses) – not a cottage, but hardly a mansion either.

Crowley bought the house with its extensive grounds in November 1899, for around twice its market value. Then only twenty-four and still wealthy, in many ways he was the archetypal pleasure-seeking laird, enjoying walking, climbing and entertaining, and putting on airs by styling himself Lord Boleskine. He hooked a large salmon in the loch (in his 'autohagiography', *The Confessions of Aleister*

Crowley [hereafter *Confessions*] he wrote: 'Salmon fishing on Loch Ness should be remembered by people who are praying for "those in peril on the deep". It is a dull year when nobody is drowned.') The house also became a sexual playground. But the purchase wasn't just the whim of a rich rake. Crowley had scoured the country for a very specific building, finally finding it on Loch Ness.

It is a complete myth that Crowley was a Satanist – he regarded the idea of the Devil as absurd, a ludicrous, outdated offshoot of the Christian religion he so despised. There were no Black Masses here. He was, however, very much interested in contacting Otherworld entities, for which the words spirit, angel or demon could equally apply. In 1898 he read *The Book of the Sacred Magick of Abra-Melin the Mage*, which had recently been translated into English by Samuel Liddell Mathers, one of the founders of the magical group the Hermetic Order of the Golden Dawn, of which Crowley was a member (at least before he engaged in a tempestuous spat with virtually everyone involved). The grimoire was supposedly written in 1458 by Abrahim the Jew, who had learned its magical secrets from a North African adept. In *Do What Thou Wilt,* one of Crowley's several biographers, Lawrence Sutin, says 'the original Hebrew manuscript has never been found and scholarly opinion now places *Abra-Melin* as an eighteenth-century pseudony-mous work.' Irrespective of provenance, the book had a huge impact on Crowley. In contrast to most magical textbooks, which tended towards flamboyant and sometimes grotesque ritual, *Abra-Melin* offered a yoga-like, quietist approach to magical attainment. There were no magic circles, pentagrams, robes, or long Latin chants – just an intense six-month period of meditation and prayer in a conse-crated room, after which the magician would encounter a higher being called The Holy Guardian Angel, who would give instructions on the summoning and control of both good and evil spirits and the consecration of talismans that would allow the magician to acquire an ever-full purse, a phantom army, sexual irresist-ibility, and the ability to create and quell storms or raise the dead. According to *Abra-Melin*, good magic and spirits were superior to their evil equivalents, so under the influence of the former, evil spirits could be bidden to do good – but if the magician failed to complete the operation successfully, he was at risk from malevolent forces.

The *Abra-Melin* text was very precise on every detail of the ritual, right down to the correct occult architecture of the location – which was why Crowley had bought Boleskine. He set up an 'oratory', a wooden structure hung with mirrors, in the south-west part of the house, and installed a north-facing door as instructed in the grimoire. This sacred space opened out onto a terrace, covered with sand two fingers deep, which he collected from the lochside. At the end of the terrace was a lodge for the good and evil spirits. The operation was due to commence in spring 1900, Easter being the time specified in *Abra-Melin*. He swore a great oath to commit himself to the operation. Had the ritual been successful it would have changed his life forever. He commenced the operation but – distracted by sex, infighting with his magical rivals, and his own volatile, abrasive personality – he did not complete it. At the time, Crowley was a force of nature – a whirlwind of energy, lust, intellectual curiosity and ego – and in retrospect it was never on the cards that he was going to take a six-month sabbatical devoted to meditation and chastity.

It is now commonplace in modern fantasy films and books that if a spell is not completed properly, the entities summoned will break out and do Bad Things. According to his own account in the *Confessions*, the danger was there as soon as he started the preparations: 'The demons connected with Abra-Merlin do not wait to be evoked; they come unsought.' The demons attack in the hope of overcoming the magician before he achieves power over them. An earlier attempt to commence the operation at Crowley's former London flat hinted at what was to come – the flat became populated with semi-materialised beings whose malevolent ambience hit visitors with nasty symptoms for months to come. As for Boleskine, Crowley said in the *Confessions*:

> I have little doubt that the Abra-Melin devils, whatever they are, use the place as convenient headquarters and put in some of their spare time in terrifying the natives. No one would pass the house after dark. Folk got into the habit of going round through Strath Errick, a detour of several miles.

The lodge and terrace became filled by shadowy shapes, 'sufficiently substantial… to be almost opaque. I say shapes; and yet the truth is that they were not shapes properly speaking… It was as if the faculty of vision suffered some interference; as if the objects of vision were not properly objects at all.' (*Confessions*). Presumably these were the demons he identified as Oriens, Paimon, Ariton, Amaimon and their 111 servitors.

A heavy, oppressive atmosphere settled over the house, with the lights being needed even at noon. Winds blew through the rooms. Bad Things, apparently, started to happen to people associated with the house. Friends and employees, unable to bear the atmosphere, fled. The lodge keeper, a teetotaller, went on a three-day drinking spree and tried to kill his own wife and children. A workman tried to kill Crowley. When the local butcher's ringing of the bell broke Crowley's concentration, he distractedly scrawled the meat order on the nearest piece of paper, which either had a spell written on it, or the symbols of two demons. Shortly afterwards the butcher accidentally sliced through his fingers with a cleaver (or, depending on the gore score of the variant being told, cut off the whole hand or even chopped through his femoral artery and died). We can't take all these stories at face value – some may be apocryphal, and violence, accidents and desertion can easily result from causes other than bad magic. But what was real was the house's evil reputation with people locally – Richard Frere's father told him tradesmen did not approach the house but left the orders at a safe distance. Boleskine is called Skene House in Somerset Maugham's 1908 novel *The Magician*, where Crowley is the model for the sinister magician Oliver Haddo.

In 1904, open magical warfare broke out between Crowley in Boleskine and Mathers in Paris. Again according to the *Confessions*, Mathers killed most of the Boleskine hunting dogs and rained illnesses on the servants. Hundreds of large stag beetles infested the property. A workman was magically controlled to violently attack Crowley's pregnant wife – Crowley had to subdue him with a salmon gaff and lock him in a coal shed. Crowley responded by using the *Abra-Melin* talismans to obtain the services of Beelzebub, one of the Eight Sub-Princes of the *Abra-Melin* spirits. Beelzebub and his forty-nine servitor spirits then attacked Mathers, and presumably the war was won. Crowley's wife Rose participated in the rituals and clairvoyantly saw the (to Crowley) invisible demons, such as Holastri, a large pink bug, Nimorup, a dwarf with greenish-bronze, slobbery lips, and Nominon: 'A large red spongy jellyfish with one greenish luminous spot. Like a nasty mess.' This whole episode is typically inconsistent: as Crowley had not completed the *Abra-Melin* operation, how could he control *Abra-Melin* evil spirits, and how was his wife entitled, under the strict terms of the *Abra-Melin* text, even to participate? Crowley does not say how or if these demons were banished; if evil did lurk in the house thereafter, it is possible it came from this episode. On the other hand, he could have just made the whole thing up. It's classic Crowley: self-contradictory, self-aggrandising – he's powerful enough to control the mighty and infamous Beelzebub – and possibly self-created.

Another hard-to-corroborate story is that in 1904, just before his daughter was born at Boleskine, Crowley tried to magically arrange for his wife to give birth to a monster: the infant was born normal, and the story may just be local gossip.

Among all the magic and darkness, there are stories of the lighter side of Aleister Crowley. He 'was one of the greatest practical jokers ever known in these parts. He… owned a wonderful collection of skins and weapons, and would often "scare the daylights" out of the community by appearing fantastically garbed on the open highway, accompanied by servants similarly clad.' (Kenneth MacRae, *Highland Ways and Byways*). Under the banner of the Laird of Boleskine Manor, he wrote to the Vigilance Society in London (which was to prostitution what the Temperance Society was to alcohol) complaining that the streetwalking in tiny Foyers was 'unpleasantly conspicuous'. When the Society wrote back saying they could find no evidence of this he fired back a mocking retort: 'Conspicuous by its absence, you fools!' He erected signs stating, 'The Dinotheriums are out today', 'Beware of the Icthyosaurus,' and, 'This way to the Kooloomooloomavlock (does not bite).' The latter was an invisible monster that terrorised the good people of Foyers. One wonders if Crowley had caught a whiff of the local stories about a creature in the loch…

One morning he awoke to find a large jar of illicit whisky on his doorstep – a gift from the illegal distillers in the hills, who were worried his walks over the hills might expose them (they were in no danger there); he planned to build a flying bicycle and launch it from the slopes above Boleskine, with a boat waiting on the loch to retrieve the aerocyclist (nothing came of this); he convinced a visiting

Swiss mountaineer to go on a hunt for the haggis, described as a large, danger-ous, feral sheep. After an expedition through the gardens and hills behind the house, accompanied by Crowley's ghillie, the Alpinist got his elephant gun out and bagged the creature (actually a tethered ram, deliberately put in place), which was ceremonially served to him at a mock banquet. Another story says Crowley had a crucifix beneath the front doormat, so visitors would blasphemously tread on the Cross when they entered; it's impossible to tell if this is true. What does seem like an obvious tall tale (especially as it was propagated by Crowley himself) is the story of the head of Simon, Lord Lovat, executed after the 1745 rebellion, rolling around the corridors at night. It's difficult to divine how a man gets to haunt a house that was not built when he was alive and with which he had no connection.

In the summer of 1909 Crowley returned from more of his endless travels. He was joined by two younger men, Kenneth Ward and Victor Neuburg. The former just wanted to enjoy himself; the latter regarded Crowley as his holy guru and was there to undertake a 'magical retirement' under Crowley's tutelage. Over ten days Neuburg – who kept a 127-page magical record of the process – practiced yoga, meditation, astral travel and magical ritual techniques, studied Crowley's writings, and experienced a series of visions and heightened mental states. During the days Crowley went skiing and climbing with Ward; in the evenings he tutored Neuburg, which sometimes involved scourging the student with a gorse switch or stinging nettles, and, once, a vile anti-Semitic tirade. The relationship between Crowley and Neuburg was clearly intense – a mix of sex, master and pupil interdepend-ency and sadomasochism. After further magical adventures together Neuburg, like so many of Crowley's friends and associates, later became alienated from him.

Crowley frittered his fortune away. In 1913 he mortgaged Boleskine. The fol-lowing year he put it up for rent, legally transferring any income to a magical group he had set up, the Mysteria Mystica Maxima, or M.M.M. The idea was that the group would pay off the mortgage, run the place, and provide it as free accommodation when their leader required. Meanwhile he went to America for the duration of the First World War. It was the last time he set foot in Boleskine.

As a way of staving off financial disaster it was an abject failure – four years later the estate was sold off and Crowley did not receive a penny from the sale. He had also left behind the majority of his library in the house. In the 1930s the library was off-handedly sold by the owners at auction in Inverness. After his time at Boleskine, Crowley's life degenerated, morally, financially and even magically. Several writers have tried to pinpoint when it all went wrong. C.R. Cammell, in his book *Aleister Crowley, the Man, the Mage, the Poet* believed it was when Crowley broke the sacred oath he had taken in preparation for the *Abra-Melin* ritual – an oath in which he swore to use his magical powers for good: 'To me Crowley appeared thenceforth to have been a man accursed: he lost all sense of good and evil, he lost his love, his fortune, his honour, his magical powers...'

Although he was probably in residence for, in total, no more than two of the fourteen years he owned the house, Crowley had both emotional and occult affection for Boleskine. It is mentioned in several of his rituals and to this day followers of the Beast are required to align their temples and altars towards Boleskine. Before he died in 1947 he left instructions that the urn containing his ashes be placed on the edge of the cliff behind Boleskine. This did not happen and the location of the ashes is unknown.

Boleskine had a number of different owners during the rest of the twentieth century. Several of them came to bad ends, prompting much press speculation about the residual evil in the place. (A good example is the headline from the *Scottish Daily Mail*, 18 May 1965: 'Did Evil Linger On In The Beautiful House By The Loch? Black Magic And Butchery.') Edward Crane, a retired Army major and member of a well-known family, shot himself in the house. In *The Other Loch Ness Monster*, a 2000 television documentary for BBC Scotland's Ex:S series, Anna MacLaren, a former housekeeper at Boleskine, recalled absent-mindedly throwing the dog a bone – which turned out to be part of the dead man's skull. Another owner was involved in a financial scandal in which Government money had been misappropriated – a pig-rearing scheme had been camouflage for a love nest 'which it seems was feathered more often by others than himself.' (Alan Lawson, *A Country Called Stratherrick*). Another undetailed, unconfirmed and undated story says several people entered the 'secret chamber' (possibly the oratory?) sometime after Crowley left. One of them blew on a ceremonial goat's horn which supposedly set off a chain of inexplicable and demonic events in the area.

In 1969 the alternative film director and iconoclast Kenneth Anger stayed at the house and told rock star Jimmy Page it was up for sale. Page, guitarist with Led Zeppelin, then the biggest band in the world, was a Crowley obsessive, with a growing collection of Crowleyana. He also worked on the soundtrack for Anger's Crowleyan film *Lucifer Rising*. Page owned the house from 1970 to 1992, during which time he spent a total of around six weeks there. He can be seen in the grounds of Boleskine, climbing up a rock face and meeting a mysterious hermit on the summit, in the Led Zeppelin film *The Song Remains the Same*. Stephen Davis' 'excess all areas' Zep biography *Hammer of the Gods* – which may not be entirely reliable in all matters – claims Page had Boleskine redecorated by a 'renowned Satanist named Charles Pierce', although I can find no further reference to this. The heady world of 1970s rock superstardom and the hellish reputation of Boleskine were a marriage made in heaven for the press, and soon stories circulated of Page signing a pact with Satan in the house, and the terrible curse which stalked Led Zeppelin. Yes, the band suffered tragedies – Zep's singer Robert Plant lost his young daughter to an illness, and his wife was badly injured in an accident, and notoriously hard-living drummer John Bonham died of too much alcohol – but this is hardly evidence of some kind of demonic death-stalking.

In the 1970s a rites-of-passage tradition grew up among local teenagers – camping overnight in the woods as close to the house as possible, staying awake to see if the bogeyman would turn up. This developed into 'devil tourism' – throughout the 1970s and '80s the house was plagued by unwanted visitors seeking to commune with Al's spirit, or at least try to steal some kind of souvenir. The brunt of this was born by Malcolm Dent, who was installed by Page as a kind of caretaker. In several newspaper interviews Dent decried the selfish thoughtlessness of the trespassers, who often made the lives of himself and his family a misery. Dent also described some of the paranormal phenomena supposedly still current in the house. For example, in the *Highland News* of the 8 February 1997 and the *Inverness Courier* of the 3 November 2006, there are descriptions of disturbances caused by construction work, as though the house didn't like it – doors would slam all night and carpets and rugs would be piled up. At other times all the doors would suddenly open as if someone was running through them. 'We just used to say that was Aleister doing his thing,' said Dent. Page bought a number of chairs from the Café Royal in London, a favourite hang-out for Crowley. Each chair had a name-plate from a famous customer – Crowley, Marie Lloyd, Billy Butlin, James Agate, Ruldolph Valentino, William Orpen and Jacob Epstein. Crowley's chair was, of

Boleskine graveyard: hexagram graffiti in mort house.

Boleskine graveyard: symbols of mortality.

Boleskine graveyard: tombstone
with bullet holes.

course, placed at the head of the table, but each morning it was found to have
swapped places with Marie Lloyd's. It transpired that during repairs the respective
nameplates had been accidentally transposed. Dent and several friends, during a
pause in an evening's conversation about the occult, saw a small porcelain figure
of the Devil rise off the mantelpiece, move to the ceiling, then smash into the
fireplace. On another occasion Dent heard the 'snorting, snuffling and banging' of
some huge beast outside the bedroom door. Petrified, he lay awake all night, only
opening the door in the daylight – 'Whatever was there, I have no doubt, was
pure evil.' Dent moved out before Page sold the house in 1992. During the move,
he heard a great booming voice saying, 'What are you doing?'

In *The Other Loch Ness Monster* documentary, Dent says that Boleskine 'responds
to people.' At the time of its production (March 2000) there were press claims that
the programme was 'cursed', with equipment failures, a key member of the production team dropping out, and everyone having recurring dreams of Crowley.
Apparently the situation became so bad that a minister was called in to bless the
proceedings. I have no way of telling if any of this is a) real b) imagination attrib-
uting routine problems to the 'Curse of Crowley' or c) PR flimflam.

Ronald and Annette MacGillivray bought the house from Page, and successfully ran it for several years as an upmarket guesthouse, although it took three
years of renovations before they could move in. In a piece in the *Daily Record*, Mrs
MacGillivray categorically stated that they had not experienced a single paranormal event in five years. Boleskine is now a private house.

BOLESKINE GRAVEYARD★★ ᴥ

NH50772216. Of all the old graveyards in the Loch Ness area, it is no surprise that this is the most visited – it is on the B852 directly opposite Boleskine House. It has suffered so much from inconsiderate Crowley-seekers that the nineteenth-century anti-bodysnatching watch house has been closed up to prevent the current magical graffiti inside being further extended. The medieval church is long gone, and was replaced in 1777 by the present church several kilometres further east at Druim an Teampuill (NH508183, see next chapter). Alan Lawson quotes both Bishop Forbes, who in 1762 described the church as 'the poorest Edifice of any kind I ever looked upon', and Boswell in 1773: 'the meanest parish Kirk I ever saw.' The story that the church caught fire and the entire congregation were trapped inside and burned alive was either invented by Crowley or propagated by him, because there is no historical record of this (although churches elsewhere were set on fire during clan warfare). Another one of Crowley's fictions may be the alleged tunnel between Boleskine House and the graveyard – I was told a story that Jimmy Page once tried to dig for this imaginary tunnel, although I have no confirmation of the tale.

Until well into the eighteenth century few churches had pews or seats. In 1684 Thomas Houston, also known as Huison, the minister of Boleskine from 1648 to 1705, reported that 'all persons of all ranks indifferently buried their dead within his church, not only his own parishioners, but some others of the neighbouring parishes, so that several coffins were hardly under ground, which was like to be very dangerous and noisome,' and dogs fought over the human bones that protruded through the earthen floor (*Records of the Presbyteries of Inverness and Dingwall 1643-1688.*) This same minister supposedly had to 'exorcise a savage water demon which terrorised the good folk about Achadiach' (Lawson) and lay to rest the spirits of the dead raised in the graveyard by a magician called An Cruinair Friseal, the Fraser Crowner, a maker of magical circles and owner or servant of a familiar spirit. Achadiach is above the Falls of Foyers. A number of books say the graveyard was the haunt of witches, but I can find no detail of any kind, so the Houston story may be the forgotten source.

The tale is also told by Revd Thomas Sinton in 'A Day at Boleskine and Foyers' (*TGSI*); entering the graveyard, Sinton's friend James Smith of Erchite Wood, known as James Gow, whispered, 'the silent folks are here.' Gow was the repository of the area's folklore; he died at the age of 100 in 1903, and is buried in Boleskine, although his gravestone incorrectly gives the date as 1906. James Gow was also the main source for the booklet *Tales from Aldourie Estate*, compiled by Neil Fraser-Tytler in the 1920s (see DORES). Just southeast of the mort house is a tombstone with three clear bullet holes. The story (told in, among others, Kenneth MacRae's *Highland Ways and Byways*) is that some time after Culloden, a cart carrying military provisions passed through a funeral party. One of the mourners lifted a loaf of bread and threw it to some dogs: he was arrested and

taken to Fort Augustus. Before leaving, the soldiers fired an indiscriminate vol-
ley at the party, but only hit the tombstone. The next morning the minister of
Boleskine used his known support of the Government to persuade the Duke of
Cumberland to release the miscreant.

In June 1969, three American students found a ritual object in the graveyard
– a tapestry wrapped around a conch shell. It was shown to author Ted (F.W.)
Holiday, from whose account in *The Dragon and the Disc* the description is taken
(there is also a photograph of the tapestry in the book). The tapestry was about
4 by 5ft (1.2–1.5m) and had the appearance of an altar cloth, with serpentine
symbols embroidered in gold thread, and reddish stains as if objects had been
placed at each corner. The white conch was about five inches (12cm) long and
inscribed with two parallel grooves and a lotus blossom. It produced a harsh bray-
ing sound when blown. The objects were not mildewed or damp and had clearly
been hidden just a few days earlier. The finder took them to the Victoria and
Albert Museum, where the tapestry was identified as coming from Turkey.

The meaning of this strange find has never been clearly established – on no
evidence whatsoever, Holiday claimed it had belonged to Crowley, but he was
on stronger ground in suggesting that 'someone unknown' had been interrupted
in some kind of ritual. 'Whoever he was, he used every possible method to get
back his unholy trappings. He even had the police hunting up and down the glen
for the tapestry although, when asked, none seemed to know the name of the
owner.' Richard Freeman (*Dragons: More Than a Myth?), following 'Doc' Shiels,
suggests the instigators were Patrick Kelly and his father, Laurence. Shiels had met
Patrick when he was working on the 'Monstermind' ritual (see URQUHART
CASTLE). He made a series of astonishing claims – to have photographed a lake
monster in Lough Leane in 1981, seen Nessie on 1 May 1969, and to be a direct
descendant of Edward Kelly, the notorious scryer and medium of the Elizabethan
magus Dr John Dee. Laurence Kelly had apparently met Crowley in Paris and, it
being 1933, they discussed the hot topic of the moment, the Loch Ness Monster.
Crowley reportedly was very interested in the creature. Of course, some people,
taking the lead of Ted Holiday, suggest Crowley's misapplication of magic actually
created Nessie (the supernatural monster, not any putative zoological specimen).
It has to be said there is little actual evidence to support the link between the
Kellys and the altar cloth and conch.

INVERFARIGAIG

A steep narrow and winding road climbs northeast from Inverfarigaig. It gives
superb views of the Iron Age hill fort Dun Dearduil, probably the most spectacular in the Highlands (NH526239). The name, Deidre's Fort, takes us into the
world of Irish mythology and different versions of the same story, although all
variants agree that the beautiful Deidre, daughter of the royal harper and the
intended wife of King Concobar/Conacher, fell in love with Naisi/Naoise, son

of the champion Uisnech, and the couple eloped to Scotland with Naoise's two brothers. Thereafter the versions diverge, but usually after a great deal of fighting, betrayal, scheming and warrior-society power struggles it all ends tragically for the young couple. Note that climbing Dun Dearduil is dangerous.

In 1907, Revd Thomas Sinton, in 'Places, People and Poetry of Dores in Other Days' (*TGSI*), identified several spots further up the road which are not now very easy to locate. An Sithean Buidhe, the Yellow Fairy Knoll, had a rowan tree and was in the angle between the road and the track to Ballagan Farm (NH536249); Preas a Chonochair, the thicket of the hiding place of Conachar, was somewhere north of the farm; somewhere nearby was Sithean an Losaid, the Fairy Knoll of the Trough, underneath which a pair of ploughmen heard two women violently quarrel over a broken griddle. One of the men fashioned a new griddle and put it on top of the knoll: when he returned with his team of horses it had been replaced with a bottle of ale and a bannock. He ate and drank but soon died; the other man had refused the fairy food and lived. The deep tree-shaded ravine of the River Farigaig is Glaic n h-Amair, 'an eerie locality', reputed to be haunted. Omas Ruadh Friseil, a ploughman at Ballagan, drove his horses into Glaic an Amair to graze there for the night in a grassy bottom. Having shackled one of them, he turned round and said, 'where is the other fetter?' A weird voice replied 'it is here' and he saw 'a mannikin in a red cloak, apparently headless, who threw the fetter towards him and then disappeared in the darkness.'

This was the Bodach a' Gharbh-Dhùin, aka The Old Man of Inverfarigaig, who lived on Dun Garbh, the hill on the other side of the Farrigaig (NH533241). His cry was a death omen for a member of the tribe of Frasers to whom he was attached. One summer gloaming Sinton's friend James Gow (see BOLESKINE GRAVEYARD), on an errand with his brother, heard the Bodach's moaning cry, so they ran home as fast as they could, task forgotten. There is also a Loch-a-Bhodaich (NH552245), described by Lawson as 'an eerie patch of water surrounded by reeds and floating bog'.

Now difficult to find on the south bank of the Farigaig in Glaic an Amair is Fuaran an Amair, a cloutie healing well, once famous, where ribbons, coins and other offerings were left (NH527242). A water sprite lived within it. James Gow saw a woman from Strathnairn coming to take water from the well for a sick friend. Before leaving she threw a green blade upon the surface. It sank, an omen of death, and her friend soon died. Some 430 yards (400m) further on from Ballagan, on the north side of the road, is Cill mo Luaig, the site of the chapel and graveyard of St Moluag (NH539251), where only prolonged study will discern a few gravestones in the turf. Long after the site was officially closed, unbaptised infants continued to be buried there. The small hill to the north hosts Caisteal Cruinn, Castle Kitchie, (NH538253) a heavily-overgrown circular stone dun. All these places benefit from being lonely, high, and giving superb views of Loch Ness.

Dun Dearduil.

BETWEEN INVERFARIGAIG AND DORES ON THE B852 ᴖᵣ

This stretch of road has provided many famous Nessie sightings. In 1919, Jock Forbes and his father were travelling home on a dark February night. About two miles (3km) north of Inverfarigaig, their pony stopped and backed away in fright, nearly sliding the cart off the road and down the bank. Then something large crossed the road about 20m in front: it had come out of the trees above the road and moved very slowly across the road, down the bank and into the water. Jock was too preoccupied with controlling the pony to notice anything other than the thing's size, fully the width of the road. His father muttered something in Gaelic and they went home, never again talking about the incident: the thing was *tabu*.

In 1933, at around 3.30 p.m. on a hot 22 July, Mr Spicer and his wife were driving when he saw, 'the nearest approach to a dragon or prehistoric animal that I have ever seen in my life.' It crossed the road in the direction of the loch. This is one of the most discussed sightings, because it is the first 'long neck' report, the first use of the word 'dragon' or 'prehistoric animal', and because it is one of the rare land sightings. Many consider what Spicer saw was a mundane animal distorted by the heat haze on the road, with the experience amplified by his recent viewing of *King Kong*, with its impressive Diplodocus. The arguments still continue.

On 19 April 1950, Lady Maud Baillie, CBE, commander of the ATS during the Second World War and sister-in-law of the future Prime Minister, Harold MacMillan, was driving between Dores and Foyers with her two grandsons, along with Lady Spring-Rice and her two grandchildren. Lady Maud pointed out Urquhart Castle and one of the children asked, 'Is that a rock out there?' It wasn't, so they pulled up. The rock moved off to the north very quickly and was soon lost behind the roadside vegetation. 'Although none of us saw it for long enough to give any real details, we all saw two separate big dark humps in the water. There is no question that it was a very large living animal.'

On 14 July 1951, Lachlan Stuart, a forester from Whitefield, took a soon-to-be-famous picture of three humps in the water. Thirty years later, local author Richard Frere revealed that shortly after the photograph was released Stuart had confessed the humps were hay bales covered with tarpaulin.

In 1963, on an August evening, Hugh Ayton from Balachladaich Farm, his son, Jim, another local farmer called Alasdair Grant and two tourists from Stirling saw something moving south in the loch. Hugh and one of the others got the boat out to follow it. Close up, he described a long neck, a head like a horse but bigger and flatter, three low humps, and rough, dark skin: the most memorable feature was an oval-shaped eye near the top if its head – 'I'll always remember that eye looking at us!' Soon afterwards the creature submerged, creating a disturbance which rocked the boat.

Opposite Urquhart Castle and at various points along the road there are well laid out picnic areas; on the other side of the road from the first layby with picnic tables is the ruined building called the Witch's House, of which the provenance is obscure. Walking the path from the layby 400m south brings you to the singularly unimpressive site of An Ithur Mhor, the Change House, where horses were changed, visited by Johnson and Boswell in 1773. An information board tells the story. In 1746 the house was run by an old woman and her beautiful granddaughter; Cumberland's men tried to rape the girl. She escaped and returned with some local men but the woman was dead – strangled. Cumberland was furious, severely punishing the officer and demanding he pay blood money, although it is not clear if this was ever handed over. Another murder at the same place was possibly connected to the first crime – a paymaster for the Fort Augustus soldiers was found dead in his bed, with the money and his horse and harness nowhere to be seen. The woman in charge of the house was a 'noted character' who hoarded her money underground. When struck by a sudden fatal illness she tried to reveal the location of the hoard – 'between the sheepfold and the goatfold… directly in line between the big stone near the house and the full moon.' Many sought the treasure, but it was never found.

The OS map shows 'General Wade's Well' at NH577314, marked with a name stone in 1922. I failed to locate it. Equally elusive was The Well of the Outstretched Hand, aka 'The Well of the Phantom Hand', where drinkers would sometimes see a ghostly hand as they bent down to the water. Somewhere nearby there apparently used to be a stone carved with '1745', marking the graves of two Highlanders who died after Culloden. I doubt it is still there.

At Allt Dail Linn (NH581323) lived an old woman called Bean-a-Charier, the carrier's wife, reputedly a witch with the Evil Eye. In 1881, attending the wedding of Lieutenant-Colonel E.G. Fraser-Tytler, she brought as presents a goose, an old spoon, and 'some magic concoction like gruel in a pot.' Apparently something of a troublesome person, her death in 1885 was a relief to the locals. According

Dores beach with monster hunter Steve Feltham's van.

to Kenneth MacRae (1953), the bridge a bit further north at Baile-a-chladaich (NH586328) is the Witch's Bridge, where hags were often seen on the parapets; there may be some confusion with the bridge at Allt Dail Linn, which is called the Witches Bridge in Neil Tytler-Fraser's 1920s booklet *Tales from Aldourie Estate* (the source for all this information).

DORES★ ₪

The beach and the car park of the Dores Inn are popular locations for Nessie spotting. The Dores post office, run out of a cupboard, is the smallest in the UK.

In 1965, at 10.30 p.m. on 15 June, Sergeant Ian Cameron and his friend saw an object like a large upturned boat which moved against the wind. The sighting went on for some time and was witnessed by several other people.

In 2006, at the Rock Ness Festival, DJ Fat Boy Slim's headline set included the song 'Monster' by The Automatic, in which the question is repeatedly asked, 'What's that coming over the hill? Is it a monster?' With the Loch Ness panorama in the background, 20,000 people sang along. Nessie did not appear. A year later, in 2007, thousands of instant cameras were distributed to the festival-goers at Rock Ness, with a prize for the best picture of Nessie. The prize was not claimed.

In 1991, Steve Feltham gave up his job and his ordinary life in Dorset to become a full-time Nessie hunter. He's still there, on Dores Beach, living out of a converted van emblazoned with 'Nessie-serry Independent Research'. He sells homemade stone Nessie sculptures – one turned out to accidentally contain a Neolithic polished axe head. Pop along for a chat if you are interested in Nessie.

In Dores churchyard★ (NH601350) is buried Hugh Fraser, 'the Man With the Iron Hand'. He was a blacksmith at Bunchrubin, and when he was working at Aberchalder, machinery crushed his hand; he walked the many miles to Inverness, where his right hand was amputated without anaesthetic because he had a conscientious objection to chloroform. He was fitted with an iron hook and after the accident worked as a mail carrier and ghillie. He died in 1901. The entrance to the graveyard has a First World War memorial archway with panels on the front in a symbolical design called 'the garment of praise', with the words:

> To give unto them beauty for ashes
> Oil of joy for mourning
> The garment of praise
> For the spirit of heaviness

The accompanying sculptures have not survived.

To the north, on a hill overlooking the village, is Old Clune House (NH605354). There is a report of the smoking room window rattling at midnight as if someone was trying to get in – a haunting attributed to young Fraser of Foyers, killed in 1776, after an argument, by MacGillivray of Dalcrombie, his host. Fraser died in the gardens of the house. A magnificent Pictish stone carved with a boar was found near Clune Farm around 1850; after being used as a slab in the chimney wall of Clune Farm, it was removed and is now on view in the National Museum of Scotland in Edinburgh.

Aldourie Ring-Cairn (NH59993587)★ is a Clava-type cairn that has at some point in the relatively recent past been relocated and rebuilt as a *faux* stone circle. Despite this, the size and number (eighteen) of the stones makes it a site worth visiting. Walk west from the road through the channel of trees and turn right at the fence.

Right: Dores churchyard: detail of gravestone.

Opposite: Looking south, down Loch Ness from Dores beach.

The oldest part of Aldourie Castle★ (NH60123721, private) dates back to the seventeenth century but it is the Victorian and Edwardian 'Scots Baronial' flourishes that catch the eye, the ostentatious multiple turrets and chimneys giving the mansion a fairytale-like quality. During one enlargement in 1850 a cement fireproof floor was laid between the ground and the first floor, the process of which apparently banished the 'Grey Lady' who haunted the area between the west bedroom and the front room. In the mid-nineteenth century the castle was the home of Mary Fraser-Tytler, wife of the artist George Frederick Watts. In the 1880s, Mary's three-year-old nephew fell from a pony near the castle grounds. The event inspired Watts to paint 'Death Crowning Innocence', in which, breaking with the standard iconography of Death as the Grim Reaper, a benign and female winged figure cradles the dead child. Watts described this Death as 'the gentle nurse that puts the children to bed.' The painting is in the Tate Gallery in London.

The minor road opposite Aldourie towards Loch Ashie via Darris climbs to the MacBain Memorial Garden (NH613358) – which contains statues of cats, the emblem of Clan Chatten. Kinchyle of Dores (NH62153896) is probably a Clava passage grave, although the cairn has been completely removed and the few remaining stones of the outer circle are badly overgrown and difficult to access. It was visited by Johnson and Boswell during their Highland Tour (30 August 1773), Dr Johnson grumpily declaring: 'that to go and see one is only to see that it is nothing, for there is neither art nor power in it, and seeing one is as much as one would wish.' Boswell recorded that, 'There was a double circle of stones, one of very large ones and one of smaller ones.' The Knocknagael Boar Stone (see INVERNESS – GLENURQUHART ROAD) originally stood by the roadside at NH657414. A local tradition says it was buried for many centuries and discovered only when the Essich Road was built.

Aldourie Castle.

To the west of the road is the eighteenth-century Borlum Farm (NH623400) (private, but open for B&B), built on the site of a medieval castle owned by the notorious Mackenzies of Borlum. In 1618, Lord and Lady Borlum plotted to murder the venerable Provost of Inverness. According to Karen Wood (*The Folklore of South Loch Ness-Side*) their plans were overheard by a servant who tried to escape to Bona to raise the alarm; the plotters took a secret passage and ambushed the girl, dumping her body. Their two sons then killed Provost Junor when he was making his usual evening stroll near the Essich Road. Lady Borlum was Bessy Innes, aka 'The Witch of Borlum', not a woman to cross. Borlum Castle was burnt by Government troops following Brigadier William MacKintosh's support for the Jacobite rebellion of 1715. After Culloden, the Fraser clan chief hid in a hollow tree in the back garden of the ruins before moving on to Fort Augustus. Karen Wood's grandfather, Hugh Fraser, owned the later Borlum House, and Wood relates that in 1937 Fraser's uncle found an upright grave in one of the fields nearby. A plough had struck the slab and exposed a skeleton in standing position. Wood claims that, 'Many similar graves have been found in the fields since', although I can find no record of these or the original find. The house was also apparently haunted by a Green Lady.

8

THE SOUTH SHORE OF LOCH NESS II: THE UPLAND ROUTE

These stones,
Memorials of the dead, with rustic art
And rude inscription cut, declare the soul
Immortal.

Michael Cruce (1746-1767) 'The Last Day'

This chapter starts from the burial ground at the junction of the B862 from Fort Augustus/Whitebridge and the B852 down to Foyers, and proceeds northeast through the 'Inverness Lake District', a lovely upland area of numerous lochs and few people, perfect for walking, cycling and exploring. The area includes much of Stratherrick and Strathnairn. According to Andrew Cumming's article 'Some Tales of Strathnairn' (*TGSI*), Stratherrick was notorious for witchcraft. A wizard lived there within living memory (Cumming was writing in the 1970s). This warlock never laughed except when planning evil; when he died, the strath was in an uproar. Cumming himself met a hag who had praised another woman's young son, thereby causing him to have a fit (a use of the Evil Eye). 'Another woman, who is not even Highland and was certainly far too modern to believe in witchcraft, had one or two alarming experiences with the "witch" which were quite extraordinary.' No further details are given.

Carmina Gadelica, Alexander Carmichael's *magnum opus* of Scottish folklore, tells the story of a 'seoltaiche,' a cunning man, who went about lifting the 'toradh,' substance from the nine best glens in Scotland. Stratherrick was the last glen to which he came. He lifted the substance of Stratherrick on his back, and was moving away, when a man more shrewd than his fellows cut the wizard's withy with his knife, and the luck of the whole nine glens fell to the ground. And that is how Stratherrick came to be the allegedly most fertile glen in Scotland. A similar story is told of the WESTERN PART OF INVERNESS.

B852/B862 JUNCTION

There is a small resting cairn, Carn Bhean Ardachy, the Cairn of Ardachy's Wife, along the B862 in the direction of Gorthleck, on the north side of the road. Here coffin parties would rest, take refreshment and change bearers, *en route* to Druim an Teampull or Boleskine.

Cnoc an t-Sidhein,
the Fairies' Hill,
Garthbeg.

LOCH MHOR

Loch Mhor (the Big Loch) was created from the artificial raising of the water levels of lochs Garth and Farraline when the aluminium factory at Foyers was built in the late nineteenth century. The southern arm (NH52091762) contains a stony crannog 40ft (12m) across which is usually submerged – it came to light when the water level was temporarily lowered during renovation of the dams in 1973. There's a good colour picture in Alan Lawson's *A Country Called Stratherrick*. 'Its particulars were taken before it sank, once again, beneath the ripples. One cannot help being reminded of J.M. Barrie and Mary Rose's island.' (Richard Frere, *Loch Ness*).

The church at Druim an Teampuill (NH508183) is relatively undistinguished architecturally but it does have a glorious (if windswept) location. The minor road opposite runs east to Garthbeg (NH518169). Revd Thomas Sinton in 'A Day at Boleskine and Foyers' (*TGSI*) writes that the best cow bolted from the milking here and headed for the hills. The tacksman followed and saw a fairy sweetly singing as it milked the cow on Sithean Ruigh Stob, which I think is Cnoc an t-Sidhein, the Fairies' Hill, a strikingly obvious hill 1.25 miles (2km) southeast at NH531154. The river entering the loch at Garthbeg is the River E, Scotland's thriftiest name.

Immediately after Culloden, the fleeing BPC stopped at Gorthleck House (NH545210, private) where Lord Lovat was in residence, a victory feast being in preparation – although due to the recent change in circumstances the reception was frosty and the Prince did not stay long. 'A little girl of five told Mrs Grant of Laggan that to be out of the way she was sent up to a little room where she looked out upon a marsh in the plain below which was supposed to be the haunt of fairies... a party of horsemen [had] entered the field below the house. She thought for a moment that she was looking at a band of fairies...' (Revd Dr John

Gargoyle sign,
Loch Mhor.

MacPherson, 'Daviot and Dunlichity', *TGSI*). This is the only example I know of where Bonnie Prince Charlie was mistaken for a fairy.

In a wood half a mile northeast is Tom a'Mhoid, the justice mound (NH531205). A minor road crosses the reedy channel between the two lochs to Aberchalder. Revd Sinton relates an incident from here. A popular dance at balls was the 'round dance', where a person lay motionless in the centre of a circle of dancers before leaping up to choose a partner, when another would take his place. Ruari Og did not rise from the floor as other young people danced around him. After chiding him for some time, they found he was dead. A case of second sight came from the quarry at Errogie. A seer from Strathnairn told a workmate to stop swearing as he had 'seen' the man's blood on the rocks. Later a rock fall seriously injured the blasphemer and the rocks were stained red with his blood.

B862 TORNESS TO DORES

Tales from the Aldourie Estate says one of the men of Sutherland became overtaken by mist on his way to communion and encountered Lucifer on a coach driven by four horses driving up Loch Ceo Glais★ or Ce-glas, (pronounced 'Keglish', NH590285). According to the same source, 'the Loch is haunted by various hob-goblins.' Revd Sinton adds that, 'The scene around is peculiarly eerie as seen even on a summer's day.' To the east of the loch is Dunchea Hill, on which sits a low pointed mound, Tom na Croich, the gallows hill (NH591280). Here the Lovat Frasers administered capital judgement under their Regality, the corpse hanging until it disintegrated, 'to the terror of others to commit the lyke abuses in tyme coming.'

Lacking a police force or a nationwide system of centrally-controlled courts, kings of necessity had to delegate justice to the powerful barons. There were three kinds of court – Sheriff Courts (for example, the one that covered all of Inverness-shire), Courts of Regality and Courts of Barony. Courts of Regality had jurisdiction almost as great as the Crown, including the power of 'fossa et furca', pit and gallows (imprisonment and execution). Most of Stratherrick was the Regality of Lovat, which meant the Lovat Frasers exercised legal powers of life and death over the people within their territory. Barony Courts had lesser powers, mostly dealing with minor civil and criminal cases and issues between landlords and tenants. On the west side of the loch, beneath the electricity lines, are two old women, once gleeful spectators of the hangings, now turned to stone for their lack of humanity.

Sinton relates another tale of supernatural punishment. Three travellers were fording a burn during a violent thunderstorm. The man in the middle asked the other two if they were afraid; they were indeed. In blasphemous terms he swore he thought nothing of it. A bolt of lightning struck him dead on the spot. The location is Drochaid na Feithe-glaise, about two-thirds of a mile (1km) north of Loch Ce-glas; the burn is now crossed by a bridge, so modern travellers have nothing to fear.

There was a stopping place for coffins at Achnabat (NH599302), where rest and refreshment would be offered to the weary men carrying their burden to the churchyard. Kenneth MacRae in *Highland Ways and Byways* writes that, 'In rough ground between the B862 before its junction with the Essich road and Loch Duntelchaig is Lag na Cailliche, Witch's Hollow, with a haunted spring Fuaran na Fuathasaich, Spectre Well.' This would be around NH6031 but I could find nothing. MacRae also identifies a standing stone on a slight promontory over-looking Loch Duntelchaig with Loch nan Geadas in the foreground: again, I'm unable to find this. There is a low cairn and kerb at NH59823110 in the woods west of the road. By the road junction is Caisteal an Dunriachaidh★ (NH601316), a very prominent Iron Age hill fort, 'a grim-looking place that doesn't encourage any day-trips to 700 BC.' (Richard Gordon, *Round Inverness, The Black Isle and Nairn.*) There was once a well by a dip in the road between Kindrummond and Balnafoich (approx. NH596337) where the body of a mother and son were found following the great storm and flood of 1826. Two local farmers lost 1,100 and 1,300 sheep respectively that night (source: Kenneth MacRae).

LOCH ASHIE★

The landscape around this loch is always lonely and frequently bleak – the perfect setting for the area's best-known story, that of the phantom battle. Or, actually, battles, for there appear to have been at least two spectral conflicts recorded. Newspaper accounts in 1870-71 described a battle seen shortly after dawn on a May morning. Vivid details were given – 'large bodies of men in close forma-tion and smaller bodies of cavalry facing an attacking army marching from the east; wounded men clapping sphagnum moss to their wounds and binding it on with strips torn from their shirts.' (MacRae). The phenomenon was 'explained', or explained away, as a long-distance 'mirage reflection' of a contemporary battle in the Franco-Prussian War.

The same (or another?) battle was also seen both during the First World War, and again sometime between the 1950s and 1973 by a group of picnicking Americans staying at the Drumossie Hotel, who took it to be a local pageant. Cumming, in 'Some Tales of Strathnairn' (*TGSI*), writing in the 1970s, said he knew two men, one now dead, who saw the ghostly battle, and another woman who lived at Insh by the lochside told him she had seen it often. Cumming named two of the witnesses as Thomas MacKintosh, tenant at Midtown, Duntelchaig, and William MacQueen of Balloon, Farr, and added the detail that the battle is normally seen in frosty weather. Although the descriptions of the battle are sketchy, they appear to be of the eighteenth or nineteenth century. This contrasts with other reports of a second conflict, possibly early or late medieval, such as that mentioned in the *Inverness Courier*, 7 July 1998. In the 1940s a mist-bound shepherd heard and saw a small-scale battle involving wild-looking, bearded, long-haired men in ragged clothes, armed with wooden clubs and short-bladed swords. The shepherd hid behind a rock, but realised the warriors were not aware of him. After about ten minutes of combat, the mist lifted and the scene disappeared. On a sunny summer evening in the mid-1980s, a local man fishing on Loch Ashie heard shouts and the clash of arms, which rose to a crescendo and then slowly faded out.

There is no historical record of a battle taking place on or near Ashie Moor, but there is a long – and entirely legendary – tradition of a set-to here between Fingal's army and a group of Vikings led by A'ishidh (or Athasaidh or Ashie), who was killed and supposedly gave his name to the loch. As part of the process of the 'landscapisation of legend', the story has also imprinted itself on the place names of the area in other ways. There was a chair-like outcrop of rock called Cathair Fhionn, Fingal's throne or seat, from which the hero watched the progress of the battle: this was at NH615336, to the south of the crossroads, but it is now just a pile of stones – one of several in the area that, in the nineteenth century, were regarded as burial cairns for the dead of the battle, but are now seen as just stone clearance heaps. South of the crossroads at NH621343, by the side of the road to Dunlichity, was the Clach-na-Brataich (Banner Stone), a flat stone with a central hole, supposedly the support for Fingal's banner. This appears to have gone missing in recent years.

Further southwest along the road is a truly spectacular monument. Climb over the gate opposite a track and walk south through a firebreak in the forestry for about 400m to reach Buaile Chòmhnard* (NH621332), a massive boulder-built circle fully 80ft (25m) across with low walls up to 11ft (3.5m) thick. The name comes in different forms, either Bual Aonarach (solitary fold), Bual-a-choranaich (fold of the funeral dirge) or Bual Chòmhnard/Chomhraig (fold of battle or strife), the latter having been favoured (and made it onto the maps) because of the association with the Fingalian battle. The assumption has been that this was

Buaile Chòmhnard, once thought to be a fort, now seen as a stock enclosure.

a fort for the home team; unfortunately for all this romantic speculation, Buaile Chòmhnard is actually a stock enclosure, used by drovers who were driving cattle on the nearby drove road. It's still a great site, though.

There have been other ghostly encounters in the vicinity, possibly connected, or possibly not. Edward Meldrum in *From Nairn to Loch Ness* says the house at Drumashie (NH634374) is reputed to be haunted, but I have no further details. A cyclist on his way to Inverness saw several horsemen in front of him on the road. Turning a corner, he ran into the group – and cycled right through them, falling off his bike in horror. C.J. Shaw of Tordarroch writes in his *History of Clan Shaw*:

> At the crossroads the road to the right goes to Inverness across Drumashie… Hereabouts the writer and his wife had the experience, in broad daylight, of slowing down at a corner where he had seen an approaching car which had signalled with his lights that he was pulling into the passing place, only to find the road empty! On telling this to a party of visitors with the [Inverness] Field Club, a local member said that recently a forest worker sitting down to his lunch looked up to see a woman and child approaching who simply disappeared.

Somewhere near these same crossroads used to be the now lost Tobar na Feosaig, The Well of the Beard, aka Fuaran na Fuathasaich, The Well of the Spectre. The origin of the first name is allegedly the deliriously bonkers idea that, as there was no dish, men dipped their beards into the water. More prosaically, a bearded packman was said to have been robbed and killed here, and so haunted the site. The well may have been near the Merchants Stone (packman = merchant), a boulder on the roadside at NH613333.

ESSICH TO DUNLICHITY

Carn Glas Chambered Cairn★ (NH649383), west of the road, is the largest Neolithic mound in the area, an unusual Orkney-Cromarty cairn 125 yards (115m) long with three separate burial chambers, possibly reflecting three different periods of construction. Most of the cairn material is lost but it is still an impressive structure.

A note in the *Northern Chronicle* of September 1910 by 'M.C.' (probably the Revd Dr Campbell) describes an episode related by Hugh Noble of Bunachton. In the 1760s, a man called Am Bard Dòmhnullach, who had the *casg fola* (see INVERNESS), was asked to staunch the flow of blood from a dog, but would not exercise his gift on a lower animal. In the moorland district of Bunachton there was a chapel, and close by is Fuaran an t-Sagairt, the Priest's Well. Andrew Cumming in 'Some Tales of Strathnairn' (*TGSI*) mentions Clach a' Bhrùinidh, the Brownie's Stone, east of Bunachton, and Clach an Duine Marbh, the Stone of the Dead Man, marking the grave of a fugitive from Culloden, behind Crask on the Loch Bunachton side of Blar-buidhe, but I can locate neither. There is a curious set of remnants in the area of Mains of Bunachton farm. There was an old chapel somewhere here and there is still (although difficult to find) Tobar an t-Sagairt, the Priest's Well, by an old stone wall at NH65773436. Other local place names include the Priest's Chair and the Field of the Chapel. Cumming says that crops showed the marks of the old graves and that a new tenant at Bunachton unknowingly ploughed the old churchyard and sowed the ground with oats. When he learned of the site's history he refused to harvest the crop. An archaeological excavation at NH65783439, southeast of Midtown, found a rectangular building with slightly rounded ends. It is not clear if this was the chapel. In the words of the description on the RCAHMS Canmore website:

> There is a stone lined entrance 0.6m wide in the middle of the southeast side; a single stone blocks the inner end of the entrance passage. Inside the building in the southwest half is a setting of stones embedded in the ground, not unlike a cist but probably bogus. The peculiar entrance and the cist like setting of stones seem out of place in this site.

Several locations have been claimed for the former Font Stone; a stone with a hollow at Clachindruin (NH65153432) may be the supposed item, although it is more likely to be a mortar for pounding corn. There are three hut-circles southwest of Clachandruim (NH645340); a small standing stone sits between the two most northerly.

Dunlichity graveyard with Clach na Faire, the Watching Stone, on the hill above.

Dunlichity graveyard, detail.

Dunlichity graveyard, with marks where swords were sharpened.

DUNLICHITY★★

The church and burial ground here (NH659331) are two of the most interesting in the area, with numerous mossy carved stones and a striking setting in which the rocks from the hillside protrude through the sloping graveyard. Marks from the sharpening of arrows can be seen on the corner stones of the walls of the burial enclosure of the Shaws of Tordarroch and the MacPhails of Inverernie, near the southeast corner of the church. Revd Dr John MacPherson in 'Daviot and Dunlichity' (*TGSI*) describes a tradition that the Presbyterian minister once admonished a group engaged in archery practice on Sunday morning and per-suaded them to go to church. No one was to leave until the service was over. After a while, one impatient fellow got up to leave. The minister took another bow, went outside and shot the ruffian in the thigh, then tied up the wound, returned to the church, and continued the service. The practice of weapon sports on Sunday thereafter came to an end. A story attached to the anti-resurrectionist watch house has one of the drunken watchers firing at imaginary grave robbers and leaving bullet holes in a tombstone. When improvements were being carried out in the churchyard, James Gow (see BOLESKINE GRAVEYARD) saw an entire arm bone from shoulder to wrist without a joint, taken out of the earth below the pulpit. It had belonged to Martuin Bàn Obar-Challadair, who was known to have no elbow joint (source: Sinton, 'A Day at Boleskine and Foyers', *TGSI*).

The MacGillivray enclosure contains several heraldic carvings and the stone of Alexander MacGillivray, tacksman of Dalcrombie (*d*. 1797, aged thirty-eight) and son Donald (*d*. 1797, aged twenty-five) – which apparently shows Alexander was thirteen years old when he fathered his son. However, the very detailed *A History of The Clan MacGillivray* by Robert MacGillivray and George B. MacGillivray states that Alexander was fifty-eight when he died, not thirty-eight – a stonemason's error which has been frequently repeated in many books and articles. The same clan history describes an event from the terrible famine of 1784: so many people had died, there was no one to bury the corpses, and a man had to carry his dead brother in a cloth on his back three miles (5km) to Dunlichity, in the hope that someone would inter the body in the graveyard.

The present church, built in 1758, is probably the third on the site – there was definitely a late medieval building here, and possibly before that an early Christian structure dedicated to the sixth-century saint, Finan. In 1643, the good folk of the Reformation seized a wooden effigy of the saint from a private house nearby and burned it at the Mercat Cross in Inverness. Burials took place inside the church building until the comparatively late date of 1800, and the floor was bare earth, so one minister could preach in anger to his congregation, 'There you are sitting and standing on the graves of your ancestors, the dogs gnawing at their bones, while their souls are rotting in eternal hell!'

A story is told that the hand bell in the vestry, inscribed 'Robert Mcconachie 1702', was used to call folk to holy service at another church on the south side of Creagan an Tuirc at Brinmore (NH665290); when plans were made to relocate the church to Dunlichity the bell was taken there but it kept reappearing at Brinmore, leading to suspicions of supernatural powers at work. The new laird wanted the church near his home at Dunlichity. He took the Brinmore bell to the new church but each time he moved it to the east, it returned to Brinmore, tolling the words Glag Fhinnan, Finnan's Bell; the laird had it secured but it broke the chain. At last, he left it at Brin and it disappeared, taking with it the fertility and health of the strath.

Another tale is that the new church was intended to be built at Cnoc Buidhe, a kilometre south, but every morning the masons' tools were found at Dunlichity, so the hint was eventually taken. The 'bell returning to its original church' and 'the fairies strongly suggest you build the church *here*' stories are widespread motifs in the folklore of Scotland and beyond.

The graveyard has a stone erected to Revd Archibald Cook, who, at the time of the 1843 Disruption, became the first Free Church minister here. The Revd was something of a seer, and Andrew Cumming records several of his predictions: although the 950-seat church was always full, the day would come when the grass would grow on the path up to it and in the cracks of the doorstep (this has come true to an extent); the day would come when there would not be a gate on the Duntelchaig road (all the gates are now replaced by cattle grids); and the day would come when Strathnairn would be nothing but trees and water and the Gospel would not be read or sung from one end to the other.

Cumming also relates several supernatural tales. A man who was born one midnight with a caul described to Cumming a huge black dog he had seen passing the churchyard. His sister was by his side and did not see it – but when he put his hand on her the dog 'exploded at the gate and disappeared.' Another man told Cumming he frequently saw the ghost dog going up the road to Blarbuie. A member of a family between Gask and Bunachton would lie on a certain flat stone in the churchyard to call up spirits for divination. On the last occasion 6,000 spirits passed in front of him, the last being his grandmother who told him he would be burned by his enemies. Within a year he was on a cattle raid when he was forced to take refuge in a hole, and the opposing clansmen heaped heather and bracken at the entrance and burnt him to death.

Clearly visible on the summit of Creag a Chlachain behind the church (NH653334) is Clach na Faire, the Watching Stone, a large upright stone used as a meeting place and beacon hill. MacRae (*Highland Ways and Byways*) claims the hill also has 'a hoof print of a horse on bare rock', but I couldn't find this. Equally elusive (to me, at least), is what has been called the old font, a stone with a large hollow, supposedly by the roadside 300 yards or metres south of the church. Sick children were cured by washing or sprinkling with the water from the hollow, which had to be rain or dew, and collected at dawn.

In 'Daviot and Dunlichity' (*TGSI*) Revd Dr John MacPherson describes the Clach Cailleach nam muc, the Stone of the Pig-Woman or Pig-Witch, a huge oblong stone near Blar Buidhe. The woman appears to have been a genuine historical personage, travelling with her pigs around Glenurquhart, the Aird, and Glenmoriston in the late nineteenth century. The large hollow at the bottom of the stone was where she and the pigs lived when visiting Strathnairn. The story handed down was that she was from Lewis, the daughter of a supposed witch: when her suitor found this out and left her she departed the Hebrides, but not before one of the sailors cut a cross in her forehead so the ship could leave Stornoway harbour safely. On the mainland she somehow acquired a sow and for rest of her life wandered with its offspring, allegedly suckling the piglets.

Ailean Mor Cheann Drochaid of Torgoill, Glenmoriston, who died in the 1910s, remembered the woman and said in the end the pigs killed and ate her, which might be a story too far. Blar Buidhe is at NH675344 – I have been unable to locate the stone.

LOCH DUNTELCHAIG★

The headline in the *Highland News* on 6 July 2006 was 'Tourists return "cursed" stone to Highlands'. A couple from the Isle of Wight posted a stone to the Inverness tourist information centre with a note: 'Rock found near Loch Duntelchaig last year. Wife feels stressed when it is in the house. Maybe from the stone, so we have sent it back.' VisitScotland customer advisor Bob Hunter-Dorans was quoted as saying the tourist had added that:

while he had picked it up from the water's edge, he reckoned it had rolled down from the site of an Iron Age or Pictish fort which once stood above the loch. It is possible he has done research on the area and thought the stone was cursed, so he decided to return it before it brought him and his wife any bad luck.

Bob was pictured returning the cursed rock to the lochside. For the return of more 'cursed' rocks, see CLAVA.

Two brothers and another man were out hunting by the loch. One of the brothers was inseparable from his dog, Frangach. The second brother, along with the other man, became separated from Frangach and his owner. In the mist they saw a figure sitting on a stone, who appeared to be the missing brother. Alarm bells went off when the dog was nowhere to be seen, and the figure abruptly disappeared. Later the two found the brother with a broken leg at Leitir chuillin, some distance away.

On a hot day at Duntelchaig a working man said he would like some buttermilk. A little old woman appeared to offer him some – he drank the milk and died within a year, while a friend who refused lived. Both these tales are related by Cumming, although exactly the same story about not consuming fairy food is told of DUNDREGGAN on the other side of Loch Ness.

West Town Ring-Cairn at NH62173258 on the northwest side of the loch is a Clava-type cairn, very badly damaged and beset with clearance stones, although the central chamber and parts of the inner kerb are still visible. Excavation revealed traces of an Iron Age smelting hearth in the cairn, which may indicate disrespect for the sacred site of an earlier culture.

STRATHNAIRN

Cumming relates a nineteenth-century event somewhere in the strath – a lad called Donald would hide in a bush and shake it and make unearthly sounds at passers-by. Duncan, 'a young swack fellow', was so frightened he kicked the bush with heavy boots and broke three of Donald's ribs.

DUNMAGLASS

The Dunmaglass Estate is the site of one of the more extraordinary stories of fairies in Scotland, and perhaps throws light on a period when belief in fairies was still widespread but was starting to wane in some quarters. The tale is repeated in various publications but for the version here I am indebted to *A History of The Clan MacGillivray*, which goes back to the early sources (the papers of Simon F. MacKintosh of Farr, 1835, and George Bain, *Stories and Sketches of Nairn*) for the details. There is also an account in the *Celtic Monthly* of 1898 by Charles Fraser-MacKintosh. In the early eighteenth-century, William MacGillivray, son of Farquhar MacGillivray of Dunmaglass, was clan captain. Captain Ban, the white or fair captain, was a handsome, much-admired man. One day Amelie, the attractive wife of MacKintosh of Daviot, disappeared. After weeks of searching,

MacKintosh was induced to ask his neighbour William for advice. William said he would ask around, and eventually through his informants he discovered that the fairies had taken Amelie to Tomnashangan (the Doune at Daviot, which I am unable to accurately locate, although it may be the Iron Age hill fort of Dun Davie, NH719392).

Attempting to enter a fairy stronghold was no easy task so Captain Ban sent a messenger to John Dubh MacQueen, laird of Pollochaik, who was reputed to have dealings with the Good Folk. MacQueen sold the messenger a magic candle and gave a warning not to look behind him on the return journey no matter what he heard. At dusk at Craiganuin near Moy Hall, the rider heard a carriage and horses following him, weird music, and voices saying 'Catch him, catch him'. He looked over his shoulder, and although he saw nothing he fell from his horse and lost the candle. The next messenger William sent was made of sterner stuff. He ignored the voices at Craiganuin but at Farr the noises were so loud he glanced back, and the candle was again lost. Finally, William sent Archibald MacGillivray, Gillespic Luath (Swift or Fast Archibald). MacQueen told him he would rather the captain had asked him for his fold of cattle than the candle. Archibald passed the first two obstacles but found the river magically engorged, so he went back to MacQueen who instructed him to return to the riverbank, dismount, and throw a stone across the river. Archibald did this and at once he found himself seated on his horse and on the opposite bank. Noises continued to follow him but he succeeded in delivering the candle to Dunmaglass in the early hours of the morning. On the next moonlit night William went to Tomnashangan, where he saw the outline of a door. As he walked in the candle burst into light, revealing Amelie enjoying a dance with the fairies. William escaped with the woman and returned her to MacKintosh of Daviot. She told her husband she thought she had been dancing for a couple of hours, not several months, and had no memory of how she got there. The candle was kept by the family 'in order to keep off all fairies, witches, brownies, and water kelpies in all time to come', but was stolen around 1805.

The fairies were peeved at the captain's actions and told him they would 'keep him in view.' Shortly afterwards, William was badly beaten by persons unknown as he rode home one evening by the west end of Loch Duntelchaig. He made it home but never recovered. The whole fairy story is elaborately conceived and filled with detail, but presumably Amelie's husband and his family saw it for the ruse that it was and took their revenge on the amorous captain.

Dunmaglass Lodge (NH592223, private), built in the 1860s in the classic crow-stepped grand style, has several gargoyles on its main tower. Andrew Cumming mentions Carn nan diolan, Cairn of the Bastards, where women with illegitimate children were forced to publicly add a stone as a penance. On Carn na croiche, the Cairn of the Hanging, (NH615257), many people met their end courtesy of William MacKintosh of Aberarder, the notorious 'black baillie'.

ABERARDER

The Laird of Aberarder sent Calum Luath, Swift Malcolm, to Edinburgh with important papers. Calum ran there and back in two days, immediately falling asleep on his return to Aberarder. The laird thought he had just not left at all, and stabbed the messenger to death. Exactly the same story is told about Ashintully Castle in Perthshire. Calum was buried in one of the Carnban (white cairn) fields near the wood by the roadside. The original house of Aberarder was supposed to have been prevented from being built for seven years by a wizard called an duine salach, the dirty or nasty man. Cumming relates a ghost story about this building (which is a kind of annexe to the present Aberarder House). About 1700 a tailor was staying here making up clothes. A herd boy threatened to shoot the tailor in fun, not knowing the gun was loaded. The tailor was killed. Thereafter the thump of his fall and the jingle and rolling sound of his thimble was often heard. Around 1968 the wife of the estate's gardener worked in the big modern house. She told Cumming that in the old part of the house she had heard a thump and jingle. She was from the West Coast and neither she nor Cumming knew the tailor's story at this time.

CROACHY

Andrew Cumming mentions Caochan an dubh chaileag, the streamlet of the dark girl, which flows into the River Nairn west of the church at Croachy (NH648277). An unfortunate young woman drowned an unwanted child here and was subsequently haunted by the infant's ghost. The garden of the wonderful Old Parsonage B&B contains two upright stones; they were erected by the establishment's owners, Isabell and Graeme Steel, as an in-joke relating to the stone 'portal' through which Claire Randall, the central character of Diane Gabaldon's *Outlander* series, travels back to the eighteenth century.

North of the village is the Steadings Hotel, also known by its long-established name of the Grouse and Trout. In 2005 a previous owner embarked on what could be seen as an ill-advised publicity stunt when he arranged for a bed that had purportedly belonged to Aleister Crowley to be exorcised. The tabloids duly responded, with articles such as 'Satan Sheets – Hotelier exorcises devil-worshipper Crowley's old bed' and 'The Evil Bed – *Record* girl's creepy night in Crowley's kip' (*Daily Record*, 11 and 24 January 2005 respectively). The then owner, Andy Pavitt, was quoted as saying:

The room with Crowley's bed always has a very strong musty smell. We had it checked for damp and there isn't any. A couple of times we have had people saying they woke up because they felt moving or shaking…Visitors have told us all sorts of stories about that bed. Some feel it shake or rise off the ground while others have heard tapping or rattling. Guests have left after one night in the bed – before we even saw them in the morning.

The room was also cold even with the fire on. There is no evidence at all that the bed was ever Crowley's – the only link is that it and other furniture were inherited from the previous owners, who also owned Boleskine House after Jimmy Page's incumbency – and in retrospect the entire episode seems rather embarrassing.

LOCH RUTHVEN*

Cumming relates some of the folklore of this area. Three boys playing by the loch met a beautiful horse. Stroking it, they found their hands stuck to his coat. The horse plunged into the waters, intent on drowning and devouring them – one boy saved himself by cutting off his own fingers. This is a classic each-uisge or water-horse story. The last wolf in the area was killed by a wife of the MacGillivrays around the year 1700. She went to Dunchia, near Torness, to borrow a griddle for baking bannocks. The woman met the wolf on her return route above Loch Ruthven and killed it with one blow of the griddle. This is one of many 'last wolf' stories told around Scotland, with the final beast supposedly having been despatched any time between 1644 and 1756, or even later.

Tom Bhuidhe*, an enigmatic mound on the south side of the loch (NH60442740), was probably an island dwelling – the ditch on its south side may have been a moat before the level of the loch was lowered in the nineteenth century. There is a crannog just to the northeast.

FLICHITY

Another tale given by Andrew Cumming is that of the farmer at Flichity Home Farm, who wanted the land of an old woman at Druim a' chala. He conspired with the laird of Flichity to have her accused of witchcraft and burnt at Clach cailleach, the Witch's Stone. At the stake she cursed the estate and farm of Flichity – as long as the Flichity Burn flowed north the laird would prosper, but the farmer would not, or the farmer would and the laird would not. Cumming says the curse was fulfilled. One subsequent laird altered the direction of the stream but a storm put it back on its old course. The story has become confused with that of the witch Creibh (see INVERNESS).

Brin Cave below Brin Rock (NH664293) is supposedly bottomless, stretching back to Loch Duntelchaig.

Leonella Longmore (*Inverness in the 18th Century*) relates the story of a funeral wake in a house near Milltown of Brin, in 1798. The corpse was laid out on boards, the ends of which hung out the open window. In tune with the custom of the time, a fiddler set up and soon the entire company were jigging and reeling. Then the corpse started to bounce up and down, as if joining in the dancing. Only when the panic-stricken group had fled outside was the cause discovered – a pig scratching itself against the protruding ends of the boards.

The entrance to the Artists Cottage, Farr.

FARR

At the south end of the village is the Artists Cottage*, an Art-Nouveau structure built to a design by Charles Rennie Macintosh, with striking outbuildings and sculptures nearer the road; a curious and delightful sight, bearing no relationship to any of the other architecture in the area.

As with elsewhere in the strath, I have drawn heavily on Andrew Cumming's 'Some Tales of Strathnairn' (*TGSI*) for the folklore of the area around Farr. Carn na Freiceadan (NH655316) and Creag na Gobhar (NH696325), two hills on each side of the strath, were each home to one of the royal sons of a witch called Bean Gheur, the Sharp Wife or Woman, who may have lived on Beinn nan Cailleach to the east (NH725325). The king of Gobhar was An righ bàn, the White King, an archer with a bow and arrows of gold. On Freiceadan lived An righ dubh, the Black King, black as soot, a great fighter, although he possessed no weapons. He could become invisible but a red spot remained over his heart. Both men loved Gnùis Aillidh, Bonny Face, who was a kind of nature goddess, blessing animals and crops, but she only loved the White King. One gloaming the goddess was at the foot of Freiceadan. The Black King used his invisibility to abduct her and take her to his dungeon. The White King could not rescue her as, like his brother, he could not leave the limits of his hill and he had already fired his daily arrow – he would not get another until dawn. All night the enemy danced and sang on his hill, wakening the wind which moaned around the strath. At dawn the White King fixed his newly-forged arrow in his bow and took aim. The Black King made himself vanish but the arrow hit the visible red spot. Gnùis Aillidh was freed, and the area was transformed with light and happiness. After lying dead all day, the Black King was revived by a magical ointment applied by his mother, and promptly commenced plotting again. This allegory of the conflict between day and night is told in many other places.

A spot on the minor road between Farr and Glen Mazeran to the east, the Carn a' Heesbach or Carn a' theasaich, was said to be haunted – horses were reluctant to pass it and had to be dragged. Seònaid Mor in Farr had the Evil Eye, and caused cows to lose milk and children to become sick; the Cnoc an òir, the hillock of gold, is somewhere on the farm of Ballone. A local man stole Cromwell's pay chest or part of it, but was wounded getting away: he died before telling his family exactly where he had buried the chest. A similar tale is told about Cnoc an airgiod, the silver or money hillock, near Invernie Lodge. Every New Year's Day there was a shinty match between the lads of Farr and those of the church of Dalarossie in Strathdearn. One year the first day fell on a Sunday. The Dalarossie team refused to desecrate the day, so the Farr boys played a game between themselves. They all died of disease before the next New Year. When New Year's Day (Old Style, 12 January) falls on a Sunday, the ghostly shinty players return to play their game.

Croftcroy Chambered Tomb (NH683331) is a very badly damaged Clava cairn incorporated into the back garden of a house. A much better site is Tordarroch Ring-Cairn★ (NH68013349), 200m north of the road, with stones up to 5ft (1.5m) high and a large fallen kerb stone with about thirty cupmarks. Nearby and next to the road is the recently restored and impressive Tordarroch House. Kenneth MacRae in *Highland Ways and Byways* (1953) says that in an overgrown pond nearby, 'relics of by-gone clan feuds were found long ago', along with a Wellington boot with a leg in it. It caused quite a stir locally and was sent to Inverness for investigation, but nothing more was heard. In 1530 the barn here was the site of a clan-warfare mass hanging of MacKintoshes by the Earl of Moray's men.

B851 TOMBRECK TO THE A9

The Clava Ring-Cairn of Midlairgs (NH714368) has just a few stones left and is close to a sand and gravel extraction pit. A church near here was lost to the quarry. If you have the time and energy you could trek out to Uaigh An Duine Bheò, The Grave of the Living Man (NH727347). In the sixteenth century there was a border dispute between the MacKintoshes and Farquhar MacGillivray of Dunmaglas. The oldest man of the two clans, Eoin MacGillivray of Achadhlodan, was asked to arbitrate. Eoin stood on the disputed spot and said, 'I swear that by the head under my bonnet [a fearful oath then] and the ground under my feet that this is MacGillivray land.' Something about the form of words aroused suspicion and one of the MacKintoshes removed Eoin's bonnet, revealing the head of a cock; in his shoes was earth from MacGillivray land. Eoin was buried alive on the spot. Nearby are Allt and Coire Eoin Rànaich, the burn and corrie of Eoin's wailing – his ghost could be heard at night, possibly complaining about being a fall guy for Farquhar MacGillivray, who clearly put him up to it. The tiny cairn on this spot is swamped by forestry and within a few hundred metres of the noisy A9; it is reached by following two miles (3km) of forest tracks from the B851.

DAVIOT

Daviot church (NH723394) is a landmark for motorists on the A9 because of its distinctive spire and golden cockerel weather vane. *Nessie's Loch Ness Times* (16 March 2002) reported the sighting of a strange light in the sky above the village. Malcolm MacKintosh, a retired businessman, saw it at 6.20 a.m. from his patio:

> I couldn't make out the shape of the craft – all I could see was lights. There were a number of reddish lights, and a very bright pure white light, and in the centre there were some dancing lights. It was in sight for about two minutes, before it moved off and there was a trail of fire coming from the back of it. It wasn't travelling that fast, I'd say its speed was more in keeping with a fighter aircraft. It was a very clear morning and I am in absolutely no doubt as to what I saw.

At the same time, an unnamed policeman in Keith, Aberdeenshire, more than sixty miles (96km) away, saw a cluster of amber lights to the west of the town, heading south. The policeman got out of his car to study the lights, several of which were circling a larger central light. Neither man reported any sound. Local RAF bases said that they had no aircraft flying in the vicinity of the sightings at the time, but the report still sounds like the misidentification of an aircraft.

One evening, following the Battle of Culloden, there was a knock on the door of a croft owned by an elderly widow at Easter Craggie (now on the east side of the A9). It was an English soldier, looking for food. The woman asked him where he had obtained the plaid he was holding. The soldier replied he had taken it from a sturdy Highlander he had killed with difficulty at the battle. The widow invited him to sit by the fire while she went to milk the cow. Once outside she went into the barn, found a sickle, climbed onto the low wall of the house above the door, and called out to the soldier to help her. As he bent down coming through the doorway she cut off his head with one blow. She had recognised the plaid as belonging to her only son. The cottage is now a ruin, but has been claimed to be haunted, with strange noises heard at night. (Source: Revd MacPherson, 'Daviot and Dunlichity', *TGSI*.)

B861 TOMBRECK TO INVERNESS

With a 90ft (27m) diameter, the Mains of Gask Ring-Cairn★★ (NH679358) is the largest of the Clava group, and one of the surviving monoliths is an incredible stone, 11ft (3.4m) high by 10ft (3m) wide, but only 8in (20cm) deep. There are cupmarks on a prostrate stone on the north. The site is easily visible and accessible from the road. Further north in forestry is the Clach an Airm★, the stone of weapons (NH68103663), where the Clan MacGillivray gathered before Culloden and sharpened their weapons on this 1.5m high standing stone. Tomfat Plantation Chambered Cairn★ (NH67803742) is badly damaged but it does have a large

2.1m slab at the end of a chamber. Approach from the car park further north at NH677378 then go right and right again through the forestry. There is a large standing stone at NH68323795.

The road travels north over the moorland of the Black Wood of Leys. Here the Cailleach of Leys would take a traveller's bonnet and rub it hard; as it became worn, so the traveller became tired or fell into a bog, and so died. In *Scottish Healing Wells*, Ruth and Frank Morris describe the versatile well which used to exist near Leys Castle (NH680410, private) before being ploughed over. It had relocated itself from Lochaber after the *genius loci* had been insulted there, and could cure several diseases, especially diarrhoea. A piece of wood with a stone on it placed at the bottom of the well told the patient's fate: if it bobbed up, all was well, but if it remained submerged death was inevitable. It also had the unique ability to detect faithless lovers: a nail or pin which sank head first (as distinct from point first) confirmed your worst fears about the love-rat.

The B861 joins the Inverness bypass at Lochardil. Turning right (east) the road passes Castleheather, originally Castleleather or Castlelezar. Part of the old house was built with stones from the ruined castle 200m to the west. Turning south onto Old Edinburgh Road leads to Glendruidh House Hotel, with a distinctive tower added in the 1850s. Kenneth MacRae says the circular drawing room is haunted but gives no details. Further south is Druid Temple Farm, which gives pedestrian access (ask permission) to the atmospheric Druid Temple Chambered Cairn★★ (aka Leys, NH68514201), probably the best Clava cairn outside Corrimony and Clava. Beautifully situated in what I suspect is a romantic Victorian Druid-evoking plantation of oak trees, the kerb and outer circle of stones are easy to follow, and the tallest stone is an impressive 2.5m. A report by Daniel Wilson in *Prehistoric Annals of Scotland* says:

> A funicular rod or torc of gold was dug up within the great circle of Leys… in 1824, and was produced at a meeting of the Society of Antiquaries of Scotland as a golden sceptre or rod of office… 22' long, hooked at both ends; but one of the terminal hooks, broken off by the plough, was retained when the other portions were given up as treasure trove.

The RCAHMS Canmore website says the torc was purchased by a jeweller, and later lost, although a facsimile in lead was lent by the Inverness Museum to the Archaeological Institute Exhibition in Edinburgh of 1856. I assume these reports are of the same object, although it appears both original and copy are long lost.

9

EAST OF INVERNESS: CULLODEN, CLAVA AND FORT GEORGE

Ancient traditions, when tested by the severe processes of modern investigation, commonly enough fade away into mere dreams: but it is singular how often the dream turns out to have been a half-waking one, presaging a reality.

T.H. Huxley, *Man's Place In Nature*

INSHES AND WESTHILL

Kenneth MacRae, in *Highland Ways and Byways*, interviewed Mrs Lilian Hartley about her childhood experiences of the 'brown-suited Robertson' who haunted Inshes House (NM695437).

> My brother wakened me in the middle of the night to ask if I heard a terrible noise up in the attics of the house… I agreed it was the most terrible noise of the kind to which I had ever listened. Of course, we knew nobody was there, which didn't console us in the least. Another time my mother's maid, Jessie Grant, had been making the beds with one of the housemaids, and on her way to the bedrooms had to step aside in the passage to let the little man pass, but I don't believe the other girl even saw him… his wife shut him up in the attic with a barrel of whisky, and there he stayed until it was finished. Somehow he escaped and fell headlong down the stairs and broke his neck. My sister saw his ghost falling down the attic stairs on several occasions.

In his fictionalised childhood memoir, *Erch in Urchinage*, the writer M. Dick remembered the men telling stories while waiting for the pub to open. One of them had seen a chicken with four wings and four legs at Inshes. It belonged to 'Stewartie th' Chaffoor'.

On the B9006 in Westhill (NH714443) is the striking Raigmore Tower. Hansom cab drivers would tell visitors to Culloden Battlefield it was used as a prison for Jacobites, but it is in fact an early nineteenth-century Gothic folly.

CULLODEN VILLAGE

Culloden House Hotel★★ (NH721465) is a beautiful Palladian mansion clad with ivy and set in delightful grounds with several curiosities, such as two tree stumps

Culloden House Hotel, front view.

that have been carved into a Highland warrior with targe and sword, and a woman shackled by her wrists. Although dating from the 1780s the foundations incorporate part of the pre-1745 building and it has a deep relationship with the Battle of Culloden. BPC stayed here (before the battle) as did the Duke of Cumberland (after it). The Prince's Stone, a large boulder, said to be where BPC viewed the battle, was displayed in the house until 1897. The house belonged to the prominent Forbes family, pre-eminent among whom was Duncan Forbes (1685-1747), the Lord President of the Court of Session. Thomas Pennant, in his 1769 *A Tour in Scotland*, relates one of the most famous elements of Jacobite folklore:

> I heard of one instance of Second Sight, or rather of foresight, which was well attested, and made much noise about the time the prediction was fulfilled. A little after the Battle of Preston Pans, the president, Duncan Forbes, being at his house of Culloden with a nobleman, from whom I had the relation, fell into discourse on the probable consequences of the action: after a long conversation, and after revolving all that might happen, Mr Forbes suddenly turned to a window said 'All these things may fall out; but depend on it, all these disturbances will be terminated on this spot.'

The Battle of Prestonpans, the first significant battle of the 1745 Jacobite Rising, took place near Falkirk on 21 September, and was a success for the Jacobites. If Pennant's secondhand report is accurate, Duncan Forbes predicted the Battle of Culloden seven months before it occurred. The president was a staunch Hanoverian and so had not been at home when BPC came calling; he was, however, a patriot and a humanitarian, and his protests at the bloody aftermath of Culloden caused him to be shabbily treated by the Government. Duncan's mansion was replaced in 1772-83 by a new house built for Arthur Forbes, which remains the core of what we see today. The nearby dovecot and stables date from this time, as do the four Classical statues at the rear – Cato and Scipio (two Romans of great moral integrity who opposed Julius Caesar) and Odenetus and Zenobia, a husband and wife team who were entrusted with the protection of Rome's Eastern empire in the third century AD. The symbolism is subtle: the latter two may hint at the Forbes' political role – trusted advisors at a distance from the centre of power – while the former pair alludes to Duncan's moral stance and his criticisms of the Government.

The Forbes were noted for high living. J. Cameron Lees (*A History of the County of Inverness*) tells how, at the burial of Mrs Forbes of Culloden, her two sons and their friends drank so much that when the cortège arrived at the churchyard they found they had forgotten to bring the coffin. The Forbes line came to an end in 1897 and the contents of the house were sold by a four-day public auction; many Jacobite relics were dispersed at the sale. Kenneth MacRae describes how at this time a locked and barred room that had been out of bounds to servants, guests and owner alike was entered. Within was an old wooden or stone coffin with instructions to bury it at Chapelton graveyard. Chapelton had long since vanished into arable land so the coffin was taken to the vault in the family graveyard three-quarters of a mile (1km) away.

R. Macdonald Robertson, writing in *Selected Highland Folktales* in 1961, says that 'some years ago', when the house was open to public in season, the owner, returning late, was surprised and annoyed to see a man walking along the corridor and into the library. She hurried after him to find the room empty. There were no other exits. The servants then told her the last of the tourists had left before 6 p.m. The man was described as tall and was wearing tartan with a plaid of hodden grey (a coarse cloth of undyed wool). Robertson also quotes Miss Myra K.G. Warrand, of No. 43 Bury Walk, Chelsea, a relative of the late owner, who said her eldest sister, staying at the house, saw a man in 'some kind of dark cloth' cross the second-floor landing. She was alarmed, as all the rooms on that floor were occupied by women, and she was then relieved when he suddenly vanished. Both these sightings were said to have been of BPC, but there is nothing in the descriptions that justifies this. I think this is just another example of the power of celebrity – the ghost could be of anyone at all, but it becomes identified as BPC simply because he is famous. This tendency to assume ghosts must be the shades of dead celebs must really hack off the more humble spectres.

St Mary's Well★★ in the woods to the south of the village is one of the best cloutie or rag wells in Scotland. From the Forestry Commission car park (just north of where the road to Westhill goes over the railway line) proceed along the yellow route uphill then turn right over the railway bridge; the well is another 500m straight on (NH72354523).

Its use as a healing well is long-standing. The Synod of Moray attempted to suppress pilgrimages to this and other wells on 26 April 1626 and 4 October 1642. In 1678 the Synod told the Presbytery of Inverness 'to intimat that persons goeing to superstitious wells are to be censured' (William MacKay, *Records of the Presbyteries of Inverness and Dingwall 1643-1688*). The traditional procedure was for visitors to approach the well at dawn, 'silver' the water with a coin, sip the water, cast it round, and then tear a shred from their clothing – it was important that you were wearing it – and attach it to the nearest tree. As the shred or clout decayed, so would the supplicant's illness or troubles. Anyone stealing a clout acquired the

St Mary's Cloutie Well,
Culloden Woods.

Clouties, St Mary's Well,
Culloden Woods.

Bathing/healing pool, St Mary's Cloutie Well, Culloden Woods.

ill it represented as well. In 1896 the well was still visited on the first Sunday in May by hundreds from Inverness, and the *Daily Record* for 7 May 1934 reported: 'Buses heavily laden were run from Inverness almost every hour yesterday, and there were motoring parties from all parts of the North... County policemen regulate the traffic.' Janet Honnor of Westhill B&B told me the practice in the 1950s was to wear an old shirt under your kilt, listen to the service, then tear a strip off your shirt and tie it to a tree. If the strip was gone the following year your wish would come true. The Gaelic scholar Ronald Black has commented on the remarkable popularity of this pre-Reformation 'superstition' in an area strongly associated with evangelical Protestantism from the seventeenth to the twentieth centuries.

The well is variously named Tobar Na Coille, the Well of The Wood; the Culloden Well; Tobar Gorm, the Blue Well (although its iron-rich waters are reddish); and Tobar na h-Oige, the Well of Youth. The clues to its origins are probably in the names St Mary's Well or the Well of The Lady. The *Name Book* of 1868 says it is named after a chapel in the neighbourhood dedicated to St Mary. Donald Anderson, in 'Local Folklore' (Field Club), relates the tradition that St Mary was a local cailleach or wise woman who lived at Chapelton and healed the sick with water from the well as she travelled around. Mary may well have been a real local person, or, just as likely, the well, as were so many others in Scotland, was named after the Virgin Mary.

The well as it stands today is a natural spring surrounded by stone flags enclosed within a two-yard (2m) tall circular wall. It is not known when the wall was built – Kenneth MacRae gives the charming story that the wife of one of the Forbes of Culloden persuaded her husband to build a wall around it so she could take a bath in private. Once there were wooden seats around the interior and a woman who acted as a combination priestess-caretaker, providing dishes for the visitors and looking after the place. The basin of the spring was once kept under lock and key. Twenty-five paces from the west of the wall (that is, opposite the entrance on the east) brings you to a water-filled stone-lined pool, which was once fed by piped water from the well – an elaboration of the basic procedure which allowed the sick to bathe in the healing waters. The well continues to be venerated and on my visit many clouties dated with the first Sunday in May 2007 could be seen. The only downside is that these days many people leave non-biodegradable materials, which, as well as being unsightly, rather misses the point of the ritual.

Donald Anderson mentions another healing well named after another cailleach, Eppie. I have searched for this along the railway embankment but although there are two possible candidates I fear Eppie's Well may have dried up or been diverted. Retracing your steps back to the first forest crossroads and turning right (east) and then left brings you to the Prisoners' Stone★, a large glacial erratic. There is a tradition that seventeen Jacobite officers remained hidden in the cellars of Culloden House for three days before being discovered and executed on this spot. In the woods to the west (NH718455) was the former private mausoleum of the Forbes, recently demolished because of the irresistible attraction that crypts have for teenagers.

BALLOCH

Fuaran a' Chleirich, or Tobar nan Cleirach, the Well of the Priests, supposed to be where priests washed themselves before taking part in religious ceremonies (NH73294717), is now encased in a metal grille and incongruously located in a small public stone patio deep within the gentle embrace of suburbia. From the post office at the bottom of the village go east to a small park, strike up Wellside Road then turn right into Wellside Place.

Culloden Battlefield – The Well of the Dead.

Culloden Battlefield
– The field of the
English.

Culloden Battlefield.
Did the Jacobite and
Hanoverian cavalry
know about this?

CULLODEN BATTLEFIELD★★★

Here on 16 April 1746 the Hanoverian forces under the Duke of Cumberland decisively defeated Prince Charles Edward's Jacobite army, changing the face of Scotland and the Highlands forever. Like many battlefields, you need to allow some time to get to grips with the place – a fleeting visit merely gives the impression of bleak moorland, but if you take the trouble the site will start to reveal itself to you. The details of the battle are very well covered in a series of guidebooks and the superb new National Trust for Scotland visitor centre, so this section will concentrate on the stranger aspects of the site. It is, however, worth countering all the cheap anti-English comments made by some parts of the local tourist industry by pointing out that a large part of the 'English' Hanoverian forces were actually Scottish. Culloden was also one of many battles ostensibly fought for a grander political purpose which provided the perfect excuse for various clans to pursue grudges against their traditional enemies – that is to say, not the English, but other clans. History – and especially warfare – is rarely neat and simple, and the continuing weepy underdog myth, where brave romantic Jacobites were overcome by dastardly English thugs, does a disservice to both the complexity of the events and the actions of the participants on the day.

War is the crucible of folklore and as a site of great slaughter Culloden duly has its full share of the contra-mundane. To begin with, the landscape of the site itself has been shaped to meet a Victorian romantic ideology. Duncan Forbes of Culloden House (1851-97) performed a great service to the nation by documenting the battle site, marking some of the graves and the locations where particular actions had taken part, but he also imposed a mythic structure onto the battlefield beyond which it is now hard to see. The key elements of this mythic structure are the Great Cairn and the clan graves. The former, at 20ft (6.5m) in height, is the visual focus of the battle site. Erected in 1881, it includes a stone with the inscription 'Culloden, 1746 – E.P. fecit 1858', carved by Edward Power, a commercial traveller and enthusiastic Jacobite who had intended it for another, unfinished cairn. Originally the rough stones of the cairn were given a skein of ferns and ivy – instant antiquity. The main slab on the structure is inscribed 'The Battle of Culloden was fought on this moor, 16 April 1746. The graves of the gallant Highlanders who fought for Scotland and Prince Charlie are marked by the names of their clans.' Note the way our emotions are manipulated – the Highlanders are 'gallant' and they all 'fought for Scotland'. The Scottish clans who took the field on the Hanoverian side might dispute that last all-encompassing phrase. Forbes erected other memorials, in the form of standing stones, to mark the clan graves: MacKintoshes, Camerons, Frasers and Stewarts, and so on. It all seems so orderly, and even though Forbes collected traditions passed down through family generations as to where each fallen Jacobite was buried, the idea that each clan stone is anything more than a symbol rather than a geographically-precise marker for the fallen is fallacious. Given the chaotic nature of warfare and subsequent disposal of the bodies, probably the only stones which are accurate in depicting who lies beneath are the ones marked 'Mixed Clans'. Another stone names a little spring as 'The Well of the Dead'. It marks the spot where Alexander MacGillivray of Dunmaglass, Commander of Clan Chattan was found – one of the few locations which is reliably documented. MacGillivray was a great warrior and fought fiercely on the day. For more on his fate, see PETTY CHURCHYARD.

Culloden's stones do have a function for the modern visitor, for without them there would be nothing to see other than a stretch of moor, and, as with memorials elsewhere, the stones act as a focus for emotion and remembrance – it is common to find flowers, pieces of tartan, small stones and other items left on them. Psychics often sit near the stones in an attempt to 'heal' the battlefield. The stones also may provide a locus for perceived paranormal events. In August 1936 a woman on holiday from Edinburgh was alone on the battlefield. In her own words: 'when I lifted a square of Stuart tartan, which was blown down from the stone to the mound which is the grave, I distinctly saw the body of a very hand-some, dark-haired Highlander lying, as it were, at ease, on top of the mound.' His clothes were dirty and muddy and old-fashioned, and his tartan was red. She had the impression he was dead and dropped the square of cloth over his face. At this point she realised she was '*seeing things*' (her expression) and fled the scene. The account is from a letter she wrote in 1941 to the splendidly-named Committee for the Recording of Abnormal Happenings, and is reproduced in Alasdair Alpin MacGregor's *Phantom Footsteps*. Note that the exact stone and 'grave mound' is not identified; this has not stopped several writers claiming the location for this encounter as the Great Cairn.

Other ghosts supposedly sighted include a weary Highlander who says the word 'Defeated', although I have been unable to find the source for this. Many phantoms are supposedly sighted on the anniversary, 16 April. I can find no relia-ble source for a definite anniversary ghost army, and offer two observations: firstly, on at least one occasion, visitors reported hearing the shouts and cries of battle – which were actually the sounds of a re-enactment group practicing out of sight (this was told to me by one of the re-enactors in 2006). And secondly, the British calendar was adjusted six years after the battle: 2 September 1752 was followed by the 14 September. Are we then to assume the ghosts of Culloden have made the same calendrical adjustment as the rest of us? Or do they turn up on 25 April, and no one notices? Culloden also shares in the same sentimental folklore of other battlefields, where nature is seen to be in sympathy with the human horrors of the site. Birds are said not to sing here and heather is said never to grow over the graves. Both fallacies are simply disproved by observation.

Stories of people having strange experiences relating to the battle, even though they were far away at the time, are found throughout Scotland: women 'saw' their menfolk killed, great stones were split in two, and ministers preached the out-come to their flocks long before they could have heard the news. The collective implication is that Culloden was an event of such magnitude that it somehow irrupted into the psychic world. Two examples will suffice here: MacCrimmon, the great Skye piper, had a premonition of death and so before leaving home composed the famous pibroch 'No more returning'. He was killed at Culloden. And (as reported in Pennant's 1769 *Tour in Scotland*), when the Earl of Loudon was forced back to Skye by the Jacobites, a common soldier there proclaimed the victory of Culloden at the precise moment BPC fled the field. The man had the vision 'by looking through the bone', that is by 'reading' the shoulder blade, a procedure which was usually used for divination.

Writing in the *TGSI* in 1890, Alexander MacBain, in 'Gaelic Incantations', described a powerful *sian* or protective charm placed on men about to go into battle. The recipient of the charm had to kneel while the charmer laid his hand on his head and circled in a sunwise direction twice while speaking the first part of the charm, then completing two circuits anti-sunwise while uttering the second part. The recipient then departed but the charmer had to stand with eyes shut until the other was out of sight. From that moment the charmed one was protected against harm in battle until the charmer saw him again. MacBain commented: 'Men so protected, for instance, at Culloden, had only to take their plaids off their shoulders and shake out of them the bullets that hit them.'

Alexander Carmichael's monumental collection of Gaelic lore, *Carmina Gadelica*, includes a specific example. A woman in Bearnasdale, Skye, put a *sian* on MacLeod of Bearnaray, Harris. At Culloden 'the bullets showered upon him like hail, but they had no effect.' When MacLeod threw off his coat in the retreat, it was picked up by his foster-brother Murdoch Macaskail, and found to be riddled with bullet holes.

'Battlefield Curse Strikes Again' was the headline in *Nessie's Loch Ness Times* on 6 May 2000. Battlefield manager Ross Mackenzie was quoted as saying:

We get all sorts of strange things through the post here, none more so than this parcel which just arrived from anonymous persons containing what looks like part of a fir tree root... There was no signature or return address, only a request from a lady to return it to the field without delay, because she and her husband had had nothing but bad luck since taking it home. She didn't specify what sort of bad luck.

The package was postmarked Yorkshire, and the soggy root was probably from a tree from the now-cleared Forestry Commission plantation, of no historical significance whatsoever. Mr Mackenzie noted this was not the first time this kind of thing had happened – 'The last package contained stones, sent all the way back from Australia with the same story of ill fortunes.'

In *Haunted Scotland*, Norman Adams describes a colour photograph taken on the battlefield on 16 April 1996, the 250th anniversary of the battle. In the lower right-hand corner is what appears to be a face or skull with a wig and a Highland bonnet, and possibly a shoulder and arm ending in a fist. It could of course be a simulacrum, an accidental arrangement of heather and stones that we see as a human face (this is part of the psychology of expectation and perception, where we actively look for patterns that are perceived as something meaningful, although they have no objective reality). The woman who had taken the picture, however, was convinced the photograph had invited in some presence, as her house became the focus of mild poltergeist activity and strange noises. A clairvoyant identified the spirit as a Jacobite chief from Skye, killed assisting BPC escape from Culloden and miffed that he had been ignored by historians.

A broadside, a cheap popular sheet, published in Edinburgh in 1820, claimed to contain: 'A most Wonderful and true Prophecy, which was found in an iron box in a Subterraneous Cavern, near the memorable field of Culloden, and was written three hundred years ago, and contains many Discoveries of what is to take place in various kingdoms of the World betwixt the years 1822 and 1826.' The prophecy was apparently written on a large roll of parchment kept in an iron box which had been hidden behind a square stone, only coming to light when workmen employed by a Mr Grant repaired a cave on his land. Grant showed the parchment to two or three clergymen, who determined it was written 'in the Celtic language… [and] was wrote by some great prophet, when the Celtics inhabited the kingdom of Scotland.' Nowhere does the broadside quote any of the original text of the parchment, even in translation, and the broadside is one of many from the period in which mysterious ancient documents apparently foretell the future.

Firstly the prophecy's credentials are established – it correctly predicted the rise and fall of Napoleon, and the trial of Queen Caroline in 1820, the year of the broadsheet's publication. The Battle of Waterloo in 1815 and the Queen's much-publicised acquittal for adultery were still fresh in the public mind at the time, so they were the obvious candidates to demonstrate the veracity of the seer. Then came the predictions for the future: the British economy would collapse in 1823, between 1821-6 there would be great slaughter in the sister kingdom (France? Ireland?) and the Turkish Empire would fall. The whole document is remarkably indistinct, without any obvious purpose. If the location is a fake, why mention it was found near Culloden of all places and then not shoehorn in some mention of the battle? If (as is often the case) the 'prophecy' was designed to provide a spurious legitimacy for a contemporary political or religious viewpoint, this seems oddly lacking.

Near Death Experiences (NDEs) have been widely reported by people who have been close to death in hospital. The typical NDE involves travelling along a tunnel, encountering a bright light, and perhaps meeting loved ones who have previously passed on. Of course there is great variation in this standard pattern, but I have never heard of anyone whose NDE involved viewing the Battle of Culloden from an elevated position as if on a gantry. But that is what one elderly American experienced when recovering from a near-fatal accident. He recounted the vision in precise detail to his son, who eventually realised his father was describing the Battle of Culloden. When the elderly man eventually visited the site, he was disappointed at the state of the battlefield – he had expected it to have more standing water. And, indeed, research has shown that at the time of the battle, Drumossie Moor was indeed a very waterlogged place when compared to today.

There is a monster associated with Culloden – the Great Skree. This awful bat-winged creature, with burning red eyes and the head of a man, was apparently seen screeching and hovering over the Jacobite forces the night before the battle. It was later viewed as a harbinger of doom, and has been linked with other alleged sightings of the entity on occasions when Scots have headed for disaster. Sometime around 2004 or 2005 a group of re-enactors – burly, macho types – were crossing part of the battlefield one evening when they heard a strange screaming. Proceeding to investigate they saw a black, leathery shape on the ground which moved into the air and proceeded to fold up like an umbrella, before disappearing. Whether this was the Skree or not, it had a profound impact on the witnesses. The episodes of the 'umbrella beast' and the NDE 'eyewitness', along with many other supernatural stories, can be found in Hugh G. Allison's

Culloden Tales: Stories from Scotland's Most Famous Battlefield (2007). Hugh Allison is a guide at the visitor centre and the book contains stories visitors have told him about their experiences on the site.

Turning right from the visitor centre and going through the crossroads takes you to, on the right-hand side of the road, Cumberland's Stone★ (NH74974526). You can climb the metal rungs onto the surface of this enormous glacial erratic and read the huge letters carved into it that claim the Duke of Cumberland used it as his vantage point during the battle. It may have been his breakfasting point on the day, and he may have stood beside it on horseback to watch the battle.

Kenneth MacRae reports a belief that Cumberland stood on it and left an imprint on it. This is an echo of the widespread belief that rocks bear the footprints of saints or devils; it is not hard to guess which the Duke would have been classed as.

Culloden Battlefield – The Cumberland Stone.

Clava, Southeast Cairn.

Clava, Southeast Cairn, cupmarks.

Clava, Northwest Cairn..

Clava, Northwest
Cairn, cupmarked
stone on kerb.

CLAVA CAIRNS★★★

Here, you are entering a prehistoric ritual landscape. The interpretation at the main site (NH752439, signposted and parking) is not very fulsome so it is worth downloading the visitor's guide from www.historic-scotland.gov.uk. The main site at Clava (from the Gaelic for 'the good stones') is a truly amazing place. It consists of three large cairns on a northeast-southwest line, and a smaller, much less obvious kerb cairn slightly to the north. The two cairns at the ends are passage graves, where a low passage led to a central burial chamber which was originally roofed but is now open to the sky. The central monument is a ring-cairn, with no external access to the central burial area, which appears never to have been roofed. Each of the three large cairns is surrounded by a circle of standing stones, and each has examples of the enigmatic rock art known as cupmarks. The small kerb cairn also has cupmarks. The numinous setting is enhanced by the mature trees planted during the Victorian craze for Druidic groves – quite a difference to the description in the 1845 *NSA*: 'the place is the most dreary and bleak the imagination can conceive – dark stinted heath, without any other vegetation whatsoever… four of them [circles] have been diverted from their original design into cairns of remembrance of either good or evil.' All the cairns are aligned on solar events, which make them unique among all the cairns of this type, which tend to be oriented on lunar cycles. A DVD available locally, *The Clava Cairns* by Douglas Scott, gives video and photographic examples of the solar alignments, such as the shadows of standing stones falling on cupmarked stones at particular times, and particular sunrises and sunsets aligned on specific stones. The DVD also shows the spectacular effect at the winter solstice – in 2005, the unroofed chambers were temporarily covered over, revealing how during the Bronze Age the midwinter sun penetrated along the low passages to illuminate the rear of the central chambers. Douglas Scott interprets this as the sun god impregnating the earth goddess to cause plants and crops to flourish in the following spring.

Mains of Clava – monolith from damaged ring-cairn, possible medieval chapel, and Victorian viaduct.

Nessie's Loch Ness Times for 22 January 2000 reported the return of a 'cursed' stone to Clava. An anonymous Belgian tourist had picked up a souvenir from the site then posted it back after it had apparently cursed his daughter (broken leg), his wife (fell seriously ill) and himself (broken arm and made redundant). Bob Hunter-Dorans, a visitor services assistant at the tourist office in Inverness, returned the stone to Clava. Barbara Fraser from Historic Scotland was quoted as saying, 'this is not the first stone to come back from Clava. There was one instance a few years ago when a chap took a stone but eventually took it back to the National Trust with a donation asking them to return it.'

The *Highland News* (2 November 2006) posed the question 'Is Clava crow find a Hallowe'en sacrifice?' prompted by the discovery of a dead crow arranged in 'an unusual way' on the standing stone apparently connected to the Samhain/Hallowe'en festival. John Ray, of Inverness, who found the crow, said, 'I've seen offerings left at the stones before at Hallowe'en, midwinter and midsummer solstices over the years – flowers, mistletoe, crystals, that sort of thing. This was different. The person that did this must have known what they were doing... Could somebody have been using it for some kind of black magic?'

Following the road west from the main site and taking a signposted path through a kissing gate takes you to Milton of Clava ring-cairn★ (NH75254397). This is damaged but does have one huge monolith nearly 8ft (2.4m) high. Next to it to the west – and also within the Historic Scotland guardianship site – is an unexcavated rectangular ruin which may be a medieval chapel dedicated to St Bridget or St Dorothy, possibly built here to combat the pagan power of the place.

There are several more chambered cairns in the immediate area, reinforcing the sense that this river valley and its edges were regarded as a centre of ritual activity. A large, 6.5ft (2m) high single standing stone★ at NH75944461, visible in the north from the road east from the main site, may be the sole remains of the circle of another cairn. An overgrown circular feature south of the road and opposite the main site (NH75854441), was formerly regarded as a hut circle but in 1996 was identified as an almost-destroyed Clava cairn. In 1994 another very badly damaged Clava cairn was discovered 1.5m (2km) south at NH75554285. Culdoich ring-cairn (badly damaged) lies southwest of Milton of Clava at NH75114378; on the valley ridge to the west are Leanach (NH74244434, two monoliths standing) and Culchunaig (NH74204418, three standing stones left). That's at least nine chambered cairns within four square kilometres.

ALONG THE A96

The garden wall at Ashton Farm (NH701455, private) incorporates two marriage lintels dug up on the site, one with the date 1699 and the second featuring a thistle and a rose. Milton Farm (NH707469), a former inn, had an underground tunnel under the house for use by smugglers delivering illicit whisky by boat. There are three chambered cairns in the area – Allanfearn★ (NH71624761), on the north side of the A96 just east of the junction to Alturlie; Cullernie★, 800m to the east, south of the A96 (NH72504769); and Newton of Petty a further two thirds of a mile (1km) northeast (NH73484858). All are badly damaged but are easy to visit (if you can park your car and avoid the traffic).

Somewhere in the area of the huge factory at Morayhill (NH75454940) used to be Tom-a-mhoid, the Courthill, and Tom-a-chroich, the Gallowhill, also the home of fairies. A farmer's wife stayed with them a year, returning safe and well, but entirely unaware of the passage of time. In the account for Petty in the *NSA*, Revd John Grant wrote, 'about the commencement of my predecessor's incumbency, the fairies endeavoured to steal a new-born infant from its mother, at Lag-chree. Of this nefarious attempt, and of the sensation which it occasioned, there is a history in MS by a venerable person who was parish schoolmaster at the time.' I am unaware of this manuscript. There is a Cnoc an t Sidhean (Fairies Hill) at NH765510, immediately southwest of the airport, but I can find no tradition directly attached to it.

The *Third Statistical Account* mentions Tobar na Gul, the boiling fountain, at Tornagrain 'where, on a level flat there are various intermittent spouts, and with every ejection of the water, the purest sand rises and spreads around the orifice from which the water is thrown… between Culblair and Mid Coul is Bruach na fuaran, or Brae of the Well, [NH778509] where the old inhabitants say Lochandunty empties its waters.' Revd McLeod, the author of the chapter on Petty, says, 'when the writer came to the parish over 20 years ago the springs were regarded by the older people as magic wells.' Tobar na Gul is now covered by a pump house. There are good nineteenth-century gravestones in the cemetery at Ballasgan (NH796528, off the B9006 to Ardersier) although the peace of the graveyard is disturbed by the nearby Inverness Airport.

The Abban Stone, Petty Bay.

ALTURLIE

If the tide is out you can walk along the coast from Alturlie in the direction of Castle Stuart. From the seventeenth to the nineteenth centuries there was in Petty Bay a sea-mill, a watermill powered by the ebb and flow of the tide. Out in the bay is Clach-an-aban★, the Abban Stone, visible at low tide (approx. NH730495). It once marked the boundary between the Moray and Culloden. There are two stories about it. One says Revd John Morrison, the Petty Seer (see PETTY CHURCH), incensed at his flock, cried out, 'Ye stiff-necked, sinful people, God will, unless you repent, sweep you soon into a place of torment, and as a sign that what I say is true, the Abban Stone, large though it is, will be carried soon without human interference a long way out to sea.' The other attributes the prediction, perhaps inevitably, to the Brahan Seer. During a great storm on the night of Saturday 20 February 1799, the stone did indeed relocate from the land into the sea, leaving a large hole visible in the original position. Two theories were proposed at the time: (a) it was pushed by the Devil (b) a large sheet of ice 18in (45cm) thick had collected around the stone, raising it sufficiently above the ground and floodtide for the gale and waves to shift its 8-ton bulk some 250 yards. I invite Fortean-minded engineers to attempt to replicate the incident. The most accessible account of the mystery is in the *NSA*; a more detailed report was written by Sir T. Dick Lauder for the *Edinburgh Wernerian Transactions* for 1817-20.

The *NSA* also dubiously suggests the (now extensively quarried) sands of Petyn (Petty) are derived from 'Pait' or 'Pit-Ian', from the Fingalian heroes Pipan and Ian Beag nam Fion. The latter, who left behind giant bones when buried in the area, was 14ft (4.25m) tall, and the *NSA* identifies him with Little John: 'the histories of Robin Hood make his friend Little John to retire like a smitten deer from his gay green wood and companions, in order to rest his weary bones in the dry sands of Petyn.' The original source for all this silliness is Hector Boece's 1527 *History of*

Castle Stuart.

Scotland, an almost entirely unreliable work, although here Boece has been misinterpreted, as he was describing a man called 'little' John, not Little John of Sherwood.

CASTLE STUART★★

Dating from 1625 and succeeding two earlier castles on neighbouring sites, the recently restored Castle Stuart now provides upmarket accommodation. Large paintings illustrate events from the '45. The website asks: 'Can you find the secret revolving door to the Drawing Room? It saves walking the long way to get a dram of whisky from the bar… The whole castle is full of secret stairways, alcoves, priest-holes and hidden doorways. We have not yet had time to explore them all.' You are also dared to spend the night in the 'Three-Turret Haunted Bedroom at the top of the East Tower.' The story of the room – which is told in a booklet, *The Mystery of Castle Stuart*, available at the castle and locally – has the Earl of Moray offering £20 to anyone who succeeded in spending the night in the room, which had the reputation of being haunted. Several local men tried but were assailed by a variety of grisly phantoms. Finally Big Angus, the local poacher and a man with no fear of man, beast or bogle, took up the challenge. The following morning, Angus was found dead in the courtyard below, having been defenestrated through the high tower window.

Of course, ghostly phenomena have been recorded by some guests in this room, but this may be a case of expectations fulfilled. The owner, Charles Stuart, informed me by email that on one occasion an elderly woman reported at breakfast that she had been kept awake by a door which kept opening and closing and banging. Her husband later told Mr Stuart that he had tied a length of string to his toe and attached it to the door – so he could give his wife the satisfaction of having slept in a genuine haunted room.

Big black cat:
Mackintosh Mausoleum,
Petty churchyard.

PETTY CHURCH AND CHURCHYARD★★

Although the church is now closed and starting to decay, this is a superb site with much of interest. Tradition, legend and wish-fulfilment insists Columba landed here after a miraculous demonstration of his powers, when he confounded King Brude's mocking Druids by successfully sailing into the teeth of a gale. The anti-bodysnatching watch house is complete and there are several carved stones in the graveyard. The seventeenth-century Mausoleum of the MacKintoshes of Moy has two iron upright feline guardians, unintended echoes of the big black cats that stalk the region. Four chiefs of Clan Chatten and two of their ladies are buried in the vault. The *NSA* relates a tradition that when the Jacobites were at a loss for ammunition they considered digging up the coffins to convert their lead into bullets. The *NSA* also mentions that at funerals in Petty it was for some reason the custom to run as fast as possible – which meant that people often fell when carrying the body. In the nearby parishes speeding up a funeral was therefore called 'taking the Petie step to it'. The haste may have been related to the belief that the most recent person buried in a graveyard had to act as a spectral watcher, so the party had to get there quicker than any competing funeral. In the nineteenth century some lads were running with Camronach-na-peasairach's wife, a woman long thought to be a witch, tripped and dropped the coffin, and the lads spent the rest of their lives fearing she had cursed them.

Petty churchyard: angel detail, gravestone.

Among the gravestones is that of John Morrison, minister 1759-1774, known as the Petty Seer. John Maclean's *Reminiscences* describe one of Morrison's examples of second sight. He told an elder that a godless fisherman was 'at this moment drowned at the new pier of Inverness, and his body will be taken to the Gaelic church and remain there during the night.' The fisherman's relations, hearing the story, immediately went to Inverness to claim the body; they had no doubt about Morrison's abilities. A.B. MacLennan's book *The Petty Seer* gives more examples: on two occasions his premonitions took him some distance to intervene with unmarried mothers contemplating infanticide; twice he provided music for poor drunken women because he wanted to give them some pleasure before their imminent deaths; he could tell when a servant had lied about checking on the cows, because he could 'see' one animal had broken its legs; and he correctly predicted the time of death of an innkeeper at Milton of Culloden, who broke his neck falling down stairs.

When Alexander MacGillivray of Dunmaglass fell at Culloden, the Hanoverians prevented the body (and those of other Jacobites) from being recovered (see

Ardersier: owlish
weathervane.

CULLODEN BATTLEFIELD). The elements of what follows may have been
subject to a degree of legend-making. The standard description is that Alexander
was thrown into a mass grave at Culloden with fifty others. But in the *History
of the Clan MacGillivray*, there are the sworn statements of two local men, both
named William MacKintosh, one a smith at Dalcross and the other a miller at
Kinrea, who said they buried Alexander two days after the battle, 'putting the end
of a standard into the ground at the head of the grave and the part of a sheath
of a sword and some stones on top.' This clearly-marked lone grave may explain
why the body was so easily recovered once the guards had left. Despite six weeks
having passed, Alexander's corpse was said to be perfectly fresh and the wound
bled anew. At the time this was put down to the preserving action of the moss in
which he was buried, although to me it sounds like a hint towards sanctification.
Another account says several ankers of whisky had to be emptied into the grave
to enable the body to be removed, presumably to mask the smell of decomposi-
tion. It was considered too dangerous to take him to the family burial ground at
Dunlichity so the corpse was brought to Petty. He was supposedly interred over
the threshold of the church, but investigation has not been able to identify the
grave. A modern commemorative plaque is on a buttressed wall east of the watch
house. Kenneth MacRae's *Highland Ways and Byways* says that in the early 1900s
Charlie Campbell, a mason from Kerrowgair, left instructions that he should be
buried in his own vault, the door locked and the key thrown into Petty Bog.
Immediately west of the graveyard is a motte.

Excellent views of Castle Stuart can be obtained from outside the graveyard.
At the road end leading to Lonnie, south of the castle and graveyard, is a small
stone bridge (NH742492). Here a practical joker lay in wait under a white sheet
for a young ploughman who had gone to Newton smithy with his plough irons.
The 'ghost' rose up in his spectral sheet. 'Speak or I will strike you with these

Ardersier: signs of
the times.

irons,' said the ploughman. The prankster remained silent so the ploughman hit
him with the irons, killing him – he now haunts the bridge. (Source: Kenneth
MacRae, *Highland Ways and Byways*).

ARDERSIER

According to Peter F. Anson in *Fisher Folk-Lore*, 'The fisher folk at Ardersier were
very primitive and much given to superstition.' This was once a divided village,
with one part, Campbeltown, owned by the estate of Cawdor, and the other side,
Stewarton, owing allegiance to the Earl of Moray. The distinctive mound of Cromal
Mount (NH782555), with a circular earth rampart on top, is of undetermined age
– guesses range from the Iron Age to a Cromwellian fortress. *Nessie's Loch Ness Times*
(17 March 2001) reported that a storm had revealed a circular structure 20m in
diameter in the sands off Ardersier. Suggestions included a Bronze Age or Iron Age
hut circle, a crannog, or a more recent structure connected to the fishing industry.

FORT GEORGE★★★

An amazingly well-preserved eighteenth-century fortress, this Historic Scotland
site is huge and impressive, with much to explore. The fort juts out into the waters
of the Moray Firth on a cuspate foreland – a peninsula formed by two shallow
arcs of a circle meeting at a sharp point. A second cuspate foreland can be found
at Chanonry Point, on the opposite side of the Firth. Dolphins are frequently
spotted from the northern battlements and seagulls nest on the walls. There is an
excellent guidebook for sale and many parts of the fort have been interpreted,
so rather than reiterating this historical material here we will concentrate on the
strange and the supernatural.

Fort George Chapel.

In the entrance passageway before the parade ground, a right turn takes you into the cells where military miscreants were locked up. One room has an extensive piece of graffiti carved by a trooper who calls himself Abernethy. This name has been applied – with what accuracy I cannot say – to various ghostly sightings, although the details are scant. Tales of a phantom piper might be just standard 'frighten the new recruits' fare (the fort is still an active military training garrison). The casemates – bomb-proof shelters – hidden in the thick walls of the fort are certainly sufficiently dark, dank and drippy to set off the imagination. The chapel★ has a stained-glass window with an angel playing the bagpipes, and a memorial on which a mermaid appears to have just torn the head off a snake or monster.

I take the view that pretty much any museum collection, no matter how specialised, will contain something of interest for those whose fancy turns to quirks, strangeness and charm, and the Regimental Museum★★ is no exception to that rule. It goes into exhaustive detail on all the regiments who have been based at Fort George, and every campaign and operation they have been involved in. Looking beyond the endless weapons, medals and imperial paraphernalia, however, there are some real curiosities.

Fort George Chapel: making a joyful noise unto the Lord – angelic bagpiper.

Fort George Chapel: memorial with a mermaid tearing the head off a monster(?) snake(?).

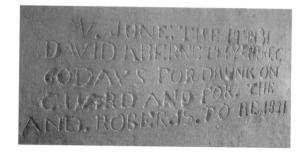

Fort George: the 'Abernethy' graffito.

On the landing of the stairs to the first floor. The carved stone 1662 marriage lintel of Kenneth, 3rd Earl of Seaforth and Countess Isobel, of Brahan Castle. The decoration includes a long-haired wild man with a club and loincloth, chained eagles, and a coat of arms supported by an animal.

Room 3, 72nd Duke of Albany's Own Highlanders, Afghanistan Campaign 1878-80: A heavy brass clock, three inches (8cm) deep and seven inches (18cm) across, which the orderly to the commanding officer carried on his back, face outwards, so the CO could see the exact time to give the order to advance. Also the enormous stuffed head of 'Seaforth', the regimental mascot ram, with silver ends on the huge horns.

Room 10, the First World War. A strikingly strange painting called 'An Incident at Arras April 1917'. The 1st/4th Battalion Seaforth Highlanders were involved in an action at Arras on the night of 8/9 April, after heavy snow. An officer crossing the former German second line came across two Seaforths who had been killed by a shell bursting overhead. One man was kneeling with his New Testament in his hand, while the other sat with his arms outstretched. Both remained with their eyes open, frozen in life-like positions as if in a photograph.

Room 11: The articulated metal arm made for a wounded corporal in 1917, with artificial hand, hook, shaving brush, and three other attachments.

Room 13, the Second World War: Hitler's dispatch box, taken from the infamous bunker, along with a piece of Hitler's desk from the same place. And a rifle lost at St Valery en Caux, Normandy, in 1940, found in the sea in 1993 encrusted with seashells and stones.

Room 16, after the Second World War: Human skull with a red star painted on the forehead, 'found in a Communist terror camp' in Malaya.

Room 17: A model of a deer's head, presented by a local headman in Brunei. And, absolutely best of all, a human skull gifted to J.J.G. Mackenzie – 'the Restless Skull of Fort George'. As part of SAS operations in Brunei and Borneo during 1962-65, Lt Mackenzie had worked with scouts from the Murut tribe, and at the end of his tour of duty the headman of a longhouse in the Tutong district honoured the British soldier by giving him the skull. For the rest of the story I am indebted to the detailed account in Norman Adams' *Haunted Scotland.* The skull was not that of a revered ancestor but of a Chinese man killed by a blowpipe during the period of the 'White Rajah', Sir James Brooke (1803-68). Like the other skulls which hung in baskets in the longhouses, it had been smoked to preserve the bone. By 1996 Lt Mackenzie was General Sir Jeremy Mackenzie KCB OBE, Deputy Supreme Allied Commander Europe (from 1999 he was Governor of the

Kirkton of Ardersier graveyard: the death symbols on the table-top grave are under the slab rather than facing outwards.

Royal Hospital Chelsea). Sir Jeremy wrote to Adams with a description of the customs surrounding the skulls:

> once every six months or so they would all be taken down and walked round the longhouse with due ceremony. This allowed the spirit attached to the skull to see any new additions to the building, and thereby not become restless... They firmly believed that if this process was not followed through the spirits would break up the longhouse.

The skull was left in Dorset with Sir Jeremy's mother, who promptly plonked the vile thing in the attic. Over the next few days several valuable objects in the house were smashed or damaged, with the result that the skull was banished to Fort George. There it lay in a box until 1978, when the souvenirs of the Borneo campaign were brought together for a new display in the museum. The apparent consequence of this disturbance to the skull's slumber was, in Adams' words, 'a series of unfortunate mishaps to museum personnel and property', and the skull was relegated to its box again. Some time later Colonel Angus Fairrie, the museum curator, met the skull's donor, who explained the spirit in the skull simply liked to know where it was. So Colonel Fairrie duly gave the skull a full tour of the museum, and there were no further disturbances thereafter. Adams leaves the last word to Sir Jeremy, and so shall I: '[the skull's] physical properties belong to the museum, but I am sure that my Borneo headman firmly believes that one day I will be in need of a Chinese orderly in the next world, and he has made the necessary arrangements for this!'

THE CARSE OF ARDERSIER

This is the low-lying rural area east and southeast of Ardersier and Fort George. Kirkton Cemetery★★, close enough to the rifle ranges to hear the crack of gunfire while exploring the graves, has a superb collection of table-topped graves and old-school death symbols, as well as a watch house. Many of the graves are of soldiers from Fort George. The *Third Statistical Account* (1985) elaborates a story told in the *NSA* of 1845. In first part of the sixteenth century (or, alternatively, in the 1640s) the Thane of Cawdor fell off his horse and died at Druimadeobhan on his way home from the ferry. Witchcraft was suspected and a withered old woman 'who looked not like an inhabitant of the earth!' was interrogated and found to bear the Devil's mark. She was burned at the crossroads near the present farmhouse of Baddock (NH796561). The *NSA* mentions the case of a man called Munro who around 1730 left his child overnight on the conical knoll of Tom Eanraic, Henry's knoll (the natural mound of Tom Eanruig, NH814557, visible from the road through the trees). The infant was supposedly a fairy changeling, and Munro wanted to reverse the original exchange, where the fairies had abducted his child and replaced it with the sickly fairy. The following morning the infant was found dead, and Munro was prosecuted.

In July 2003 the Paterson family of Upper Carse (NH806558) captured a big cat on video from their front room. The *Press and Journal* reported the creature was about the size of a Labrador with a distinctively cat-like tail. The cat was seen by Mrs Tracy Paterson and her two daughters, Rebecca (eleven) and Michaela (fourteen), for more than five minutes. A week earlier a big black cat had been seen by a local man when he was driving to work, and in around 1993 a local woman had reported a large black cat which jumped over the bonnet of her car.

The Kebbock Stone★ is a Pictish Class II cross-slab in a croft garden (NH826555, ask permission). Although the stone is an impressive six-footer, the carving is almost invisible. The *NSA* gives three dubious origin stories for the stone: 1) it is a boundary marker between Inverness and Nairn; 2) it is the place where the Danes were sent packing after a battle; 3) (my favourite) it is the grave of a chief killed in a dispute over a cheese.

10

LOCH NESS AND POPULAR CULTURE

To log all sightings of Nessie in the mediascape, from adverts to zoology, would take an entire book, so here are just a few morsels worthy of further investigation.

Loch Ness's reputation is an easy win for scriptwriters of popular series, and everyone from *The Tomorrow People* and *The Goodies* to *Doctor Who* (twice) and Scooby-Doo has turned up on the loch shores. My favourite LNM TV moment is in *The Simpsons*, when the nasty Mr Burns takes Nessie back to Springfield and unveils the monster to the public in a *King Kong*-style presscall. When it all goes pear-shaped, Nessie gets a job at Burns' casino.

I have a soft spot for *The Private Life of Sherlock Holmes* (see TEMPLE PIER) but most of the films about Loch Ness are dire. The exception is *Incident at Loch Ness,* in which the truly great director Werner Herzog plays a director called Werner Herzog who is making a documentary to disprove the legend of the monster, while dealing with a producer who wants to create a sensationalist blockbuster. Then something large and animate hits the boat… A feature film pretending to be a documentary about the making of a fictional documentary, this puckish piece piles on layer upon delicious layer of fake realism, and is enjoyable both for its own sake and for its acerbic comment on the sometimes looking-glass world of Nessiemania.

In the novel *The Curse of Loch Ness* by Peter Tremayne (the pseudonym of Celtic scholar Peter Berresford Ellis), wicked Druids entice the intelligent dinosaur into the flooded cellars of a castle to mate with a woman. It's full-on Bram Stoker-style Gothic horror, and none the worse for that.

In the PC game *Secret at Loch Ness* you are Alan Cameron, Chicago PI, it's 1932 and you've got to negotiate a perplexing mystery around Loch Ness that reveals a magical conspiracy to destroy civilisation. There are many deft touches, my favourite being the opportunity to take your own 'surgeon's photo' of Nessie.

Nessie turns up in a few bucolic folk songs, but much more worthwhile is the reggae track 'Loch Ness Monster' by King Horror, originally issued in 1970 on the brilliant Trojan record label, and now reissued on a CD of the same name, which includes other examples of the short-lived horror-reggae genre as 'The Vampire' and 'Dracula Prince of Darkness'. For proper nuttiness, check out 'The Loch Ness Monster' on *The Weird World of Lionel Fanthorpe & Jon Downes*, a CD of cryptozoology-themed songs by two stalwarts of the Fortean canon.

LEVIATHAN

Canst thou draw out leviathan with an hook? Or his tongue with a cord which thou lettest down?

Canst thou put an hook into his nose? Or bore his jaw through with a thorn?…

Who can open the doors of his face? His teeth are terrible round about…

Out of his mouth go burning lamps, and sparks of fire leap out.

Out of his nostrils goeth smoke, as out of a seething pot or caldron.

His breath kindleth coals, and a flame goeth out of his mouth.

In his neck remaineth strength, and sorrow is turned into joy before him.

The flakes of his flesh are joined together: they are firm in themselves; they cannot be moved.

His heart is as firm as a stone; yea, as hard as a piece of the nether millstone.

When he raiseth up himself, the mighty are afraid: by reason of breakings they purify themselves.

The sword of him that layeth at him cannot hold: the spear, the dart, nor the habergeon.

He esteemeth iron as straw, and brass as rotten wood.

The arrow cannot make him flee: slingstones are turned with him into stubble.

Darts are counted as stubble: he laugheth at the shaking of a spear.

Sharp stones are under him: he spreadeth sharp pointed things upon the mire.

He maketh the deep to boil like a pot: he maketh the sea like a pot of ointment.

He maketh a path to shine after him; one would think the deep to be hoary.

Upon earth there is not his like, who is made without fear.

He beholdeth all high things: he is a king over all the children of pride.

Job 41:1-34

BIBLIOGRAPHY

Items marked with an asterisk★ have been particularly useful.

TGSI = *Transactions of the Gaelic Society of Inverness*, published by the Gaelic Society of Inverness in Inverness.

NEWSPAPERS AND MAGAZINES

The *Daily Record*
Fortean Times
The *Highland News*★
The *Inverness Courier*★
Nessie's Loch Ness Times★
The *Press and Journal*
The *Scottish Daily Mail*

TRAVEL, HISTORY AND ARCHAEOLOGY – LOCAL

Barron, Hugh (ed.) *The Third Statistical Account of the County of Inverness* Scottish Academic Press, Edinburgh 1985

Burt, Edward *Burt's Letters from the North of Scotland* Birlinn, Edinburgh 1998 (Originally published as *Letters from a Gentleman in the North of Scotland to His Friend in London* S. Birt, London, 1754)★

Dick, M *Erch in Urchinage* Albyn Press, Edinburgh 1985

Fraser-Mackintosh, Charles 'Minor Septs of Clan Chattan: An Account of the Confederation of Clan Chattan; Its Kith and Kin' in *The Celtic Monthly* 1898

Frere, Richard *Loch Ness* John Murray, London 1988★

Glenmoriston Heritage Group *Glen Moriston: A Heritage Guide* Glenmoriston Heritage Group, Glenmoriston 2007★

Gordon, Richard *Round Inverness, The Black Isle and Nairn: Walks and History* Boar's Head Press, Buckie 2003★

Henshall, A.S. and J.N.G. Ritchie *The Chambered Cairns of the Central Highlands* Edinburgh University Press, Edinburgh 2001★

Inverness Field Club *The Hub of the Highlands: The Book of Inverness and District* Inverness Field Club and James Thin, Edinburgh 1990 (first published 1975)★

Inverness Museum & Art Gallery *Graveyards Old and New in Inverness District* Inverness, n.d.

Lawson, Alan B. *A Country Called Stratherrick* South Loch Ness Heritage Group, Loch Ness 2006 (1ˢᵗ Edition 1987)★

Longmore, Leonella *Inverness in the 18ᵗʰ Century* Courier Publications, Inverness 2001★

MacDonald, Mhairi A. *By the Banks of the Ness* Paul Harris Publishing, Edinburgh 1982

McGillivray, Robert and George B. Macgillivray *A History of The Clan MacGillivray* G.B. Macgillivray, Thunder Bay, Ontario 1973★

MacKay, William (ed.) *Records of the Presbyteries of Inverness and Dingwall 1643-1688* The Scottish History Society, Edinburgh 1896

Mackay, William *Urquhart and Glenmoriston: Olden Times in a Highland Parish* Inverness, The Northern Counties Newspaper and Printing and Publishing Company, Inverness 1914 (1ˢᵗ edition 1893)★

MacLauchlan, Revd F.J.L. *The Old High Church* leaflet, n.d.

Macleod, Malcolm C. (ed.) *The Celtic Annual 1913,* Dundee 1913

Maclean, John *Reminiscences of a Clachnacuddin Nonagenarian* Donald MacDonald, Inverness 1886★

Maclean, Roddy *The Gaelic Place Names and Heritage of Inverness* Culcabock Publishing, Inverness 2004★

MacRae, Kenneth A *Highland Ways and Byways* Cullernie Crafts, Inverness 1973 (originally published in
   3 vols 1953-1955)★

——————— *Highland Doorstep* Moray Press, Edinburgh 1953★

Meldrum, Edward *From Nairn to Loch Ness: Local History and Archaeology Guidebook No. 1*
   Inverness 1983★

——————— *From Loch Ness to The Aird: Local History and Archaeology Guidebook No. 2* Inverness 1987★

New Statistical Account of Scotland: Vol XIV Inverness-Ross and Cromarty William Blackwood and Sons,
   Edinburgh and London 1845★

Pollitt, Gerald A *Historic Inverness* The Melven Press, Perth 1981

Shaw, C.J. *History of Clan Shaw* Phillimore, London 1983

Sinton, Revd Thomas 'Places, People and Poetry of Dores in Other Days' in *TGSI* Vol. XXVI
   1904-1907★

Stewart, Katharine *A Garden in the Hills* The Mercat Press, Edinburgh 1995

——————— *Abriachan* Abriachan Forest Trust, Abriachan 2000★

——————— *The Story of Loch Ness* Luath Press, Edinburgh 2005★

——————— *A Croft in the Hills* Mercat Press, Edinburgh 1991 (1st edition 1960)

——————— *A School in the Hills* Mercat Press, Edinburgh 1996

——————— *The Post in the Hills* Mercat Press, Edinburgh 1997

——————— *A Garden in The Hills* Mercat Press, Edinburgh 2006

——————— *Crofts and Crofting* Mercat Press, Edinburgh 2005 (1st edition 1980)

Tytler-Fraser, Neil *Tales from Aldourie Estate* 1920s (revised Iain Cameron 2002, online at
   http://southlochnessheritage.co.uk)★

TRAVEL, HISTORY AND ARCHAEOLOGY – SCOTLAND

Anderson, Alan Orr & Marjorie Ogilvie Anderson (ed. and trans.) *Adomnan's Life of Columba*
   Thomas Nelson & Sons, London, Edinburgh, Melbourne & Johannesburg 1961

Brander, Michael *The Making of the Highlands* Book Club Associates, London 1980

Broun, Dauvit and Thomas Owen Clancy (eds) *Spes Scotorum: Hope of Scots* T & T Clark, Edinburgh
   1999

Gordon, Seton *The Highlands of Scotland* Robert Hale, London 1951

Graham, Cuthbert *Portrait of the Moray Firth* Robert Hale, London 1977

Pennant, Thomas *A Tour of Scotland and a Voyage to the Hebrides* 1772

Skene, William F. *Celtic Scotland* 3 vols David Douglas, Edinburgh 1876-1880

Wilson, Daniel *Prehistoric Annals of Scotland* 2 vols MacMillan & Co., London & Cambridge 1863

MYSTERIOUSNESS

Alexander, Marc *The Devil Hunter: an Account of the Work of Exorcist Extraordinary the Reverend Dr Donald
   Omand* Sphere, London 1981

Allison, Hugh G. *Culloden Tales: Stories from Scotland's Most Famous Battlefield* Mainstream, Edinburgh
   2007

Anonymous, 'Ancient Prophecy', broadside, 1820, held at National Library of Scotland, shelfmark L.C.
   Fol. 73 (087)

Barron, Hugh 'Verse, Story and Fragments from Various Districts' in *TGSI* Vol. XXXXVII 1971-72

Bauer, Henry H *The Enigma of Loch Ness* Johnston & Bacon Books, Stirling 1991★

Baumann, Elwood D. *The Loch Ness Monster* Franklin Watts, London 1973

Binns, Ronald *The Loch Ness Mystery Solved* W.H. Allen, London 1983

Booth, Martin *A Magick Life: A Biography of Aleister Crowley* Hodder and Stoughton, London 2000★

Bord, Janet and Colin *The Enchanted Land: Myths and Legends of Britain's Landscape* Thorsons, London
   1995

Cameron, John *The Mystery of Castle Stuart* Castle Creations 1998

Campbell, John Gregerson (ed. Ronald Black), *The Gaelic Otherworld: John Gregerson Campbell's
   Superstitions of the Highlands and Islands of Scotland* and *Witchcraft and Second Sight in the Highlands &
   Islands,* Birlinn, Edinburgh, new edition 2005

Campbell, John Gregerson (ed) *A Collection of Highland Rites and Customes, copied by Edward Lhuyd from the manuscript of the Rev James Kirkwood (1650-1709) and annotated by him with the aid of the Rev John Beaton,* DS Brewer/The Folklore Society, Cambridge 1975

Campbell, Steuart 'False Report From Loch Ness' in *Flying Saucer Review* Vol 26, No.6 March 1981

———————— *The Loch Ness Monster: The Evidence* Aberdeen University Press 1991★

Carmichael, Alexander (ed. C.J. Moore) *Carmina Gadelica* Floris Books, Edinburgh 1994 (first published 1900)★

Cornish, Vaughan *The Churchyard Yew and Immortality* Frederick Muller, London 1946

Costello, Peter *In Search of Lake Monsters* Panther, St Albans 1975★

Coventry, Martin *Haunted Places of Scotland* Goblinshead, Musselburgh 1999

———————— *Haunted Castles & Houses of Scotland* Goblinshead, Musselburgh 2004

Cumming, Andrew 'Some Tales of Strathnairn' in *TGSI* Vol LI 1978-1980★

Dalyell, John Graham *The Darker Superstitions of Scotland, Illustrated from History and Practice* Waugh and Innes, Edinburgh 1834★

Davis, Stephen *Hammer of the Gods: Led Zeppelin Unauthorised* Pan, London 1995

Dinsdale, Tim *The Leviathans* Routledge & Kegan Paul, London 1966★

———————— *Project Water Horse: The True Story of the Monster Quest at Loch Ness* Routledge & Kegan Paul, London 1975★

———————— *The Loch Ness Monster* Routledge & Kegan Paul, London 1976

Dieckhoff, Dom Cyril 'Mythological Beings in Gaelic Folklore' in *TGSI* Vol XXIX 1914-1919

Ellis, W.S. 'Loch Ness: The lake and the legend', in *National Geographic Magazine* vol 151, No. 6, 1977

Fort, Charles *The Book of the Damned* John Brown Publishing, London 1995

Freeman, Richard *Dragons: More Than A Myth?* CFZ Press, Exeter 2005★

Harrison, Paul *The Encyclopaedia of the Loch Ness Monster* Robert Hale, London 1999

Henderson, George *Survivals in Belief Among the Celts* J. Maclehose and Sons, Glasgow 1911

Holiday, F.W. *The Great Orm of Loch Ness* Faber, London 1968★

———————— *The Dragon and the Disc* Sidgwick & Jackson, London 1973★

———————— *The Goblin Universe* Xanadu, London 1986★

———————— 'Exorcism and UFO Landing at Loch Ness' in *Flying Saucer Review*, Vol. 19 No. 5 Sept-Oct 1973★

Hutchinson, Roger *Aleister Crowley – The Beast Demystified* Mainstream, London 1998

King, Francis *The Magical World of Aleister Crowley* Weidenfeld and Nicolson, London 1977

Love, Dane *Scottish Spectres* Robert Hale, London 2001

MacBain, Alexander 'Gaelic Incantations', in *TGSI* Vol XVII 1890-91

MacDonald, Alexander 'Scraps of Unpublished Poetry and Folklore from Glenmoriston', in *TGSI* Vol XXI 1896-97

———————— *Story and Song from Loch Ness-Side* Northern Counties Newspaper and Printing and Publishing Company, Inverness 1914★

MacFarlane, Revd A.M. 'Myths Associated with Mountains, Springs and Lochs in The Highlands' in *TGSI* Vol XXXIV 1927-1928

MacGregor, Alasdair Alpin *Phantom Footsteps* Robert Hale, London 1959

McHardy, Stuart *Scotland: Myth, Legend & Folklore* Luath Press, Edinburgh 1999

———————— *The Well of the Heads and Other Tales of the Scottish Clans* Birlinn, Edinburgh 2005

Mackal, Roy *The Monsters of Loch Ness* Futura, London 1976★

Mackay, William 'Saints Associated with the Valley of the Ness' in *TGSI* Vol XXVII 1908-1911

Mackenzie, Alexander *The Prophecies of the Brahan Seer* Constable. London 1998 (1st edition 1877)

MacKenzie, Donald A. *Scottish Folk-Lore and Folk Life: Studies in Race, Culture and Tradition* Blackie & Son Glasgow 1935

MacKinlay, James M. *Folklore of Scottish Lochs and Springs* William Hodge, Glasgow 1893

Maclennan, A.B. *The Petty Seer* The Highland News Printing and Publishing Co., Inverness 1906

McNeill, F. Marion *The Silver Bough Volume 1: Scottish Folk-Lore and Folk-Belief* Canongate, Edinburgh 1989 (first edition 1956)

McPherson, J.M. *Primitive Beliefs in the North-East of Scotland* Longmans, Green & Co., London 1929

Marsden, Simon *Phantoms of the Isles* Guild Publishing, London 1990

Matheson, William 'The Historical Coinneach Odhar and some Prophecies Attributed to Him' in *TGSI* Vol. XLVI 1969-1970

Maxwell-Stuart, PG *An Abundance of Witches: The Great Scottish Witch-Hunt* Tempus, Stroud 2005

Meurger, Michel with Claude Gagnon *Lake Monster Traditions: A Cross-Cultural Analysis* Fortean Tomes, London 1988★

Miller, Joyce *Magic and Witchcraft in Scotland* Goblinshead, Musselburgh 2004

Morris, Ruth and Frank, *Scottish Healing Wells* The Alethea Press, Sandy 1982★

Omand, Donald *Experiences of a Present-Day Exorcist* Kimber 1970

Polson, Alexander *Scottish Witchcraft Lore* W Alexander & Son, Inverness 1932

Pugh, Roy J.M. *The Deil's Ain*, Harlaw Heritage, Balerno 2001

Robertson, James *Scottish Ghost Stories* Warner, London 1996

Robertson, R. Macdonald *Selected Highland Folktales* Oliver and Boyd, Edinburgh and London, 1961

Ross, Anne *The Folklore of the Scottish Highlands* BT Batsford. London 1976

Rowling, J.K. (writing as Newt Scamander) *Fantastic Beasts and Where To Find Them* Obscurus Books, Diagon Alley, in association with Bloomsbury, London 2001

Searle, Frank *Nessie: Seven Years in Search of the Monster* Coronet Books, London 1976

Shiels, Tony 'Doc' *Monstrum! A Wizard's Tale* Fortean Tomes, London 1990★

Shine, Adrian *Loch Ness* Loch Ness Project, Drumnadrochit 2006★

Sutherland, Elizabeth *Ravens and Black Rain: The Story of Highland Second Sight,* Constable and Co., London 1985★

Sutin, Lawrence *Do What Thou Wilt: A Life of Aleister Crowley* St Martin's Griffin, New York 2000

Swire, Otta *The Highlands and their Legends* Oliver & Boyd, Edinburgh, 1963★

Symonds, John *The Great Beast: The Life and Magick of Aleister Crowley* Mayflower, St Albans 1973

Symonds, John and Kenneth Grant (eds) *The Confessions of Aleister Crowley: An Autohagiography* Penguin, Harmondsworth 1989★

Thompson, Francis *The Supernatural Highlands* Luath Press, Edinburgh 1999 (first edition 1976)

Underwood, Peter *Exorcism!* Robert Hale, London 1990

Wilson, Colin *Mysteries* Granada, London 1979

————— *Poltergeist! A Study in Destructive Haunting* New English Library, Sevenoaks 1981

————— *Aleister Crowley: The Nature of the Beast* Aeon Books, London 2005 (1st edition 1987)

Witchell, Nicholas *The Loch Ness Story* Penguin, Harmondsworth 1975★

Wood, Karen *The Folklore of South Loch Ness Side,* private document (The Girls' Brigade, 2nd Inverness Company, Queen's Award 1995/1997), 1996. Copy in Inverness reference library★

WEBSITES

Survey of Scottish Witchcraft, www.arts.ed.ac.uk/witches★

'Canmore', the Royal Commission on the Ancient and Historical Monuments of Scotland, www.rcahms.gov.uk★

The Modern Antiquarian, www.themodernantiquarian.com★

TELEVISION AND DVD

BBC Scotland *The Other Loch Ness Monster* (television series: *Ex-S*), 2000

Scott, Douglas *The Clava Cairns* DVD, 2006

INDEX